MONTANANS
in THE GREAT WAR

MONTANANS
in THE GREAT WAR

Open Warfare Over There

KEN ROBISON

THE
History
PRESS

Published by The History Press
Charleston, SC
www.historypress.com

Front cover images: Lieutenant Colonel George S. Patton, commanding the tanks at St. Mihiel, with a Renault FT light tank. *World War I Signal Corps Photograph Collection*; remarkable Métis and Little Shell nurse and homesteader Louise Lafournaise, one of two Montana native nurses to serve in World War I. *Nicholas Vrooman*; Master Sergeant Horace W. Bivins, a Buffalo Soldier in the Great War. *Author's collection*; "The Rock of the Marne" combat poster. *U.S. Army*.

Back cover images: *Spirit of the American Doughboy*, World War I Centennial Fort Benton's Veterans Park, sculptor E.M. Viquesney. *Author's photograph*; image from rare Charles M. Russell letter to Bumpsky Goodman, dated September 6, 1918, with World War I battle scene. *Private collection (anonymous)*.

First published 2019

Manufactured in the United States

ISBN 9781467140997

Library of Congress Control Number: 2019943511

Notice: The information in this book is true and complete to the best of our knowledge. It is offered without guarantee on the part of the author or The History Press. The author and The History Press disclaim all liability in connection with the use of this book.

To those who rang bells throughout Montana and the nation on the 11th hour of the 11th day of the 11th month, 2018, in commemoration for Montanans who went "over the top," carried the wounded from fields of fire and nursed the living back to health.

Map of Montana, 1917. *Author's collection.*

YELLOWSTONE
NATIONAL PARK

CONTENTS

CONTENTS

ACKNOWLEDGEMENTS

As I've searched the collections of many fine Montana libraries and archives, I've enjoyed the help of many along the way. My thanks to Cindy Shearer, Gallatin Historical Society; Jan Thomson, Gary Goettel and the Great Falls Genealogy Society; Megan Sanford and The History Museum, Great Falls; Alan Archambault, Fort Lewis Museum; Director Tate Jones, the Rocky Mountain Museum of Military History; Director Ray Read, Montana Military Museum; Director Ellen Crane, Butte/Silver Bow County Archives; Administrator Joren Underdahl, Montana Veterans' Home; and Nancy Watt, Fergus County Library.

To Kim Briggeman, Aaron Parrott, Kristen Inbody and Ed Kemmick; to Kevin Kooilstra, Western Heritage Center; to Kathryn Kramer, Charles M. Russell Museum; and to Bruce Whittenberg and everyone at the Montana Historical Society. To Jon Arneson, Aaron Flint and Tom Halverson, who opened their airways to history discussions; to the Van Voast family; to Marijke Taffein at St. Mihiel American Cemetery, France; and to Bethany Monroe DeBorde and her splendid newspaper, the *River Press*.

And to my colleagues, Henry Armstrong, Dan Van Voast and Dan Nelsen, at the Overholser Historical Research Center. Finally, great thanks to Karin and Ian, Pippi and Astrid.

INTRODUCTION

World War I, the "war to end all wars," continued with fury in the spring of 1918, setting the stage for decisive battles to come. As America entered its second year in the Great War, the Germans commenced a massive Spring Offensive designed to break French and British forces before the American Expeditionary Forces (AEF) could engage in large numbers. This became a dramatic race against time. Could the accelerating flow of Yanks from the sixteen draftee training camps spread across the United States arrive in time to become *the* key factor in deciding the fate of the war? Could inexperienced AEF Yanks hold their own against hardened German soldiers? Was General John J. Pershing capable of leading his burgeoning army, not only against battle-tested German generals but also against Allied leaders determined to replenish their own depleted ranks with American soldiers? Could the U.S. and Royal Navies contain the growing German submarine threat to vital transport supply lines of food, weapons and soldiers crossing the Atlantic?

The first of these tests, the U-boat threat, accelerated with U.S. entry in the war and was taking a toll. The torpedoing of the *Tuscania* in early February 1918, with the loss of 210 soldiers and crewmen, shocked the nation. The critical land war tests would come in the early summer and autumn of 1918 at places that became household names, some even rising to legendary status, across the United States and around the globe: Belleau Wood, Cantigny, Château-Thierry, the Second Marne, St. Mihiel, Argonne Forest, Flanders and others. Yanks went "over the top" to break out from

World War I Montana: The Treasure State Prepares. Author photo.

the trenches into "open warfare" in battle after battle, defying death with their bravery and vigor, stunning the German foe and confounding Allied expectations at heavy cost in lives and limbs. The battle cry of both draftee and National Guard Montanans, "Powder River, Let 'Er Buck," resonated over the battlefields of France throughout the decisive year of 1918 in this seemingly endless war.

This Great War would have profound effects at home and abroad. For Montana, it was a war of opportunity for many, trouble for some and change for all. The story of the first year of the war is told in *World War I Montana: The Treasure State Prepares* in the voices and words of many Montana participants.

This is a story that emphasizes the vital role of the Treasure State's mining, smelting and refining to the national war effort. It tells of the critical importance of Butte copper and Great Falls refined copper wire for the war's bullets and lines of communication. Montana's amber waves of grain helped to feed a starving world despite the onset of serious drought in 1917. Montana's cowboys, miners, foresters, farmers, nurses and other women marched to war in disproportionately larger numbers than any other state due to grievous census miscalculation.

In that first year after America's declaration of war on April 6, 1917, the nation raced to overcome its unpreparedness as it moved forward with a draft to raise a "million-man" army, later to become a 4-million-man army. Every community and aspect of American society mobilized in support of the war effort, and Montana strengths came into play: mineral wealth, grain production and frontier-hardened men and women.

The scale of manpower required for the war effort opened exceptional opportunities for women and minorities. Montana women became essential in the production lines and in filling selective roles in the armed forces as army and navy nurses, Navy Yeomanettes, telephone operators, entertainers and in the Red Cross, YMCA and other non-military support organizations. Hundreds of Montana women served in the military during the war.

The Soldiers' Military Record. *Author's collection.*

World War I Montana presented the story of the United States and Montanans as they mobilized and prepared for their first European war. *Montanans in the Great War* begins with nine dramatic days in late March 1918, as the German High Command launched a massive Spring Offensive designed to smash British forces while breaking through French lines to capture Paris and end the war. Heavily reinforced by forty-four divisions rushed westward from the Russian front, the Germans boldly gambled that they could prevail before the AEF could gain the numbers and experience to tilt the balance of power in favor of the Allies on the Western Front battlefields.

AEF commander General John J. Pershing immediately offered his most available troops, engineer regiments to the British, the 1st Infantry Division (the "Big Red One") to join the French on the front lines, as well as four other AEF divisions to replace French divisions in quiet sectors. With this dramatic action, the AEF Yanks began to enter the war in strength. From this desperate beginning, over the next eight months the AEF engaged in the "war to end all wars" with increasing strength and experience. General Pershing developed the essential infrastructure for millions of Yanks; built his divisions, corps and armies; and developed his concept of "open warfare" to replace the stalemate of trench warfare.

Meanwhile "Over Here" in the United States and Montana communities, all aspects of life assumed a wartime posture. Draft contingents steadily boarded trains en route to sixteen massive training camps spread across the country, with Camp Lewis, near Tacoma, Washington, serving the Northwest with many Montanans being integrated there into the newly formed 91st "Wild West" Division. The 2nd Montana National Guard, mobilized in 1917 as the 163rd Infantry Regiment, arrived in France in early 1918, joining a "replacement" division, meaning that most Montana soldiers quickly engaged in the earliest AEF battles with the 16th, 28th and other regiments.

At home, President Wilson's wartime program centered on funding the war through Liberty Loan drives and tax increases, promoting war materiel production and stifling dissent and labor unrest. War information, at home and abroad, was carefully controlled by his Committee on Public Information. Harsh sedition laws were enacted to regulate and limit free speech and dissent as patriotic fervor and anti-German sentiment built across the country. The spring of 1918 brought to many communities a virulent form of influenza, striking troops in Europe as well as in a wave across the United States. As 1918 progressed, it became clear that much of Montana would enter a second severe year of drought, endangering wheat and other crop production at the very time demand was at its greatest.

This book moves through the course of the war, featuring the stories and experiences of many Montana men and women. They will answer many questions along the way. What was it like to be stationed with your regiment in Butte while enforcing labor peace in that tumultuous mining town? How would Montana celebrities like "cowboy artist" Charlie Russell find ways to support the war effort? What would be the political fate of the nation's first congresswoman, Jeannette Rankin, after her vote against the declaration of war? How would Montana women perform in their vital new roles in the military, many in combat zones, as telephone operators, nurses and entertainers, as well as at home on production lines, roles never before open to adventurous women? You will meet these women and hear their stories.

What role would Montanans play in new war technologies, aviation and tank warfare? What about the role of Montana foresters in the spruce production camps in the Northwest, vital for aircraft production? What role did horses play as the military began to transition to combustion engines? Follow young officers Douglas MacArthur, George C. Marshall, George Patton, Eddie Rickenbacker, Omar Bradley, John Hoover and others as they gained the experience and innovated new tactics critical for them to become the leaders of the military in future wars. Read the words of Brigadier General MacArthur's tribute to his men of the 42nd Rainbow Division killed in action at St. Mihiel: "They have but passed beyond the mists that blind us here—and come to the end of the Rainbow." What was it like for black Montanans to serve in the segregated military under white officers or under French command in combat? With President Wilson's theme of "democracy for all," what were their hopes in returning to Jim Crow America? For Montana Native American warriors, many of them non-citizens, what were they fighting for? For Chinese Montanans facing exclusion from Great Falls and other towns, why were they fighting?

Follow Montanans as they engaged increasingly in combat roles from their first major battle at Cantigny, a day to remember in history. What was it like for Montana nurses and doctors to treat the wounded from these battles? Join Montana Marines in the bloodiest day in their history, as they earned the respect and admiration of allies and foe alike and the nickname "Devil Dogs" while charging through hell on earth at Belleau Wood. Blunt the vital German surge toward Paris with Montana Yanks of the 3rd Division while earning accolades from the grateful French and the sobriquet "Rock of the Marne." Find yourself behind German lines with Montanans in the Lost Battalion, facing death at every moment. Wounded and captured, learn the fate of Montana Yanks who entered German prisoner of war camps.

Join Montanans of the 91st "Wild West" Division as they went "over the top," yelling "Powder River, Let 'Er Buck" as they entered the fury of combat at the Argonne Forest. Serve with Seaman Mike Mansfield, the youngest Montanan to serve in the war, onboard the USS *Minneapolis* on convoy duty protecting transports from lurking German U-boats.

For these many questions, Montanans will relate here the stories of their experiences. Many will provide answers to these provocative questions. When available space limits their words, you can read more online at this author's website (www.kenrobisonhistory.com/world-war-1). In addition, this site presents names and details on Montana's minorities serving in the war, as well as Montana's known casualties.

With the Armistice of November 11, the "war to end all wars" ended with a peace conference that seemed almost endless. At last, as a troubled peace was arranged, an even deadlier influenza pandemic raged unabated in communities large and small at home and abroad for many months. At peace, what was occupation duty like for Montanans in Germany? What would unfold from the Peace Conference? Would democracy come to replace the authoritarian European empires that led the world into the global conflict? Would the United States return to isolationism? Would the nation return to normalcy?

At home, what would women and minorities find in the postwar future? Montana continued in its third year of severe agricultural drought, bringing on depression a decade before the rest of the nation. Monuments to the Great War rose in tribute at Fort Benton, Kalispell and Missoula; soldiers formed new organizations, such as the American Legion.

The war and the times brought profound change to the nation and to Montana. The nation followed Montana's lead in passing both women's suffrage and prohibition. Change came to women with their right to vote and their wide participation in essential wartime services both at home and abroad. Change came in the political climate through hyper-patriotism and suppression of free speech—Bolshevism soon replace the kaiser as the "mortal enemy." The war would lead to change for Native Americans, as their wartime service hastened citizenship. Sadly, change would not come for African American Montanans, as Jim Crow lingered on for almost half a century.

Montanans in the Great War is the story of a young and vibrant Montana and Montanans of all ethnicities and races as they fought abroad to win the war and at home for an elusive democracy for all.

PART I

★

MOVING INTO THE TRENCHES

The Yanks Go to War

Chapter 1

APRIL 1918

The Great German Spring Offensive;
The Big Red One "Over the Top"

On March 21, 1918, the German High Command launched its Spring Offensive along a fifty-mile front with three German armies (seventy-one divisions) in a massive assault on the British-held Somme front in the direction of Amiens. A breakthrough at this point would separate the French from the British, push the latter into a pocket in Flanders and open the way to the Channel ports. Also, it would open the way to Paris through French lines. Could this drive be stopped?

Operation Michael, the first and the main of five German offensives, began with a massive artillery barrage at 4:40 a.m. on March 21. The bombardment hit targets over an area of 150 square miles, the biggest barrage of the entire war at more than 1,100,000 shells fired in five hours.

For nine dramatic days after Offensive Michael began, it seemed that the Germans would prevail. The British Fifth Army was shattered, losing two hundred guns and sixteen thousand prisoners under an overwhelming attacking force. On March 24, American Expeditionary Forces' (AEF) 6th, 12th and 14th Engineers rushed to aid the British on their front lines. The French held more firmly but were forced also to withdraw.

Typical of the experiences of the AEF Engineer Regiments in support of the British in this offensive was that of the 14th Engineers, which worked in the thick of the artillery fire, hauling wounded British soldiers, evacuating forward ammunition dumps and even blowing up railway equipment to keep it out of German hands.

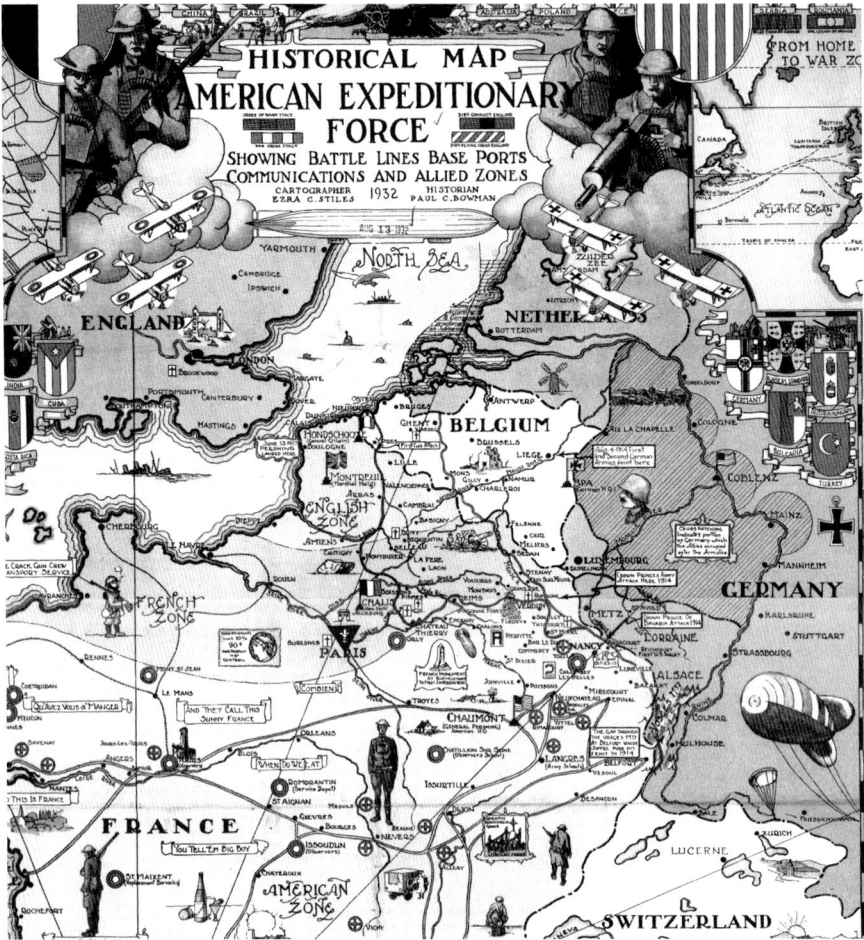

Historical map of the American Expeditionary Force. *Library of Congress.*

Opposite: Map of the German Spring Offensive, Operation Michael, March 21 April 5. *From the* Montreal Gazette *(Canada), September 6, 1918.*

General Pershing reported on the "gallant conduct" of the American engineer troops with the British Fifth Army in helping to check the German advance in the early days of the great offensive. The report was made public by Secretary of War Newton Baker on April 19, with this comment: "It will make splendid reading for Americans."

American losses in the period from March 21 to April 3, during which the engineers consolidated and held a sub-sector of the British lines against

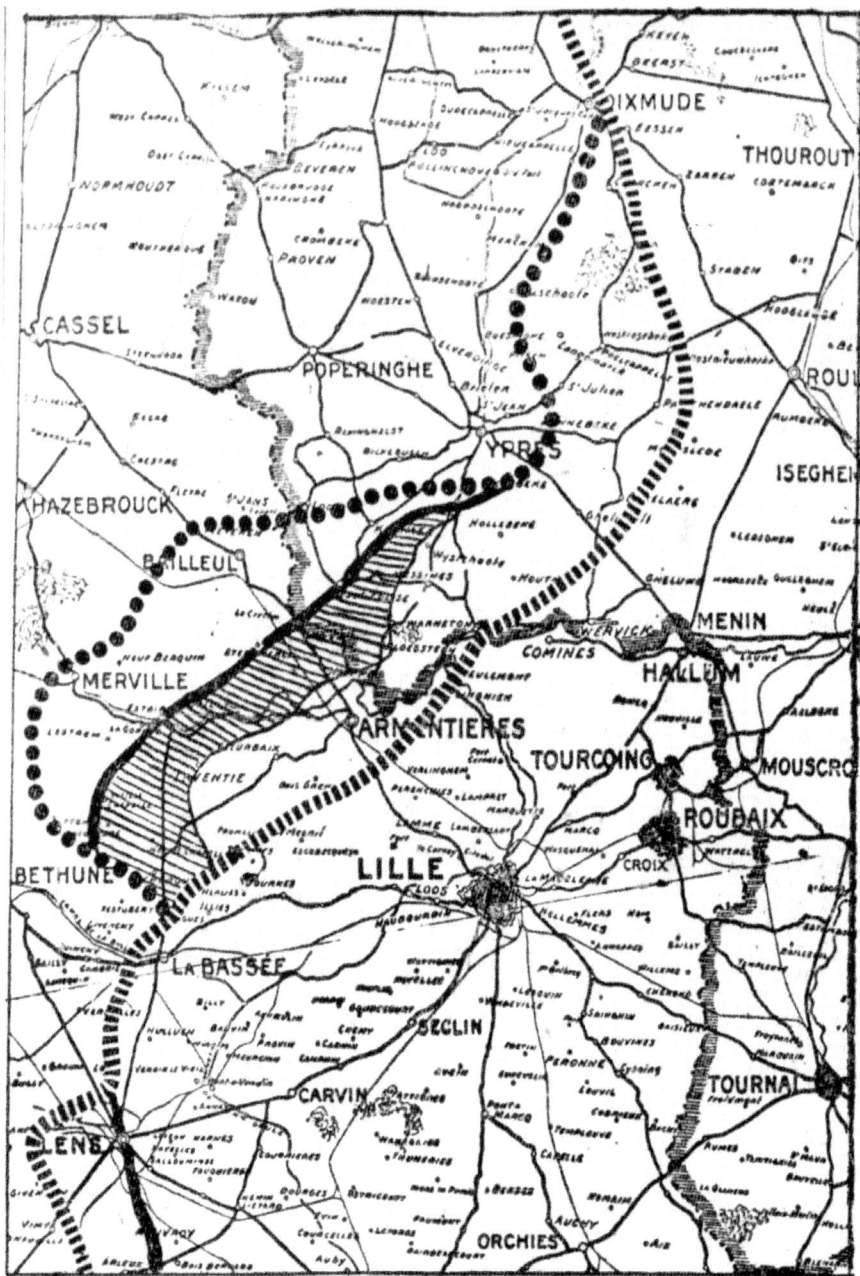

KEY TO

Old battle lines as at March 21, prior to the German spring offensive, shown by square dotted lines.
Farthest German advance up to July 18 shown by round dotted lines.

repeated assaults, were given as two officers killed and three wounded, twenty men killed and fifty-two wounded and forty-five missing. It is believed by the British authorities that all of those reported missing were not captured, but that many were separated from their command and were then with other British organizations.

The Allies realized that the only hope of beating the Germans was in unity of command, to place all Allied forces under the command of one man, who could use them to the best advantage, instead of depending on conferences to decide the course of action. The Allies agreed to accept newly promoted French marshal Ferdinand Foch in overall command with an Allied War Council, meeting in Paris to advised Foch on general strategy for the war.

On March 26, at the height of the German drive, General John J. Pershing paid a late-night visit and dramatically notified Marshal Foch and French prime minister Georges Clemenceau, "I have come to tell you that the American people would consider it a great honor for our troops to be engaged in the present battle. I ask you for this in their name and my own."

The 1st Division, the "Big Red One," was ordered immediately to the German offense battle line, while the 2nd, 36th and 42nd Divisions were deployed into "quiet" sectors to replace French divisions badly needed at the front. Pershing ordered the AEF 26th Division to relieve the 1st at Seicheprey. The 17th, 22nd and 148th Aero Squadrons also were brought into forward combat positions.

Soon after Marshal Foch took command, the German drive was slowed and finally stopped. The enemy had advanced on both sides of the Somme River, regaining in nine days all the territory which the Allies had taken from the Germans in a year and a half of fighting. Every foot of ground that the Germans had been obliged to yield a year before was recovered plus two hundred square miles in addition. The enemy had gained some thirty-nine miles on the front of fifty miles and claimed to have taken 150,000 prisoners.

The apex of the German drive was a little beyond Montdidier and Cantigny, the last place being noteworthy, for it was here that a major American victory would be won two months later.

The German armies had suffered huge numbers of casualties and were unable to maintain supplies for their advancing troops. The Germans had planned to capture the city of Amiens, a key railroad center through which British armies maintained communication with French armies and with Paris. If Amiens had fallen, the Allies would have to rely on a complex method of communication and mutual assistance, endangering the entire Allied front. Critically, the Germans were halted nine miles east of Amiens.

Unable to take the city, the Germans vented their wrath with a massive bombardment by long-range guns and aircraft bombing.

The German Michael offensive would continue until April 5, while follow-on locally targeted offenses continued for four more months until the end of July. Casualty losses during Michael were staggering on both sides. German losses were estimated at more than 240,000 men, while the British suffered almost 178,000 and the French 77,000 casualties. The minor scale played by the AEF in this early German Spring Offensive is reflected in the loss of just 77 Yanks.[1]

The *Fort Benton River Press* of March 27 reported on this great German Spring Offensive:

GREATEST BATTLE IN HISTORY
Over a Million Men in German Offensive Along Front of Fifty Miles
  British Army Headquarters in France, March 22.—The Germans today continued their assault against the positions in the Cambrai sector. At least 40 divisions have been identified on the battle front. No such concentration of artillery has been seen since the war began.
  On the southern battlefield a bitter struggle was waged today. The enemy had one thousand guns in one small sector—one for every 12 yards. Severe fighting was proceeding this morning in St. Ledger, southwest of Croiselles. At several points the enemy made gains against the British, but at others he was repulsed in counter-attacks, according to the British official communication issued tonight.
  The statement says the British losses inevitably have been considerable, but not out of proportion to the magnitude of the battle. The enemy's losses continue very heavy, all his advances being made at great sacrifices. The greatest courage is being shown by the British troops.
  Washington, March 24.—The German offensive, says the war department's weekly communique issued today, proves that German militarists, no longer able to control the German people by political maneuver, have been forced to attempt a gigantic feat of arms to maintain their domination.
  While the great attack has been able to make headway, no definite enveloping movement has been outlined, and it would be premature to express opinions on the tactical phases with a combat situation inevitably changing in a battle of such magnitude.
  The advance is being accompanied by a terrible slaughter of the Germans, who in their massed formations are being cut to pieces by British

guns of all calibers. The British casualties, too, have been heavy and Berlin claims the taking of 26,000 British prisoners and 400 guns.

Military experts say such an effort as the Germans are making cannot be continued long. Every foot gained means added difficulties of transportation and the consequent slowing up of the forward movement. A day or two more of bitter resistance, even including further British retirement, it was thought, would see the impetus of the German thrust lost and its power diminished. Then would come opportunities for counter blows on a major scale.

It has been definitely ascertained that considerably more than a million Germans have been brought to the western front in an endeavor to crush the British army holding the line from the region of Arras to the south of St. Quentin, but it daily becomes increasingly evident that the enemy in his drive has met with opposition not counted upon and been unable to realize to the full his objective.

The withdrawal of the British forces along the battle front in France was long ago planned in the event of the Germans attacking in great force. This announcement comes from the British front through the Associated Press correspondent, who describes the operation of the British army as a masterly withdrawal, made possible by gallant shock troops in the front

German soldiers resting during the Michael Offensive. *Wikimedia Commons.*

lines, who checked the advance of the Germans, while artillery, machine gun and rifle fire worked appalling slaughter among the masses of German infantry as they were sent forward thus enabling the main body of the British to fall back deliberately and without confusion.[2]

YOU NEVER KNOW

Bartle Hayfield was convicted of burglary in Valley County in April 1912 and sent to the Montana State Penitentiary in Deer Lodge with a ten-year sentence. In 1916, this Ontario-born gardener stepped from his convict's cell in the state prison to glory on the battlefields of France. His sentence was commuted by Governor Sam Stewart on the condition that Hayfield leave Montana and never return. Hayfield agreed to the terms and, upon release, went directly to Canada, where he enlisted in the army. In March 1918, Hayfield wrote to Warden Frank Conley at the prison telling him that he had been decorated for bravery in action on two occasions.[3]

In addition, First Lieutenant Larry Brennan, a former student at Montana State University (today's University of Montana), was killed in action in France in late March. Lieutenant Brennan enlisted in the Canadian army and was assigned to the British Royal Flying Corps. Killed in aerial combat, Lieutenant Brennan became the second university student to lose his life in the war, the other being Marcus Cook, who was killed in action with nine other Montanans when the transport *Tuscania* was torpedoed and sunk in early February 1918.[4]

DAYLIGHT SAVING

For all Montana animals and residents not fond of Daylight Savings Time, be aware that Congress passed "An Act to Preserve Daylight and Provide Standard Time for the United States" as a World War I cost-saving measure on March 19, 1918, to take effect March 31. The *River Press* reported the measure "to effect a change in the business life and domestic affairs of American citizens. By the innocent subterfuge of changing the clock we are advised to get up an hour earlier in the morning and retire an hour ahead of our accustomed time."[5]

THE "BIG RED ONE"

As April 1918 began, the German assault Operation Michael continued in full force. This massive Spring Offensive, code-named *Kaiserschlacht* ("Emperor's Battle"), had led to the commitment of AEF troops to the front lines well ahead of earlier planning. Because of the urgent situation, AEF divisions would be integrated with the French army rather than fighting as separate U.S. Army corps. The most experienced AEF division, the 1st Division, was ordered to the German offense battle line at Cantigny.

Moving the "Big Red One" from its Seicheprey sector westward to the Cantigny sector proved a major undertaking. First, the AEF 26th Division had to move into the front lines to relieve the 1st Division. Once relieved, the 28,000 men, 1,700 horses and 1,000 wagons of the 1st had to move over roads and railways already clogged with movement of French army units to reinforce the sectors under German attack. The 1st Division marched more than seventeen miles to the train station at Toul. There, fifty-car trains loaded with 1st Division troops, weapons and supplies departed toward the front every hour around the clock.

En route to Cantigny, the troops assembled northwest of Paris to undergo open warfare training. On April 9, in the midst of this training, the Germans launched a second offensive in Flanders against hard-pressed British lines. With this, the 1st Division immediately ceased training and moved forward, arriving April 17 for a final three-day march to the front lines. As it approached its destination, it came within range of German artillery and began to suffer casualties. The night of April 24, the 1st Battalion (16th and 18th Regiments) moved through wheat fields and wooded areas to relieve French Moroccan troops on the front lines near the town of Cantigny, a hilltop village on the farthest east flank of the German offensive. These Moroccan soldiers bravely had stalled the German advance and held firm, but their ranks were depleted and exhausted.

The soldiers of the "Big Red One" arrived to find a weak defensive position consisting simply of a succession of shell holes connected by shallow ditches. Their immediate task was to dig in with the help of the 1st Engineer Regiment, working tirelessly during hours of darkness to strengthen the defensive posture. Meanwhile, the Field Signal troops began laying miles of concealed telephone lines.[6]

THE GERMAN OFFENSIVE

During the month that it took to reposition the 1st Division, the spring German offensive went through several phases. Operation Michael, the initial offense begun on March 21, had captured much Allied territory but at great cost. The one hundred German divisions had suffered casualties estimated as high as 300,000. War reports from the front were carried in the *River Press* of April 3 and 10:

GERMAN DRIVE HALTED
British and French Lines Present Unbroken Front.
  With the American Army in France, April 1.—The acceptance by France of General Pershing's offer of all American men and material for the present emergency has in effect virtually resulted in French army command, so far as the French army and American forces are concerned. This is shown by the fact that the orders issued to the American troops are of French origin.
  Definite official announcement that American troops will actually fight side by side with the French and British in northern France, reached the American troops tonight in Paris newspapers. It was greeted with cheering. The men who will go are envied by the rest of the American forces.
  While the advance of the German armies in Picardy has come almost to a halt, there has been savage fighting in the extreme edge of the western battle zone. Encounters in which large forces have been engaged have occurred north of Moreuil, but there seems to be no decided advantage gained by the Teutonic invaders. They claim to have taken heights and to have carried a woods in advance of their line near Moreuil, but the British say that they have driven back the enemy from positions they have occupied elsewhere in this sector.
  The French lines further south have stood firm against savage assaults, especially in the region of Montdidier, and eastward of that place, along a part of the line which was subjected to a terrific strain for two days late last week. In a number of sectors the French have surged forward and taken ground from the Germans and have established their line solidly against the Oise river. The expected allied counter-offensive has not yet come, but the Germans, who are reported to be entrenching along the French front, evidently expect it there.[7]

WITH STORM OF FIRE
Terrific Attack by 100,000 German Troops Was Repulsed.

Paris, April 4.—German troops numbering well over a hundred thousand delivered a terrific attack today against the French along a front of nearly nine miles from Grivenes to north of the Amiens-Roye road. They were met with a storm of fire from the French guns, and although the assaults were repeated time after time, they succeeded in gaining only a small section of ground.

The announcement by the war office tonight of this new offensive also says that by a powerful counter attack the French made progress at this point.

London, April 4.—Field Marshal Haig's report tonight from British headquarters in France says:

"After heavy artillery preparation the enemy launched a strong attack this morning on the whole front between the Somme and Avre rivers. On the right and center of the British lines the attacking German infantry were repulsed, but on the left the weight of the assault succeeded in pressing back our troops for a short distance in the neighborhood of Hamel on the south bank of the Somme. The fight is continuing in this area."

Washington, April 4.—Renewal of the German assaults against the British and French Lines in Picardy today indicated to military observers here that the Germans, having gathered strength during the lull of the past few days, might now be ready to launch their greatest effort. Some officers think the allied commanders realize that only the first phase of the gigantic battle has passed, and that this probably accounts for the fact that no extensive counter movement has been undertaken as yet.

It is pointed out that the previous record of the German high command argues against any possibility that it would be content with the minor strategic advantages already gained by their costly enterprise, or with the abandonment of its plans without making further attempts to force a part of the French and British armies.[8]

GREAT BATTLE CONTINUES
German Wedge Fails to Reach Object of Attack.

London, April 5.—The Germans who yesterday resumed their attempt to reach Amiens and to separate the Anglo-French armies and who are still fighting for those objectives, have, according to official reports, thus far failed to widen the salient which is necessary for their security. The Teutons have, however, made some slight advance on the direct road to Amiens.

Both the British and French official statements admit slight withdrawals southeast of the city of Amiens, but on both wings of the battlefront the entente troops have succeeded in repulsing all German attacks.

England is calmly watching the maps for the result of this latest offensive and every scrap of news about it is read eagerly.

"Our difficulties and those of the enemy are fairly obvious," says the Standard. "We are suffering from a very heavy blow dealt to General Gough's army. The enemy on his side finds that the salient created through that local success is too narrow for his purpose. A good many people no doubt experienced a certain disappointment that no great reaction on the part of the allies followed the exhaustion of the German effort. It should be remembered that the battle is only in its earliest stages and nothing would please the enemy commanders better than a premature employment of his reserves."

In the great battle to the south of the Somme the contending armies fought with various fortunes, the French giving some ground in a northerly sector of their battle area but closing the engagement with their line not only standing where it was along its southerly course, but even advancing to one or two places where the Germans had been violently thrown back.

How well the valiant Franco-British forces withstood the enemy onslaughts is shown by the fact that on a front of nine miles north of Montdidier the Germans used more than 100,000 men.[9]

CHARLIE AND NANCY'S WAR EFFORT

Cowboy artist Charlie Russell and his wife, Nancy, continued their support for the war effort. In early March, Nancy Russell contributed to the Great Falls Auxiliary to American Girls' Aid of New York for a local project to care for fifteen French and Belgian orphans or destitute children of France. Four large boxes of clothing were sent and money raised. By the fall of 1918, Nancy had continued support for this effort, which had led to eighteen children being cared for by the people of Great Falls. A member of the local community served each child as a "Godmother," and many of these women received letters directly from their "children" expressing gratitude for their care and assistance.

In addition, Nancy Russell was one of the active leaders for the United War Work campaign and served as chairman of the Women's Division of that big drive during the fall of 1918.[10]

Meanwhile, the Montana Stockgrowers Association invited Charlie Russell to man the "chuck wagon" at its annual convention in Great Falls on April 16 and 17. Charlie accepted the invitation and promised to decorate the chuck wagon with pictures of ponies and herds from the pioneer days. The local committee welcomed Charlie's participation as one of the strong features of the coming convention. Charlie served on the Entertainment Committee for the convention with Lee Ford, Victor Ario, W.K. Floweree and others. He assembled a special art exhibit for the Stockgrowers members to view in the Palm Room of the Rainbow Hotel.[11]

On April 16, the Russells subscribed $500, helping Great Falls raise more than $1 million in less than one hour for the Third Liberty Loan campaign.[12]

ARMY NURSES IN ACTION

With the massive buildup of American troops in France, which by April was approaching the arrival of 200,000 soldiers each month, came an acceleration in deployment of army base hospitals and nurses. About 200 Montana women are known to have served as army nurses during the Great War, with about 80 of them serving overseas.

Many more Montana women, perhaps another 150, served in other military jobs or with nongovernmental agencies overseas. Several Montana women joined Canadian and French forces before the United States entered the war, including three young Missoula women who served in the French Red Cross. They likely were the first Montanans to serve in World War I.

Three Missoula women—Bess Epperson and Ruth and Edith Greenough—were attending school in France when World War I began in July 1914. On August 30, the Germans conducted their first air raid on Paris, while ten days later, on September 9, the German invasion of France was stopped in the First Battle of the Marne as German troops were forced back to the north side of the Marne River, causing the German "Schlieffen Plan" to fail. That German war plan had been many years in development and called for the German invasion of France in a two-front war against France and Russia.

The three young ladies were in a private school in France when the war broke out. The conflict came so suddenly that they had no time to escape. With hundreds of other Americans stranded in the French capital, they became partners of the French as invasion came. The *Missoulian* of November 27, 1914, carried their story:

> *EXPERIENCES OF THREE AMERICAN RED CROSS VOLUNTEERS IN FRANCE*
> *The Misses Bess Epperson, Ruth and Edith Greenough returned to Missoula…from a trip abroad which was marked by thrilling experiences, narrow escapes and harrowing scenes. The three girls, all natives of Missoula, were in Paris on August 2, when mobilization of the French army was ordered and for five weeks they were actually within the war zone and served as Red Cross nurses in the French army. Their story of the trip is fascinating and substantiates the trite old saying that truth is stranger than fiction.*
>
> *Miss Epperson for four weeks was actively a Red Cross nurse in a hospital at Houlgate.* [Houlgate, a town in northwestern France, on the English Channel.] *To this haven wounded from the battle of Liege were brought by the trainload and in her division of the hospital 143 patients were quartered. Miss Epperson did all the work required of any nurse. She had trained for a time for the work before going into the hospital and hers was the*

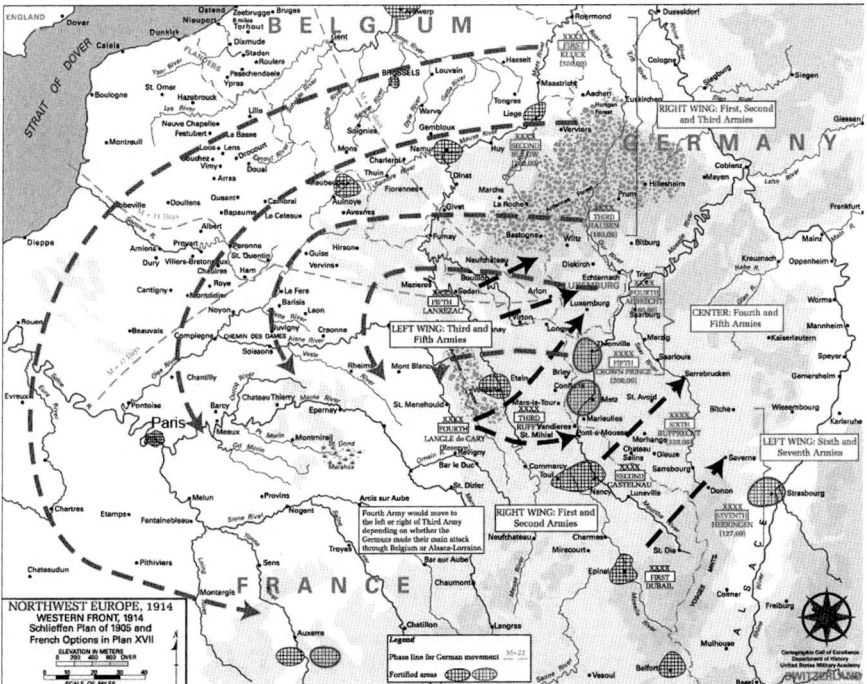

German Schlieffen Plan of Attack in 1914. *United States Military Academy.*

33

Ruth Greenough of Missoula,
French Red Cross Worker
in 1914. *From the* Missoulian,
September 10, 1922.

task of assisting the head nurse attending to the dressing of wounds. The suffering, sickness and horrible injuries seen by this young Missoula woman are seldom crowded into the lifetime of one person. The relieving of pain, the joy of serving humanity for love, the pleasure of finding missing sons of old and feeble parents has been Miss Epperson's privilege.

Ruth and Edith Greenough were actively enlisted in the Red Cross work, but, because of their years [twenty-two and nineteen, respectively], *they were not allowed to enter a hospital to active nursing. Their part in assisting the work was great however. These sisters made shirts for the men at the front; did scrubbing and other hard work about the hospitals.*

Miss Epperson and the Misses Greenough were in Paris just before the mobilization of the French Troops. They had intended going on a cruise in the North Sea. The declaration of war by France made this impossible, so, in order to get out of Paris, they decided to return to Houlgate, where they had been visiting previously.

…When the first carload of wounded soldiers arrived in Houlgate the entire populace of the town was at the station. The wounded heroes were showered with flowers, songs were sung in their honor and every possible tribute was paid.

The men were brought from the front in terrible condition. They were loaded—rather dumped—into cars and hauled to Houlgate like wood. Many of the men had been on the battlefield for hours and their clothing was blood-soaked and ghastly. The injuries, too, were terrible. Some of the soldiers had been shot three or four times…

Despite their hurts, every soldier who had been brought from the front was in a hurry to get well, so that he would be able to return to the battlefront. Such patriotism, such hatred for the foe and such longing to return to face the whistling bullets was a revelation to the tourists from Missoula.

Bess Epperson and sisters Ruth and Edith Greenough finally succeeded in securing berths on a ship departing Le Havre. They sailed from France September 19, ending their great adventure in wartime France.[13]

Let the Sun Shine…and the Letters Come

Chaplain William Pippy of Shelby went overseas on December 15, 1917, with the 163rd Infantry. While in France, Chaplain Pippy exchanged letters with Methodist minister William Wesley Van Orsdel, affectionately known in Montana as "Brother Van." Chaplain Pippy sent this letter to Brother Van in March 1918, reporting words of cheer about conditions and the "Boys of Montana":

> *Headquarters 163rd Inf., AEF.*
>
> *Dear Dr. Van: The United States mail brot me three letters today, and one of them from Brother Van. I assure you, my dear brother, that it was a great pleasure for me to read your interesting letter. Nothing clears the atmosphere for a soldier like a letter from home. A boy expressed it correctly a few minutes ago when he said: "Gee! How the sun shines in France when the letters come!" It is a fact, my dear brother—and I wish all the folks at home could realize it—letters from home greatly change the morale of our troops. One cheerful letter is equal to the strength of twenty fighting men.*
>
> *How are we getting along? Why, fine! How is the spirit of our boys and the morale of our troops? One hundred per cent! Germany is beginning to feel the sands shifting. Her vision of world conquest will never be able to lift itself again.*
>
> *When I write to you I feel as if it is my report—a quarterly report, if you please! Our army services are a great success. Even in the midst of war, and where the background has its horrors, there is no picture so sublime, so pleasing to heaven or earth…as an army service out in the open. As one stands in the midst of a throng of soldiers on Sunday morning, with God's blue dome above and around, everything to remind him of God's greatness, the glory of it all gets in his soul.*
>
> *…Last Sunday, March 10, 1918, I spoke to a large crowd of soldiers and officers. My theme was taken from the account of Moses and the burning bush. What a service we had! One of our generals came up to me after the service and said: "Chaplain, if we all caught the intensity of your spirit we would do wonders." He added then the finest statement that ever a soldier made, when he said: "The soldier or officer who goes up to the frontline trenches without the consciousness of God's mighty presence and of His promised help is not giving to his country the full value of his enlistment." I said: "General, that's the finest statement I ever heard." The condition changed it into gold!*

...Tell the fathers and mothers for me, as you gather with them around their hearths, and as you talk of the boys over there, that they are all faithful in the cause. And tell fathers and mothers, wives and sweethearts, that we will never suffer from fear of death or hardship; that our thot is not for ourselves, not for our comfort. We are thinking of them, and of the long days they are bravely enduring the pain of our absence. Tell the mother who almost thot her son's love lost that there is a boy over here and a mother at home whose love can never be separated.

Beloved Methodist missionary William Wesley Van Orsdel, "Brother Van." *Author's collection.*

Ah, Brother Van, our boys are great boys! Our boys are clean boys! Every one is fighting for home. And every boy wants to tell the same story David must have told his parents when he slew the giant—a story of duty, of praise for the other, a story of manliness and cleanness.

Give my best regards to all the friends in grand old Montana, and may He who keeps us in good cheer keep your hearts also in His great love.[14]

On April 10, the *River Press* editorialized about German progress during the Spring Offensive designed to force British forces back to channel ports and out of the war:

GERMANY WILL NOT WIN
In a forecast of the result of the terrific German assault upon the British and French positions on the western front, a writer in the Spokesman-Review advises American citizens to remember that a battle may be a matter of mere days, but that a campaign—the factor which makes military operations succeed or fail—may continue for months. Remember also the past of the western war.

Germany has come a bit closer to Paris in 1918, but between them now is a gap of 57 miles whereas in 1914 the distance was only 15 miles. Then the French and British were outnumbered, but at the very moment when the Germans seemed about to win they were driven back.

In 1915 Germany surprised the Canadian army at Ypres with the terror of murderous gases, and yet was balked at Calais by the heroism of its foe.

In 1916 Germany girded itself for the tremendous effort at Verdun, and France said: "They shall not pass." At first Germany won signal successes, but at the end of five months it still was miles away from its goal and afterwards was hurled helplessly back by the valor of France.

In 1917 Germany used 131 divisions against England at Arras, Lens, Messines and Ypres and yet was defeated by fewer than half that number of English divisions. Last year, too, it looked for a time as if Germany and Austria would overwhelm Italy, but this year Austria-Hungary is held by Italy.

Germany has defeated the feeble or the betrayed. It has not yet overthrown the strong and the true.

Germany never proves so effective in the west as its plans and preparations should make it. In every fight against the French and the British it has failed to realize its objects of importance. Temporary successes leave its strategic positions only slightly bettered. It has always been brought to a dead stand by the sanguinary losses it has suffered. The great contests on French and Belgian ground have always left Germany remote from its goal and weaker than before.[15]

One week later, the Germans launched another assault against the British, Operation Georgette. Field Marshal von Hindenburg swung his heaviest legions and mightiest guns far to the north on the Picardy battlefield, driving attack after attack against the British lines between Arras and Ypres. Charging across the level country behind a tempest of high-explosive and gas shells, the Germans succeeded by heavy fighting in penetrating the defenses at points over a front of nearly thirty miles to a depth of about six miles just to the south of Ypres. In the face of this latest German assault, Field Marshal Sir Douglas Haig, commander of the British Expeditionary Forces, ordered his troops to stand firm:

HAIG ORDERS STAND
Field Marshal Douglas Haig, in a special order of the day addressed to "all ranks of the British army in France and Flanders," says: "Three weeks ago today the enemy began his terrific attacks against us on a 60-mile front. His objects are to separate us from the French, to take the channel ports, and to destroy the British army.

"In spite of throwing already 100 divisions into the battle and enduring the most reckless sacrifice of human life, he has yet made little progress toward his goals.

"We owe this to the determined fighting and self-sacrifice of our troops. Words fail me to express the admiration which I feel for the splendid resistance offered by all ranks of our army under the most trying circumstances.

"Many amongst us now are tired. To those I would say that victory will belong to the side which holds out the longest. The French army is moving rapidly and in great force to our support. There is no other escape open to us but to fight it out."[16]

THIRD LIBERTY LOAN CAMPAIGN

The United States fought the Great War on the backs of American taxpayers and patriotic investment in Liberty Loan bonds. The billions raised paid not only for vital American warfighting but also for extensive loans to cash-strapped Allied nations. The Allies received large-scale loans that in turn were spent on the purchase of American food and munitions.

Third Liberty Loan poster emphasizing the importance of the Boy Scouts. *Library of Congress.*

The Third Liberty Loan, enacted in April 1918, allowed the government to issue $9 billion worth of war bonds at a rate of 4.5 percent interest for up to ten years. In the first Liberty bond drive in April 1917, Montana was asked to raise $6,768,000, and the Treasure State oversubscribed with $15 million. On the second issue in October 1917, Montana was allotted $15 million and raised $21 million. For this third drive, Montana was asked to raise $9 million, with the big drive to commence in mid-April. Liberty Loan committees in every county visited every resident to bring pressure to buy bonds.[17]

The *River Press* of April 10 lent its support for the drive with the words:

> From hundreds of Montana homes, in answer to the call of their country and in obedience to the law of their country, American boys have gone and today are fighting side by side with hundreds of thousands of other American boys, confronting danger and death.

The duty of us who remain at home in safety, to afford the means to make these boys powerful and victorious, is a most imperative one. Buy Liberty Bonds.[18]

SPRING INFLUENZA TAPERS OFF

The winter and spring of 1917–18 saw the first wave of an influenza pandemic, commonly called "Spanish flu." It struck German troops during 1917 and raged most intensively throughout Europe in several waves in the late spring of 1918. An even more deadly virus would hit both Europe and the United States in the early fall of 1918. This highly infectious flu strain turned quickly to pneumonia, with death often resulting. Yanks called it the "Three-Day Fever."

At least twenty deaths occurred from pneumonia among Montana servicemen in early 1918, including the following men:

- Private Charles Besty of Opheim, Company F, 25th Engineers, March 14
- Private Rudolph Brandmihl of Calumet, Montana, 163rd Infantry, January 13
- Private Ole Dahlen of Roundup, Company F, 362nd Infantry, January 27
- Private Thea M. Dice of Flat Willow Creek, Supply Company, 163rd Infantry, December 25, 1917
- Private Perry Dodd of Polson, 20th Engineer Regiment (Forestry), March 25
- Corporal Francis K. Dugan of Great Falls, Aviation Supply Depot, January 12
- Private John F. Flannery of Great Falls, Day Bombardment 166th Aero Squadron, March 14
- Private Albert V. Gordon of Livingston, Company B, 20th Engineers, January 10
- Sergeant Harrell H. Hibbard of Helena, Aviation Section, USMC, March 17
- Fireman 2nd Class William P. Hill of Helena, U.S. Navy, USS *New Jersey*, March 9
- Private Arthur C. Kannenberg of Wibaux, Company K, 362nd Infantry, March 19

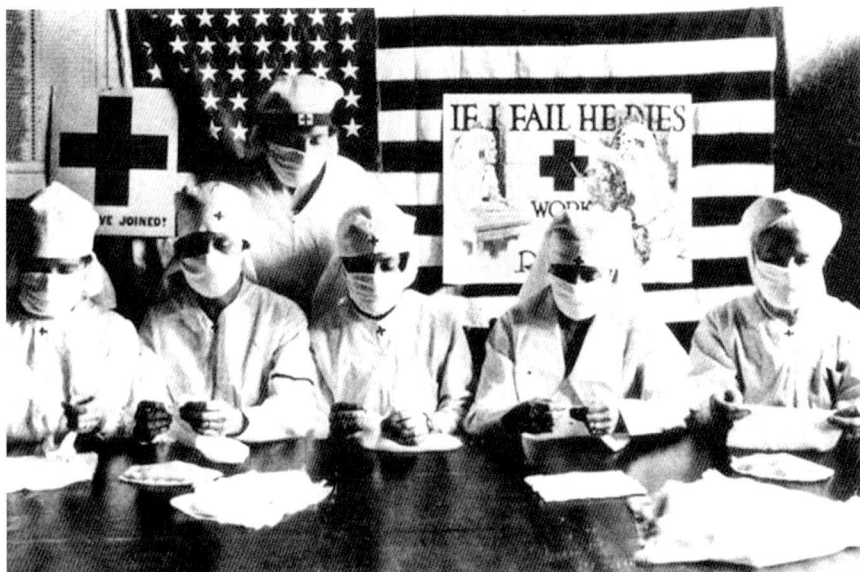

"If I Fail He Dies." Nurses treating World War I soldiers during Spanish flu pandemic in 1918–19. *Author's collection.*

- Private Albert O. Lohe of Great Falls, 66th Aero Squadron, March 13
- Private Guy Lovell of Ronan, Company B, 163rd Infantry, January 7
- Sergeant Jesse E. McDole of Chouteau County, 348th Field Artillery, March 19
- Boarswain Mate 1st Class Eugene W. McKenna of Great Falls, U.S. Navy, USS *Jason*, Januay 1
- Private Frederick W. Miller of Sweet Grass, Toole County, Company B, 362nd Infantry, February 16, 1918
- Private Montie M. Ray of Butte, Medical Department, January 5
- Private Robert Reed of Windham, Mare Island Marine Training Station, February 22
- Private William J. Simpson of Culbertson, Field Signal Corps Training Camp, February 19
- Private John Sisson Slater of Craig, Field Signal Corps, March 16[19]

THE FIGHTING MARINES

In a short article titled "Marines Suffer Casualties," the *River Press* of May 1 highlighted a major development among the AEF. The U.S. Marine Corps was moving at last into positions on the front lines:

> *Washington, April 25.—Marines fighting in France have had a total of 274 casualties, Marine Corps headquarters announced today. The casualties were divided as follows: Officers wounded, 4; enlisted men killed, 34; enlisted men wounded, 236. One company lost 21 men killed and 140 wounded out of a total of 260 men. This was the first official announcement that the Marines are taking an active part in the fighting. The marines were among the first soldiers to go to France but it had been understood they were being used for police purposes back of the fighting line.*[20]

The 5th Marine Regiment landed in France with the 1st Division, the first American troops in June 1917, while the 6th Marine Regiment and the 6th Marine Machine Gun Battalion did not arrive until February 1918. These units formed the 4th Marine Brigade now up to full strength and assigned to the 2nd Infantry Division, the Indianhead Division.

During its first nine months in France, the 5th Marine impatiently awaited combat duty, serving as police, stevedores and other noncombat duties, as well as undergoing months of training. With the arrival of the 6th Marine and formation of the 4th Brigade, the men finally began to move into the trenches. The 4th Brigade entered the front lines on the Verdun front in the Toulon sector during the night of March 16–17, just before the Germans launched their massive Spring Offensive in Flanders and western France. The 4th Brigade remained in the Verdun area until May 14, when it was suddenly shifted to the Château-Thierry sector, but that action will remain for a later day.

Among early casualties suffered by the Marines in the relatively quiet Verdun front was Morris Clark Arnold of Big Sandy, born in New York. After training, Private Arnold deployed to France with the 6th Marine Brigade and was assigned to 74 Company. On April 13, Private Arnold was gassed and forced to enter a base hospital, where he remained for several months before returning to 74 Company in September in time for the heavy fighting that followed.[21]

Private Arnold was one of three Arnold brothers serving in France. The sons of Mr. and Mrs. E.C. Arnold of Big Sandy had all served with the

"If You Want to Fight! Join the Marines." Recruiting poster from World War I. *Library of Congress.*

2nd Montana Infantry on the Mexican border during 1916. Roy Arnold, assigned to Company B, 163rd Infantry, was promoted to corporal and then sergeant. Sergeant Arnold accepted a commission as second lieutenant on July 8, 1918, completed officer training as the youngest member of his class and was assigned to the 805th Pioneer Infantry (Colored).

Kenneth D. Arnold was drafted and departed in October for Camp Lewis with the Third Contingent from Chouteau County. Corporal Arnold served in Company A, 2nd Battalion, Field Signal Corps, 1st Infantry Division.[22]

The German Spring Offensive sparked a flood of enlistments throughout Montana. The *River Press* reported this patriotic response in Great Falls in mid-April:

> *Great Falls, April 17.—Following the launching of the present German drive against the allied line in France recruiting has shown great activity in this city and at the three regular United States recruiting offices in this city 70 men have enlisted within the past 10 days. Of this number 23 went into the army, 38 into the navy and nine joined the marines. The records of the army recruiting office show that since January 1 that office has enlisted 203 men. These are not all Great Falls men, but they come from all parts of northern Montana. In addition to these, the British-Canadian recruiting office has secured many men, its results, however, not being given out.*[23]

REMARKABLE HORACE BIVINS

On April 12, a most remarkable fifty-one-year-old left his small farm at Billings and marched off to the Great War. Horace Waymon Bivins, a famed Buffalo Soldier, was born the youngest of thirteen children in a free black family on Virginia's Eastern Shore on May 8, 1866, just after the Civil War. In 1887, he left the family farm and school, joined the U.S. Army and was assigned to Troop E, 10th U.S. Cavalry (Colored). With his regiment, Bivins took part in the campaign against Geronimo during the final days of the Apache wars in the Southwest. A crack marksman, Bivins won eight medals and badges awarded by the War Department in shooting competitions from 1892 to 1894 while serving at Fort Keogh at Miles City. His marksmanship led Buffalo Bill Cody to attempt to recruit him to travel with his show, but Bivins declined, preferring military life.

In 1898, Corporal Bivins went to war in Cuba with the 10th Cavalry. During the Battle of Santiago on July 1, 1898, Bivins single-handedly operated a three-man Hotchkiss mountain gun with great effect, even after suffering a head wound as his fellow soldiers were pinned down under fire. Commended for his bravery, Bivins became a hero of the Spanish-American War for his courage and effectiveness under fire. In 1899, he wrote of his

Cuban experiences and coauthored the book *Under Fire with the Tenth Cavalry*, one of the most popular accounts of the Spanish-American War.

Now a sergeant, Bivins served six months during the Philippines insurrection in 1901. He left the Philippines and was stationed at a series of military posts in Montana, California, Wyoming, New York and Vermont. He retired from the U.S. Army on July 19, 1913, and settled down to a quiet life of truck gardening in the Billings area.

In 1917, Bivins proposed organizing a unit of volunteers in Virginia for the U.S. Army as it prepared to embark for France to fight in World War I. The army turned down his proposal but offered to commission him as a captain. He accepted, was commissioned at Newport News, Virginia, and assigned to the 413th

Master Sergeant Horace W. Bivins, a Buffalo Soldier in the Great War. *Author's collection.*

Reserve Labor Battalion (Colored) at Camp Dix, where he served until discharged on August 9, 1919.

After his retirement, Captain Horace Bivins returned to Billings and remained there for many years until 1950, when he traveled back to his home in Virginia and married the daughter of a boyhood school friend. Captain Bivins said at that time, "During my entire time in the Army I never quarreled with an officer, an enlisted man or a civilian. I don't know the taste of alcohol and I have never smoked. I have found much happiness." Captain Bivins passed away on December 4, 1960, at age ninety-four and rests at Baltimore National Cemetery.[24]

DISSIDENT VOICES

In April, the *River Press* reported two incidents being prosecuted under Montana's harsh new anti-sedition law passed by the legislature in extraordinary session in February 1918:

Red Lodge, April 16.—Ben Kahn, a salesman for a California wine house, was found guilty in the district court today of violation of the anti-sedition law. Kahn's is the first conviction under the recently enacted Measure. Kahn was convicted of ridiculing the efforts of the food administration and impeding the carrying out of its regulations. Testimony was also brought to show that he had attempted to justify the sinking of the Lusitania *and had declared that this is a rich man's war.* [On trial a month later, a jury found Kahn guilty, and the judge sentenced him to seven and a half to twenty years of hard labor. Ben Kahn served thirty-four months.][25]

Billings, April 13.—Herman Bausch, wealthy farmer residing near here, positively refused to buy Liberty bonds when interviewed by a committee today, nor would he aid the Red Cross, with the result that he was requested to appear before the third degree committee tonight for an examination. His replies were very evasive, although admitting that he had accumulated a fortune of $20,000 since his arrival from Germany. For a time it appeared as if he might be ridden around town on a rail, but calmer judgment prevailed, and he was taken to jail. He will be prosecuted under the sedition act, it being alleged he said he was against America in the war. [After a hasty trial, the judge sentenced Bauch to four to eight years in prison.][26]

Winter Wheat

The drought of 1917 in Montana could not have come at a worse time. With U.S. entry into the Great War, America's commitment to feed the Allied nations greatly increased demand for food, and to do that the United States needed to grow more wheat and reduce domestic consumption. Montana's farmers planted winter wheat in the fall of 1917 at about the same rate as in 1916, held back by high seed prices and some labor shortages. Montana's production would depend on winter conditions and whether the state would face a second year of drought.

Unfortunately, both winter wheat damage and a second dry year became major factors. The *River Press* of May 1 reported considerable winter kill in many areas as a result of chinook winds early in January, followed by a freeze, injuring the winter wheat crop. The spring showed signs of a second serious drought year throughout most of the state.[27]

Chapter 2

MAY 1918

The Red Baron; "Hello Girls"; Cantigny Sector

A Tale of Wanton Cruelty

The stories of the first two Americans captured on February 8, 1918—Montanans Privates Christian A. Sorensen and Edward "Bob" M. Roberts, both 16th Infantry—were told in *World War I Montana: The Treasure State Prepares*. Roberts had been thrice wounded and passed out in no-man's-land in the Toul Sector, only to wake up a captive of the Germans. Taken to a hospital, Private Roberts was subjected to unneeded eye surgery and blinded by the surgeon. The extraordinary experiences of Private Bob Roberts continued, as his captivity was described by World War I veteran Al Schak in the *Missoulian* of April 16, 1922:

> *Having been captured on the night of February 8 and operated upon the next night, [Roberts] was unable to leave the Guerney hospital until the following May 3. He was then put aboard a train bound for Tiben, a prison camp in the interior of Germany. When he left Guerney he was given an old undershirt, a pair of trousers that had been taken from an Englishman who had died in the prison hospital. Just before being captured he had been completely outfitted in new clothes.*
>
> *…At Tiben he was fed on black bread and coffee. The bread was made of potato peelings and sawdust, and the coffee of appleseeds and acorns mixed and ground. After three days spent in the Tiben camp, he was sent*

to Darmstadt, a larger prison camp. From the station to the camp was a stretch of seven kilometers, over which the prisoners were compelled to walk. Roberts could not stand the strain and fainted after waddling along for about one kilometer. He was picked up and sent to the prison hospital at Darmstadt camp. Here he shared food given him by a young Scot named Steve Brody, who received packages from the British Red Cross.

"Boy! Real coffee and spuds!" said Roberts, as he recalled the "feeds."

…Gaining a little strength at Darmstadt, Roberts was sent to Munster, a camp near the Holland border. The place was terribly insanitary. In fact, it was filthy and contained lice by the million. Roberts had not had a bath or shave in all the time he was a prisoner, and he was suffering from the pain caused by boils. There were 13 of them on his face and neck, and nothing was done to relieve his suffering. One of the boils on his neck became a carbuncle.

Sometime in August he was sent to a camp in Russia. Conditions at this place were far worse than at Tiben. There was not even a shed for the prisoners, who were inadequately sheltered in pits covered with tin sheets. Realizing that he was starving to death, Roberts wrote a letter, which he hoped would reach his mother, on August 25, telling her that he was starved, and that he was too weak to raise his head. On the following morning at 4 o'clock 12 Russians carried him to the railway station, and he was placed aboard a train which carried him to Rastatt, a prison camp where 2,000 American prisoners were held. Roberts was in a terrible condition. Weak, disheartened, lousy, suffering from boils and carbuncles, after existing in filth without a shave or bath for almost a year, he was ready to give up. But the American Red Cross "straightened him out." He was given clean new clothes, he was shaved and bathed, and a real dinner. His boils were treated, and the first night at Rastatt he slept in a good bed, and he wasn't hungry. He would have given anything he had for one of those luxuries a few days before.

Knowing that he was to be transferred to Switzerland soon, a number of high

Corporal Edward M. Roberts's prisoner of war card. *Prisoners of the First World War International Committee of the Red Cross Historical Archives.*

German officers visited him at Rastatt and begged him to refrain from saying a word of the treatment he had received while a prisoner, because "Germany wants to be a sister to your nation."

"It is very nice for us Americans to sympathize with Germany at the present time," said Roberts at this point in his narrative, "but the trouble with us Americans is that we forget too quickly."

Remarkable Bob Roberts lost his sight, but he never lost his fighting spirit. He was freed at war's end.[28]

THE RED BARON

When war began in 1914, the Wright brothers had completed the world's first powered flight just one decade earlier. During the war, remarkable advances were made in both the sophistication of aircraft and in their employment in warfare.

The first aircraft used in World War I were extremely basic, with open cockpits, no armaments and no navigational aids. Early in the war, aircraft became valuable "eyes in the sky" to monitor movements and activities of the armies of both the Allies and the Central Powers. Technology allowed rapid advances as airframes became more maneuverable and engines more powerful, and both machine guns and bomb racks were added. Missions expanded from aerial observation to scouting, air-to-air combat, aerial reconnaissance, artillery-spotting and bombing. The Germans developed long-range bombing attacks on London by Zeppelin balloons and Gotha bombers. Pilots were needed in large numbers to fill greatly increased aircraft squadrons and high-attrition casualties. The romantic lure of flight and a desire to avoid life in the trenches meant no shortage of volunteers as pilots or observers.

By the time the United States entered the war in 1917, the British Royal Flying Corps and the French *Armée de l'Air* (literally "Army of the Air") had kept pace with German aviation developments. The famed German fighter pilot Manfred Albrecht Freiherr von Richthofen, known as the "Red Baron," was the "ace of aces" in the war, being officially credited with eighty combat victories. Richthofen became one of the first pilots in fighter squadron *Jagdstaffel 2* in 1916 and quickly distinguished himself in aerial combat. During 1917, he became leader of the fighter

The "Red Baron," Manfred von Richthofen, in the cockpit with his Jagdstaffel 11 Squadron. *Bundesarchiv, Bild 183-2004-0430-501/CC-BY-SA 3.0.*

wing unit *Jagdgeschwader 1*, known as "The Flying Circus," with bright-colored aircraft moving like a traveling circus. By 1918, Richthofen had assumed legendary status, was regarded as a national hero in Germany and earned respect from Allies. The Red Baron was shot down and killed near Vaux-sur-Somme on April 21, 1918, as reported in the *Great Falls Tribune* of April 23:

> *LEADING GERMAN AVIATOR KILLED*
> *Winner of Eighty Victories Finally Meets End to Which He Had Consigned Many*
>
> *London, April 22.—Captain Baron von Richthofen, the famous German aviator, has been killed, Reuter's correspondent at British headquarters reports. The captain was brought down in the Somme valley on April 21. His body was recovered and will be buried today with military honors.*
>
> *Since Captain Boelke was shot down in October, 1916, Captain von Richthofen has been the most prominent and successful German aviator.*

On April 8 the German war office announced that he had achieved his 78th aerial victory...

Captain von Richthofen first came into prominence as leader of the "Flying Circus," a squadron of German aviators which fought in a peculiar circular formation following each other around so that in case one was attacked the next flyer could sweep the antagonist from the rear. Recently Emperor William conferred upon him the order of the Red Eagle.

An official statement reporting aerial operations issued yesterday at Berlin said:

"Baron Richthofen at the head of his trusty chasing squadron on Saturday gained his seventy-ninth and eightieth victories."[29]

AMERICAN AVIATION

The United States entered the Great War far behind in many essential needs of modern warfare, not least in aviation. In April 1918, one year after U.S. entry, the fledgling Aviation Section, buried under the Army Signal Corps, was struggling with problems in aircraft production. Urgently, the War Department turned to Montanan John D. Ryan to take over aircraft production, as reported by the *River Press* of May 1:

WILL SPEED UP AIRCRAFT

Washington, April 24.—Direction of the army's great aircraft production program has been placed in the hands of a civilian, John D. Ryan, copper magnate, railroad man and financier.

Secretary [of War] Baker announced the step tonight, disclosing at the same time a reorganization of the signal corps under which the aviation section virtually is divorced from the corps proper, heretofore supreme on all questions. With actual production turned over to a civilian division headed by Mr. Ryan, Brigadier General William L. Kenly is made chief of a new division of military aeronautics, to control training of aviators and military use of aircraft.

Major General Squier, chief signal officer, will confine his activities in the future to the signal branch. Howard Coffin, chairman of the aircraft board, retires in favor of Mr. Ryan, but the aircraft board itself, created by congress, will continue as an advisory body.

Throughout all the agitation over delays and mistakes in getting quantity production of aircraft underway, all critics have agreed that great fault lay in the absence of concentrated control. The power of Mr. Coffin and his board was subject to the signal corps.

…The appointment of John D. Ryan to be head of the aircraft production caused much favorable comment in governmental and congressional circles today. Speaking of the naming of Mr. Ryan for this important position Senator [Thomas] Walsh said:

"I am more than pleased that a citizen of Montana should be selected and commandeered to put ginger into the all-important airplane production, which has unfortunately lagged so much up to the present time.

"Mr. Ryan's appointment gives a comforting assurance to the country, as is evidenced by the complimentary comment in the senat today. It is to be expected that vigor and efficiency will characterize the aircraft work hereafter." [30]

One month later, on May 24, President Wilson signed two executive orders moving aviation from under the Signal Corps and creating a separate and independent Army Air Service, the forerunner of today's U.S. Air Force. In France, the air service of the AEF, under command of General Pershing, conducted the combat operations in the field, eventually with forty-five squadrons.

SPRUCE PRODUCTION DIVISION

Critical to the buildup of American aviation was organization of a new Spruce Production Division, under the Army Signal Corps Aviation Section headquartered at Portland, Oregon, and commanded by Colonel Brice P. Disque. Its mission was to produce high-quality Sitka spruce timber and other wood products essential for production of aircraft. The Spruce Division provided a remarkable 150 million board feet of spruce in just fifteen months.

Northwest spruce had been in demand by France and Great Britain from the beginning of the war. After all, Sitka spruce was ideal for aircraft production with its lightness, strength and resiliency, with tough, long fibers that resisted splintering when struck by bullets. The growing strength of the radical International Workers of the World (the IWW, or "Wobblies") presented a tough labor environment as the United States entered the war. In response, by the fall of 1917 the army had organized the Spruce Division with twenty-nine thousand soldiers, including hundreds of Montanans, many of them experienced loggers and millworkers above military draft age. Colonel Disque organized a new union, the Loyal Legion of Loggers and Lumbermen, based on patriotism and labor-management cooperation. The division, with dozens of squadrons, quickly established about sixty military logging camps, privately owned but under direction of the army.[31]

Among the many Montanans volunteering or drafted into the Spruce Division was lawyer Leslie B. Sulgrove of Butte. After training at Vancouver, Washington, Private Sulgrove was assigned to the 126th Spruce Squadron. For about six months, Private Sulgrove adjusted to his drastically changed environment and shared his experiences at Camp F. Joyce, Piedmont, Washington:

> *Lawyer's Life as Lumberjack*
> *Leslie B. Sulgrove Writes of Service in Phase of War Work of Which Little Has Been Told; Big Tasks Done.*
> *Transition from the grateful comforts of office work from the privilege of being warm…and dry…to the crude labor and surroundings of a logging camp or exploiting a shovel on a railroad dump, are circumstances which have taken place in the life of Leslie B. Sulgrove, formerly an attorney* [in Butte].
> *Mr. Sulgrove as an active member of the Butte Bar association, enjoying a lucrative practice when he entered the service and was highly esteemed in business and professional circles…*
>
> *Piedmont, Wash., Camp F, Nov. 5, 1918.—Mr. James H. Rowe, chairman local board. Butte, Mont.—*
> *Dear Mr. Rowe; For some time I have been intending to express to you my thanks with the thanks of the other Butte boys with whom I have come in contact recently in various camps for your kindness in giving us the news of home through the medium of the Butte Miner. I need hardly assure you how much this thoughtfulness has been appreciated, nor how eager the boys have been to receive the paper.*
> *…I am now more or less permanently located, my address being 126 Spruce Squadron, Camp F. Joyce, Wash., and of course I am anxious to hear from home as often as possible and hope the paper will come every day.*
> *This camp is located upon Lake Crescent, whose beauty you are familiar with. This in itself is compensation for many things.*

A section of the world's largest spruce plant, Vancouver Barracks, Washington, 1918. *Photo by Edward F. Marcell, Library of Congress.*

When the war has gone into history and attention is directed from events in Europe to how the glorious victory was accomplished our country will accord no little credit to the untiring efforts of the boys in the rear rank who far from the glamor of battlefields and the eyes of the world—and deprived of the privilege of offering their lives for their country—cheerfully and soldierly set about to accomplish the vital task of producing the spruce for airplanes to carry on the fight. Appreciating as most of us do that consciousness of having performed our duty where and when asked to do so will be our greatest reward, it is really remarkable what has been accomplished.

As one of the main tasks, for example, this railroad, 40 miles through the heart of the Olympias—an estimated 18-months' job—has been practically completed in less than five months, and the big logs started on their way to the largest mill in the world at Port Angeles, now nearly completed during the same time, all of which has been made possible by the conscientious efforts and patriotism of the boys in khaki, most of whom had absolutely no knowledge or experience in that kind of work prior to their induction into the service.

I know a high school principal who has developed into an expert spiker, a well-known automobile race driver who has been spending his time in the service driving a gang of peeve artists, a most cheerful dandy dancer who paid an income tax on $40,000, and my immediate superior is a man who made a fortune in private life in the wholesale packing business and whose ability as an executive is now being utilized in organizing logging and railroad camps.

And so it goes, each man sinking his own private ambitions and desires in the common cause...

And we all live in hope that we will be chosen in the first S.P.D. regiment and introduced to overseas service by the 1ˢᵗ of December.

Very sincerely,
LESLIE B. SULGROVE [32]

PERSHING'S "HELLO" GIRLS TO THE RESCUE

From his arrival in France in June 1917, General John J. Pershing foresaw a critical need to improve telephone communications—the French telephone system was proving woefully inadequate. By early 1918, General Pershing was ready to act by organizing Women Telephone Operators under the U.S. Signal Corps, and young Montana women were ready to serve:

MONTANA LASSIE ONE OF 150 VOLUNTEER HELLO GIRLS WHO WILL BRAVE SHELL FIRE
Some weeks ago, General Pershing issued a call for 150 young American women who could speak, read and write French and English with equal facility to go to France as "Switchboard Soldiers," as he phrased it. There was a rush of applications from girls from every state, and when the government had carefully investigated the applications, one Montana girl found that she had been honored by being selected, and that she had been chosen, too, in spite of the fact that she had never engaged in telephone exchange work. She did, however, possess all the other requirements that the government demanded in successful candidates. The young woman in question is Miss Lena Roy of Bozeman.

When she received her appointment, Miss Roy was employed at the mercantile establishment of Willson & Co. in Bozeman. Her application was sent in through Manager Connelly, of the Bozeman Telephone Company, and with the acceptance of the offer of her services came instructions to report at once at the Helena branch of the Mountain States Telephone Company for intensive training. Her training there is nearly completed, and from Helena Miss Roy will go to New York to secure instructions before taking passage to the scene of the great war.

Miss Roy is most enthusiastic about her chance to take her part in the great adventure of war. "You know, I am going to wear a uniform," she said, "and while the work is going to be hard, just think of the thrills we switchboard soldiers are going to have in active service.

Applied Patriotism

Woman has made herself indispensable to the Nation's war activities. This is being demonstrated daily in many splendid ways. The telephone operator takes her place in the front ranks of our "national army" of women.

Back of the scenes, invisible, her war work is to make telephone communication possible. Through her the Chief of Staff in Washington speaks to the Cantonment Commandant in a far-off state. The touch of her fingers forges a chain of conversation from Shipping Board to shipyard, Quartermaster General to supply depot, merchant to manufacturer, city to country, office to home.

Without her this increasing complexity of military, business and civil life could not be kept smoothly working. Hers is patriotism applied. She is performing her part with enthusiasm and fidelity.

The increasing pressure of war work continually calls for more and more telephone operators, and young women in every community are answering the summons—cheerfully and thoughtfully shouldering the responsibilities of the telephone service upon which the Nation depends. Each one who answers the call helps speed up the winning of the war.

AMERICAN TELEPHONE AND TELEGRAPH COMPANY
AND ASSOCIATED COMPANIES

One Policy   One System   Universal Service

Left: Lena Roy, of Bozeman, who was selected out of thousands of applicants to go to France as a "Hello Girl," behind the lines, where coolness in the face of danger was necessary at all times. *From the* Hardin Tribune, *May 10, 1918.*

Right: Patriotic ad for telephone operator "Hello Girls." *From the* Nonpartisan Leader *(Fargo, ND), December 23, 1918.*

"Our uniforms will be approved by the war college and must be worn at all times. The different ranks are distinguished by the different insignia on the white brassard worn on the left arm. Operators will wear a black transmitter design, supervisors a gilt laurel wreath beneath the transmitter, and chief operators the two symbols mentioned, surmounted by the gilt lightning bolts used as insignia by the signal corps. The pay is $60 per month for operators; $72 for supervisors and $125 for chief operators, in addition to which allowances will be made for rations and quarters when these things are not provided by the army.

"Of course we girls who are going understand that this is not intended for a 'joy ride,' and that social opportunities are not included in the program. General Pershing told us in a communication sent out by the war department that this is to be a task of a nature and size that would appeal only to brave

and patriotic women, and I am going to try to be brave. I am sure I am patriotic. When we applied we were told that the signal corps wanted only level-headed women who were resourceful, able to exercise good judgment in emergencies and even endure hardships if necessary. I only hope that I shall live up to all these requirements."[33]

ORISSA TORPEDOED AND SUNK

On May 1, the *River Press* reported the sinking of another transport under the headline "American Boat Torpedoed":

London, April 29.—A party of 57 American army Young Men's Christian Association workers, under Arthur E. Hungerford, arrived in London last night. The ship on which they sailed was torpedoed yesterday morning and sunk in twelve minutes. All the passengers and all but three of the crew were saved. The passengers were picked up in lifeboats and landed at a British port. The Americans are safe and well. The vessel was struck amidships while in a large convoy under the protection of destroyers. It was proceeding at about ten knots in bright moonlight when struck. There was an immediate heavy list and three minutes later the boilers blew up, extinguishing the lights all over the ship.

The British ship *Orissa* was torpedoed and sunk early Sunday morning, April 28, en route London. Onboard were about 250 passengers, including 57 YMCA workers. At that time, the army was recruiting and sending YMCA recreational directors to France. These were men who were over draft age who had experience in recreational games—men who had taken an interest in athletics and offered to work with American soldiers overseas. Among the Montana YMCA recruits serving in France were Harry Chase, Montana and Boise, Idaho; Jack Evans, Miles City; Edwin Melvin, Red Lodge; and Charles H. Hammond, Sidney. The *Anaconda Standard* initially reported that Chase and Evans were among the YMCA men rescued from the *Orissa*, although their presence on that ship was never confirmed.[34]

ON THE FRONT LINE: CANTIGNY SECTOR

On April 25, the AEF 1st Division, 1st Brigade, 16th and 18th Regiments, took over the Cantigny sector three miles west of Montdidier, relieving French colonial troops and becoming a part of the French First Army. This sector extended from Mesnil–St. Georges to north of Cantigny, a key position for planned future Allied offensive action. The defensive positions occupied by the "Big Red One" were not elaborately constructed trenches but merely a series of shell holes and shallow "fox holes" dug in the open wheat fields. There was no complete barrier of barbed wire to protect the lines, and there were no communicating trenches. The regiments of the 1st Division, including the 16th Infantry, with support of combat Engineers and Field Signal troops, immediately began reinforcing the frontline trenches. Work was practically completed in one night with very few casualties, although the soldiers were subjected to heavy artillery shellfire. During May, the Germans fired an average of 3,400 artillery high-explosive and gas shells per day into American lines, all day, every day in this sector.

CARL A. SIPHER

First Great Falls boy officially to be reported killed by Hun bullet when fighting with American forces in France.

Private Carl A. Sipher, Company D, 16th Infantry, killed in action in the Cantigny Sector. *From the* Great Falls Tribune, *May 30, 1918.*

Towns where the different regimental headquarters were established were heavily bombarded, while roads leading to them often were under interdiction fire. On the night of May 3, a very heavy bombardment was concentrated on Villers-Tournelle, while about twelve thousand shells struck the town at the rate of fifty to one hundred every minute, causing nine hundred casualties, including fifty killed. Among the Montana casualties in the Cantigny Sector in the first weeks of fighting was Private Carl A. Sipher of Big Sandy, Company D, 16th Infantry. In a letter of condolence from his company commander, Captain R. Boyd, we find some insight into his death:

Private Sipher was killed in action on May 1, 1918. The company trenches were being bombarded by German artillery throughout the day. The trenches, being very new, had no real protection against a direct hit by a German shell. Private Sipher with a comrade was off duty and was sleeping in a trench under a shelter of a few branches covered over with earth, when a German "105 mm" shell hit directly on the shelter. Both men were killed instantly. The body of Private Sipher was marked by a tiny scratch on the forehead and one on the hand, while that of his companion was mutilated by the exploding shell. There is no doubt but that both of these heroes died without even wakening from their sleep. I have seen men killed—more than I care to think about—but the death of your son was a death that all soldiers hope for—if die we must.[35]

Other Montanans known killed in action in this period included Lieutenant Bernard F. McMeel of Great Falls, who died of severe wounds on April 14; Lieutenant McMeel attended University of Chicago Law School before entering Officers Training Camp. Private Abraham Shellenbarger of Hingham, Company M, 16th Infantry, died of wounds on May 9. William Miller Van Fossen of Conrad, Company C, 2nd Field Signal Battalion, was killed on May 1. At least seven other Montanans were wounded in action.[36]

A Long War for Valant Nurse MacGregor

Katherine Jean MacGregor was born on August 5, 1866, at St. Elmo, Ontario, Canada, the daughter of John D. and Margaret MacCallum MacGregor. Her long life was dedicated to nursing, and her wartime experiences were many.

She received her nurses' training at Michael Reese Hospital in Chicago and Columbus, Ohio. Prior to World War I, she had been superintendent of Murray Hospital in Butte for many years and had served as superintendent of nurses in a hospital in Santa Barbara, California.

Nurse MacGregor was living in Canada when the war began and sailed for England in April 1915, reporting for duty as a nurse at a base hospital on Malta, located midway between Sicily and the coast of Africa. Here fighters of practically every nationality were treated, injured in the brutal Dardanelles engagements against the Turks in 1915. Germans and Turks were admitted to the hospital in a separate ward and given the same care and food as Allied patients.

Nurse MacGregor's story, acquired during a visit with her sister in Butte, appeared in the *Montana Standard* of September 14, 1917:

Nurse Katherine G. MacGregor of Butte and Canada served in the British and American Expeditionary Forces. *Find a Grave.*

"During the Dardanelles fight 20,000 men were given treatment in the Malta infirmaries, and we had our first experience in war nursing. The base there was abandoned in the spring of 1916 and the hospital staff was removed to England and later to France. I was one of the English expeditionary force which was in charge of the medical work of the war at that time," said Miss MacGregor.

Miss MacGregor minimized the privations and dangers to which the nurses were exposed, only referring to the airplane raids made at the frequent intervals by the German aviators. In the hospital base where she was a nurse, there were eight separate institutions and at one time there were 20,000 patients being cared for at this one base.

"Heroes are being made by the thousands every day of the war. Men suffering the agony of mortal wounds inflicted by shrapnel, bombs or gunshots, come into the hospital without a murmur and they endure the pain of surgical operations without wincing. The life they lead in the trenches seems to make them acquire heroic attributes.

"Every fighter is provided with a first-aid outfit, and when he is wounded either he dresses his own injury or a comrade applied the preliminary bandages. Motor ambulances then carry the man to the casualty clearing station where skilled surgeons treat the wounds. From this station ambulance trains transport the patients to the base hospitals and the patients are kept under nursing care.

"Hundreds of thousands of lives are being saved yearly by the modern medical and surgical methods being employed to minimize deaths caused by disease and injuries. I hope to be able to return to give my services to the worthy cause of the Red Cross if the war continues.

"Stories of Germanic treachery have come to us at frequent intervals. On several occasions, a white flag has been displayed by the Huns, signifying a temporary true. When allied forces have ceased firing and send out envoys to negotiate with their opponents the Prussian machine guns have opened fire, and catching the English, French and all forces off guard, have wiped out whole regiments.

"Germany is virtually beaten, but the Hohenzollern dynasty has so misled the German people that they will keep on fighting as long as they can inflict injury on their hated opponents. The allies are optimistic as to the outcome of the war and they are hopeful that it will end before another year of warfare.

"Germany has been encouraged by the dallying of Russia, but the entrance of the United States into the war has counterbalance this effect to some extent. The arrival of the first large number of Uncle Sam's troops in France will have an excellent result in rallying the entente forces in the cause of democracy.

"There will be no serious talk of peace until the Teutonic autocracy is shattered and until the democratization of the world is assured. Every Englishman and woman is doing everything possible to aid the cause. Food conservation measures have assured the continuance of ample rations for every fighting man and the resources of the allies are practically boundless."[37]

Sinking of *Moldavia*

The British armed merchant troopship RMS *Moldavia*, carrying American troops, including at least two Montanans, was torpedoed and sunk on May 23, 1918, off Beachy Head in the English Channel. The *River Press* reported the story under the headline "Americans Are Missing":

German Submarine Sinks Troopship Near British Coast
London, May 24.—The British armed merchant troopship Moldavia, with American troops on board, has been torpedoed and sunk, according to a bulletin issued by the admiralty this evening. The text of the admiralty statement follows:

"The armed mercantile cruiser Moldavia was torpedoed and sunk yesterday morning.

"There were no casualties among the crew, but of the American troops on board 56 up to the present have not been accounted for. It is feared they were killed in one compartment by the explosion."

The Moldavia was torpedoed without warning. It was a moonlight night, and although a good lookout was kept the attacking submarine was not sighted before the torpedo struck.

It is believed that the American soldiers missing from the Moldavia were sleeping on the bottom deck and were overtaken by the great inrush of water after the explosion, when they were trying to reach the main deck. It also is presumed that some of the ladders were destroyed.

The vessel was struck below the bridge. She steamed ahead for some time after being struck and at first it was hoped that her watertight compartments would enable her to reach port.

The Moldavia is the third transport carrying American troops to be torpedoed and the fifteenth troop ship sunk by the Germans. Of the vessels carrying Americans, the Antilles was the first to meet with destruction by a U-boat. She was sunk October 17 last, when returning to this country from Europe and 70 lives were lost. The second was the Tuscania, which was sent to the bottom off the north coast of Ireland, February 5, with a loss of life totaling 210.[38]

The sinking of RMS *Moldavia* resulted in the death of fifty-five U.S. soldiers, including one Montanan, Virgil C. Cook, while at least one other Montanan, Charles Cushman, survived the sinking. Private Cook, born in

RMS *Moldavia*, the third transport sunk during the war with American troops onboard.

Lane, Texas, in 1895, came to Geyser from Hobart, Oklahoma, and served in Company B, 58th Infantry, 4th Division. Companies A and B of the 58th Infantry boarded RMS *Moldavia*, while other units of the 58th were on board other ships in the same convoy.

Private Charles Cushman of Hardin also served in Company B, 58th Infantry. While he survived the sinking of the *Moldavia*, Cushman did not survive the war. He was wounded on August 6 and killed in action on October 2.[39]

MONTANA'S FIRST YEOMANETTE

Georgia Hollier became Montana's first woman U.S. Navy Yeoman on April 30, 1918, when she enrolled with a traveling navy recruiting party in Bozeman. Hollier, age twenty-six, had been working in the government forestry office in Bozeman when she enlisted. Navy Yeoman (F) 1st Class Hollier served at 13th Naval District, Puget Sound Navy Yard, for 195 days. Honorably discharged on February 4, 1919, she remained in Washington and married Fred Benedict, a draftsman at Navy Yard Bremerton.

At least nineteen Montana women served in the naval reserve as Yeoman (F) or Yeomanettes during World War I, setting the precedent for Women Accepted for Volunteer Emergency Service (WAVES) in World War II.[40]

NATIONAL SEDITION BILL

In the spring of 1918, the U.S. Congress grappled to draft a strong national sedition law. On April 2, the Senate Judiciary Committee accepted an amendment by Montana senator Thomas Walsh based on the new sedition statute enacted by the Montana legislature in February. The Montana law was one of the most drastic sedition laws in the nation.

By early May, the Senate passed the conference report on the controversial bill to severely penalize disloyal acts and utterances by a vote of 48–26. The House then passed the Sedition Act of 1918 by 293–1, with Representative Rankin voting for it and the sole dissenting vote cast by socialist Representative Meyer London of New York. The *River Press* of May 15 reported this development:

WILL PUNISH DISLOYALTY
Sedition Bill Passed by Congress Provides Heavy Penalties.

Washington, May 7.—Final legislative action was taken today on the sedition bill, giving the government broad new powers to punish disloyal acts and utterances. Adopting a conference report already approved by the senate, the house sent the president for his signature the measure which has been before congress for weeks, assailed as a menace to free speech and championed as essential to order at home during the war.

The president is expected to sign the bill promptly and through vigorous enforcement of its provisions officials of the department of justice say they will be able to do much toward checking the wave of mob outbreaks for which unpunished disloyalty and enemy activity are blamed.

Penalties of 20 years' imprisonment or a fine of $10,000, or both, are provided in the bill for those convicted of uttering or printing disloyal, abusive, scurrilous, contemptuous of abusive language about the United States or the government or the form of government, or the flag, and for those who are convicted of favoring Germany or her allies in the present war.

The debate in the house was nothing like so extended as in the senate, and while some opposition developed there, only Representative London of New York, the socialist, voted against the conference report on the final test.[41]

REPRESSION PREVAILS

On April 22, 1917, former U.S. Representative Tom Stout spoke at a Patriotic Day and Loyalty Parade in Lewistown, pronouncing, "We are done with the days of a divided allegiance in this broad land of liberty. With our sacred honor and our liberties at stake, there can be but two classes of American citizens, patriots and traitors! Choose you the banner beneath which you will stand in this hour of trial."

One year later, in a night of mass hysteria on March 27, 1918, the "patriots" of Lewistown paraded an accused "pro-German" through the streets of town in an almost lynching and held a public book-burning of German-language textbooks. A mysterious fire followed, burning Fergus County High School to the ground—a case of arson never solved. These actions resulted from a year of increasing anger and emotion as the United States entered the Great War, fueled by the government Committee on

Public Information propaganda and state and local Loyalty Councils and Third Degree Committees. All of this at the very time American troops were conducting nighttime raids in no-man's-land, with the single most valued member of each patrol being a German-speaking Yank who could collect intelligence from overheard conversations.[42]

MONTANA HORSES AT WAR

The Great War was transitional in many weapons of warfare. Submarines, aircraft, tanks, trucks—all entered fields of battle, yet horses remained of immense value, so much so that the British used more than 1 million over four years, while the AEF in just eighteen months needed almost 250,000. Horses pulled artillery, hauled vital ammunition and other supplies and operated in French mud better than the early motorized vehicles. Many horses faced a short life span on the battlefield.

Fort Keogh, an old army infantry and cavalry post in southeastern Montana, served as an army quartermaster's depot and Remount Station during World War I. There, more horses were processed for the war than at any other post in the United States. Montana cowboys served at Fort Keogh Remount Station, including Almon Hall of Ekalaka, Benjamin F. Harrison of Deer Lodge, Walter Kelley of Musselshell County, Charles Hatch of Miles City, Albert Kirch of Yellowstone County and many others.[43]

Other Montana cowboys served at the Remount Station at Camp Lewis and overseas with Remount Stations in the AEF. Major Stanley Koch, raised in Bozeman, served as executive officer of the remount service in the AEF. At the end of the war, Major Koch was awarded the Distinguished Service Medal. His citation read, "Stanley Koch, major quartermaster corps, then lieutenant colonel infantry, United States army, for exceptionally meritorious and distinguished services as executive officer of the remount service, American Expeditionary Forces. By his zeal, efficiency and devotion to duty, he has rendered great and beneficial service in the organization of the remount service....Entered military academy from Montana."[44]

The *Missoulian* announced a further honor for Koch after General Philippe Petain, the "Lion of Verdun," presented the Legion of France to Lieutenant Colonel Koch, awarding him France's highest military honor.[45]

Gasmasks for soldier and horse in the war. *National Archives and Records Administration, NAID 51643.*

THE BATTLE OF CANTIGNY

May 28, 1918, is a day to remember in American history. That is the day when the Yanks of the AEF came of age. That day, they proved to friend and foe, Allies, Germans and themselves, that they could fight and win on the battlefields of France. May 28 marked the Battle of Cantigny, the first American offensive attack, and the Yanks swept the field of battle. Despite the heavy cost, they held on through ferocious German counterattacks. For the hard-pressed French, the American pronouncement in Paris, "Lafayette, we are here," on July 4, 1917, was at last coming true—American soldiers not only were "here," but they were also proving that they could "Fight and Win." The *Glasgow Courier* captured well the essence of this small but vital battle:

> *CANTIGNY'S IMPORTANCE*
>
> *Cantigny is only a small village, but it will occupy a large place in American military annals. For Cantigny was the first village to be captured by American troops in the great world war. Just as the battle for Paris opened and the military machine of the Prussian crown prince moved toward the Marne, came news of Cantigny's capture.*
>
> *As a military achievement, it was no great feat. It was not even a major operation, judging by the meager reports as to the number of men engaged. But it marked a new phase in the American campaign. The American troops, well-seasoned by months in the trenches, baptized by fire in defensive operations and in raids, took the offensive. It was warfare to the liking of the Americans. They rushed to attack like dogs let loose from the leash. They went forward singing, shouting and yelling. And their dash terrified the Germans. In the engagement it was proved conclusively that no German is a match for an American.*
>
> *Cantigny was a good beginning.*[46]

At the time of the Battle of Cantigny, the AEF's "Big Red One" had been in France for eleven months and was the most experienced of the five American divisions. The troops occupied front lines for the French army near the village of Cantigny in Lorraine. That small village was selected for the attack, with the objective being to recapture a salient that the Germans had occupied. More importantly, this was a crucial test of AEF fighting ability, designed to instill confidence among the British and French in the ability of the AEF—and self-confidence among the Yanks themselves.

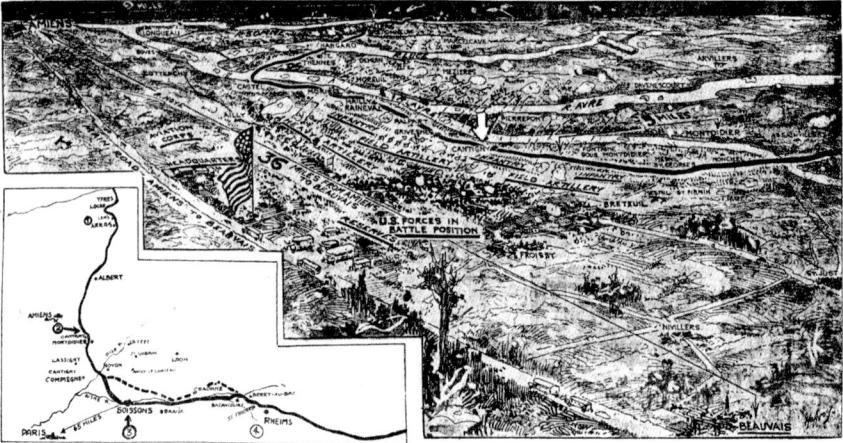

DETAILED MAP SHOWING SCENE OF AMERICAN ADVANCE

THE arrow in the center points to Cantigny, which has been captured in the first offensive undertaken by American troops. Pershing's drive extended a total distance of a mile and a quarter on either side of the village.

Below is the western front from Ypres to Rheims. No. 1 is the area of intensive German artillery fire; 2, Cantigny, in relation to the rest of the war front; 3, Soissons, taken by the Germans—the dotted line representing the allied front prior to the drive Monday. No. 4 is the extreme limit of the German offensive on the Aisne.

Map of the Cantigny-Montdider area in France. *From the* San Francisco (CA) Examiner, *May 30, 1918.*

In mid-May, the 2nd Brigade of the 26th and 28th Infantry Regiments entered the front lines, relieving the 16th and 18th Regiments of the 1st Brigade. The 2nd Brigade was greeted that night with ninety minutes of pure hell—some fifteen thousand shells fell in a mix of high-explosive and gas shells, resulting in more than eight hundred casualties, most from mustard gas. Among the casualties was thirty-year old Private Patrick O'Leary of Company H, 18th Infantry, from Anaconda, killed in action.

Lieutenant Colonel George C. Marshall, later of World War II fame, was serving on the 1st Division staff and was directed to plan the assault and capture of Cantigny without assistance of any French divisions. The mission was to capture and hold Cantigny against certain German counterattack. The 2nd Brigade launched nightly patrols to gather intelligence and prisoners to provide detailed information on defenses and possible weaknesses.

Under the cover of darkness on the night of May 23, the 18th Infantry quietly relieved the 28th Infantry on the front lines. The 28th withdrew to training areas to begin the great rehearsal of Marshall's plan for the attack on Cantigny. Over several days, the 28th rehearsed through the entire operation on terrain closely resembling Cantigny. French artillery, flamethrowers and tanks were added to the mix.

The town of Cantigny stood on a rise of ground in the center of the salient in the German lines west of Montdidier. Heavily fortified, it was strongly occupied by the German 82nd Reserve Division. Cantigny's commanding position afforded excellent observation for German machine guns and artillery. The attack was planned for 5:45 a.m., May 28, with heavy artillery bombardment; the assault was to begin one hour later. On the nights of May 26–27 and May 27–28, the 28th Infantry quietly reentered the line and relieved the 18th Infantry except for its Machine Gun Company, which remained in place.

Two German actions almost disrupted the carefully made and rehearsed plans. In the early morning hours of May 27, German artillery opened up more heavily than usual, followed by a strong raiding party trying to penetrate American lines. While the raid was turned back, serious casualties were suffered by Company E, 28th Infantry. At the same time, on May 27, the Germans began a massive third phase drive against the French and British on the front west of Cantigny, gaining five miles and taking fifteen thousand Allied prisoners in the first day. This German offensive was designed to break through over the Marne River and capture Paris.

As planned, at 5:45 a.m. on May 28 the American 6th Field Artillery and French Artillery opened fire with high-explosive and gas shells in a massive bombardment. French aircraft gained control of the sky and located German batteries for counterfire. In the words of the 1st Division history, the artillery bombardment proved highly effective, converting "Cantigny and the enemy's dug-outs into a volcano of bursting shell and flame and smoke."[47]

Ten French tanks moved into frontline positions, and the artillery changed their fire to a rolling barrage that moved ahead of the advancing 28th Infantry as they went over the top at 6:45 a.m. At this point, the French withdrew their artillery to move over to help the hard-pressed French and British hold their lines against the massive new German offensive.

The 28th Infantry moved forward swiftly over a front of a mile and a half, taking advantage of the artillery preparation and the shelter of tanks leading the center wave. PFC Horace F. Casey, assigned to the 2nd Field Signal Battalion, worked around the censor to describe briefly the action in a letter to his brother in Butte published in the June 29 *Montana Standard*:

> BUTTE BOYS GO OVER TOP. *Local Men Take Part in Battle of Cantigny According to Letter Received by Brother of One of the Fighters. Twenty-five Butte soldiers "went over the top" with American forces at the battle of Cantigny…*

American soldiers capturing the demolished town of Cantigny. *American Battle Monuments Commission.*

This is indicated in a letter received yesterday by Frank Casey of this city from his brother Horace, who says:

"Somewhere, France, May 30, 1918.

Dear Brother: Am writing these few lines in haste and will write again in a few days and tell you about the experience.

I just went over the top the other morning. Believe me, it was sure a real experience. Plenty of excitement. The Americans took their objective and are still holding it. The whole battalion was on the job and had communication all the time right up to the front line.

…It is known that there are 25 Butte boys in the same battalion with which Mr. Casey is serving."[48]

Note that Private Casey took pride in writing about the good telephone "communications right up to the front line" that his Signal Corp had put in place as the battle unfolded.

Germans who survived the artillery pounding were in deep shelters in the town and initially offered little resistance. Within thirty-five minutes, Cantigny was captured, and the mopping up operation began. German resistance was heavier on the flanks outside Cantigny, and there the urgency was to dig in to prepare for anticipated counterattacks. In the hours that followed, the Germans organized strong machine gun fire as the companies of the 28th Infantry worked to dig new trenches and build three strong points.

Mopping up in Cantigny brought hand-to-hand fighting, with invaluable support by French flamethrowers driving the Germans out of their deep dug-outs. Among the Germans captured in Cantigny were 5 officers and 225 enlisted men, and interrogation confirmed that the American attack came as a complete surprise.

Among known fatalities suffered by Montanans in the assault on Cantigny on May 28 were Private Ray A. Noyd of Madison County; Private John Czyzeskit of Glasgow; Private Theodore Kraakmo of Glasgow; Private Gotfried Axel Peterson of Missoula; Private Emmett C. Smith of Hardin; PFC Ray Q. Brent of Helena, the first Helena soldier known to die in the war; and Lieutenant Colonel Robert Jayne Maxey of Missoula.[49]

Lieutenant Colonel Maxey, the highest-ranking officer and only battalion commander to personally lead his men in the attack on Cantigny, lost his life that day of combat. He had assumed command of the 2nd Battalion of the 28th Infantry just three weeks earlier. A West Point graduate and a veteran of combat in the Philippines and the Mexican border, he met and married Lu Knowles, the daughter of prominent Montanans Mr. and Mrs. Hiram Knowles, while stationed at Fort Missoula with the 6th Infantry. Lieutenant Colonel Maxey went over the top with a revolver in his right hand, ahead of the French tanks toward Cantigny. One of his officers was killed while directing trench construction, so Colonel Maxey, who never ordered a man to do what he himself would not do, decided to take over the task with no thought of personal danger. Suddenly, an incoming German shell burst and a fragment flayed open Maxey's neck. In the words of Captain Clarence R. Huebner:

> *I was second in command of the battalion, also commanded Company G, 28th Infantry, which was in support.*
>
> *Colonel Maxey was advancing with the first line of the infantry when he was wounded in the neck by a shell fragment, which later caused his death.*
>
> *Upon being wounded he was placed upon a litter and was being carried to the first aid station by two runners, who had accompanied him, and he insisted upon being carried up to my position, as he said he had some orders he wanted to turn over to me. Upon arrival at the position of my company he ordered the litter bearer to lay him down and go and get me. I was about 200*

yards away superintending the construction of a strong point at the point the messenger found me. He stated that Colonel Maxey wanted to see me. I found the colonel lying upon a litter, helpless, but he could talk. He gave me full and complete instructions as to how to carry on. He had me get his map, showed me on the map where the positions were to be and how to defend. Told me that the adjutant had his other papers, but that the adjutant was looking for a dug-out in town to place the Post Command.

All this time we were under heavy machine gun fire and occasionally artillery shot. He showed utter disregard for his own wound, but thought of nothing but the success of the operation; nor would he proceed on his way until he was sure that I understood everything, thereby inspiring great devotion and courage.[50]

Montanan Lieutenant Colonel Robert J. Maxey, senior officer killed in the Battle of Cantigny. *U.S. Military Academy.*

Only at this point would Colonel Maxey allow himself to be carried by stretcher to a first-aid station and then to a field hospital. His wounds were too grave, and he died on June 4, leaving his widow and two sons: Curtis, age twelve, and Ratcliffe, age nine. Lieutenant Colonel Maxey was posthumously awarded the Distinguished Service Cross by General Pershing on August 29. His Distinguished Service Cross citation reads:

Citation: The Distinguished Service Cross is presented to Robert J. Maxey, Lieutenant Colonel (Infantry), U.S. Army, for extraordinary heroism in action while serving with 28th Infantry Regiment, 1st Division, AEF, at Cantigny, France, May 28, 1918. Lieutenant Colonel Maxey advanced with first wave and, in the face of heavy shell and machine-gun fire, located the objective of his battalion. He was a cool, dependable, and heroic leader. Although fatally wounded, he gave detailed instructions to his second in command and caused himself to be carried to his regimental commander and delivered important information before he died.

General Orders No. 99, War Department, 1918
Born: at Brandon, Mississippi
Home Town: Hot Springs, Arkansas or Missoula, Montana.[51]

HOLDING ON AT CANTIGNY

The great difficulty lay not so much in capturing Cantigny but in holding it. The French withdrew their counter-battery artillery to rush it to oppose the German Aisne Offensive, which had begun the previous day. On May 29, two small counterattacks were launched between 6:00 a.m. and 7:00 a.m. but failed. In the afternoon, German artillery delivered another heavy preparation, and at 5:45 p.m., a strong, determined assault was made against the left flank of the line. Combined artillery, infantry and machine guns drove the Germans back with great loss, but on the extreme left, the advance elements of the 28th Infantry were forced back to their old line.

At 5:40 a.m. on May 30, the Germans made a final effort to retake Cantigny. Two well-formed waves of infantry, preceded by a rolling barrage, advanced, but the Yanks held the line.

Among Montana wounded at Cantigny in late May were: Private Mitrofan Artuhov of Anaconda, Private Lauron Boggs of Miles City, Private Virgil T. Gibson of Ovando, PFC Charles Joseph Goodisky of Miles City and PFC Ole Gunderson of Power.

Cantigny American monument commemorates the first large offensive operation by an American division during World War I. *Warrick Page/American Battle Monuments Commission.*

As the first American offensive during the war, Cantigny inspired the confidence of the Allies and had a depressing effect on the Germans. Despite the casualties, Cantigny's success heightened morale throughout the AEF.

Meanwhile, the powerful German Aisne Offensive, launched on May 27, was moving toward Paris with alarming progress. This forced the French to take some of their divisions from the line, and one sector selected was the left of the 1st Division, so the "Big Red One" was ordered to take over this additional sector extending its front to more than three miles.

The relief of the French division was executed on the nights of June 1–2 and June 2–3.

MONTANA DRAFT NEWS

Local draft boards in Montana were directed by Adjutant General Greenan to make arrangements for the registration of men who had come of draft age (ages twenty-one to thirty-one) since June 15, 1917. The order was issued pending final passage of Congressional legislation for a Second Draft. Most of the contingents of drafted men from Montana counties, totaling 2,163 called under the First Draft, entrained May 27–30 for Camp Lewis.[52]

Chapter 3

JUNE 1918

Holding Cantigny; Birth of the Devil Dogs

Cantigny and Its Aftermath

As the first American offensive during the war, success at Cantigny was critical. Despite heavy casualties, Cantigny heightened morale throughout the AEF and among French and British allies. Marshal Petain cited this first American offense in French Army Orders:

28th Regiment of U.S. Infantry:

"A regiment inspired by a magnificent offensive spirit under command of Colonel H.E. Ely, this regiment rushed forward with irresistible dash to attack a strongly fortified village. It reached all its objectives and held the conquered ground in spite of repeated counter-attacks."

General Headquarters The Marshal of France
Commander in Chief of the French Armies of the East: (Signed) Petain[53]

Finally, on the night of May 30, the battered, exhausted, hungry, thirsty men of the 28th Infantry who had held firmly were relieved by the 16th Infantry. Eight rested companies replaced the depleted sixteen companies holding the front lines at Cantigny. A combination of very heavy German casualties and the need for manpower to support the German offensive at Chemin des Dames resulted in no more German attempts to recapture Cantigny—the battle for Cantigny was won.

While the Germans could no longer take offensive action, their heavy concentrations of 77-, 88-, 105-, 150- and 210-caliber artillery continued to rain down on AEF positions. In the words of Captain George Marshall, "A 3-inch shell will temporarily scare or deter a man; a 6-inch shell will shock him; but an 8-inch shell, such as these 210-mm ones, rips up the nervous system of everyone within a hundred yards of the explosion."[54]

The continuing German artillery fire resulted in more casualties over the next week, among them at least seven Montanans serving in a single company, Company L of the 16th Infantry. PFC Clifton M. Jordan, of Malta, was cited for heroism at Cantigny on June 2. Awarded the Distinguished Service Cross for extraordinary heroism, his citation read:

Citation: The Distinguished Service Cross is presented to Clifton M. Jordan, Private, U.S. Army, for extraordinary heroism in action while serving with Company L, 16th Infantry Regiment, 1st Division, AEF, near Cantigny, France, June 2, 1918. Private Jordan went forward, under intense machinegun and artillery fire, and assisted in the removal of a wounded soldier over a distance of one kilometer.

General Orders No. 35, War Department, 1919
Born: Hamburg, Arkansas
Home Town: Malta, Montana

Private Jordan was later killed in action on July 4.[55]

Overall American casualties in capturing and holding Cantigny totaled more than 300 men killed or dead from combat wounds and about 1,300 wounded. Throughout June, until the 1st Division was relieved from the sector on July 8, some 500 more Yanks would be killed in action while holding a much broader area. Of the 4,000 Americans in the Cantigny battle and its aftermath, almost half became casualties. German records reveal a total of more than 1,700 casualties of their own during the Battle of Cantigny.

German Aisne Offensive

Along the whole of the Western Front, the war continued at an intensified pace, and by May 31, the Third German Aisne Offensive west of Rheims had crossed the Chemin-des-Dames, captured Soissons and was heading along the Marne Valley just thirty-seven miles from Paris—the distance between Fort Benton and Great Falls. The AEF 2nd and 3rd Divisions were rushed into battle. With almost 1 million Americans now in France and 250,000 more arriving every month, the AEF was at last becoming a major force in the war.

The 2nd Division, including the 4th Marine Brigade (composed of the 5th and 6th Marine Regiments), together with elements of the 3rd and 28th Divisions, was thrown into the line in the Château-Thierry sector. The 2nd Division, which had been in reserve northwest of Paris and preparing to relieve the 1st Division, was hastily diverted to the vicinity of Meaux on May 31 and, early on the morning of June 1, deployed across the Château-Thierry-Paris road near Montreuil-aux-Lions in a gap in the French line.

On May 31, the German 231st Division moved toward Château-Thierry, a town built on both sides of the Marne River. The Germans began to cross the Marne as forward elements of the AEF 3rd Division arrived, followed by the 2nd Division. The 7th Machine Gun Battalion rushed forward to stem the German advance, arriving in the early afternoon on May 31. In desperate fighting, the German attempt to cross the Marne was driven back.

On Saturday, June 1, a short distance northeast of Château-Thierry, the Marines made a stand against the Germans at Belleau Wood as the latter entered the Wood, near the Marne River. The 2nd Division, including Marines, moved forward to block the Germans from crossing the Marne at that point. Belleau Wood (in French, Bois de Belleau) was an ancient hunting preserve heavily overgrown and in places almost impenetrable. The Marine 5th and 6th Regiments moved forward to Belleau Wood to stop the German offense.

On June 2, the French lost the villages of Belleau and Rorcy, while the Marine 5th Regiment stopped the Germans at Les Mares Farms, just thirty miles from Paris in a three-day battle. On June 3, the French attempted to take Hill 142, failed and fell back, ordering the 5th Marines to retreat with them. The Marines refused to retreat, countermanding the French order. In the face of a major German attack, the Marines used long-range rifle marksmanship so effectively at three to five hundred yards that the German attack ground to a halt.

Over the next two days, the Marines turned back successive German waves of attack. French infantry was battered by the German advance and retreated to escape the onslaught. Yet the Marine lines held. By June 5, the 2nd Division had occupied and held positions on the Marne salient

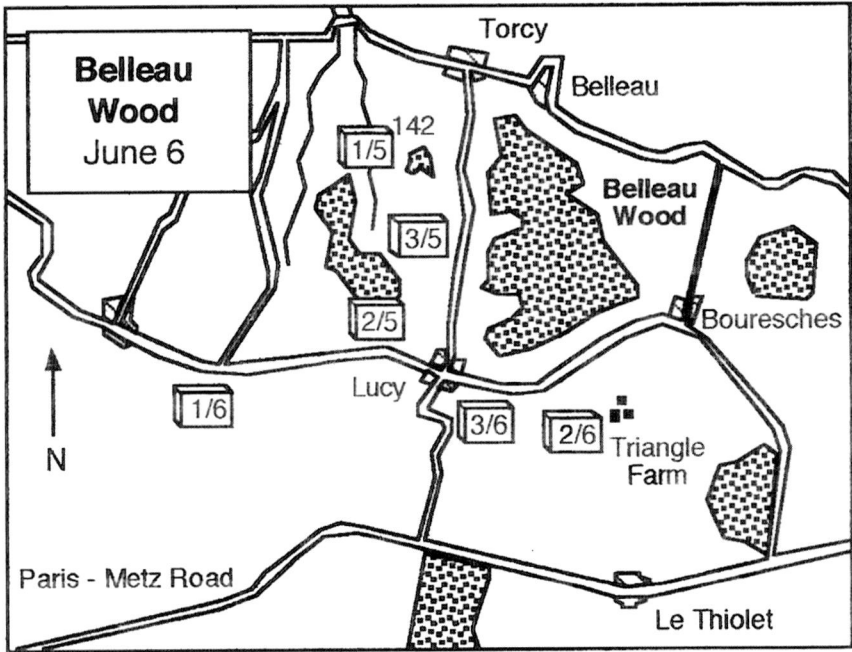

Marine 5th and 6th Regiments at Belleau Wood during their June 6 assault. *Wikimedia Commons.*

nearest Paris. The Germans held Château-Thierry on the right of Second Division, as well as Hill 142, Bois de Belleau, Bouresches and Vaux. The Battle of Château-Thierry, June 3–5, saw the Yanks defend the bridges over the Marne River and stop the German offensive advance toward Paris. Château-Thierry was the second American victory of the war, coming only days after the first at Cantigny.

On June 5, French reinforcements arrived, and a counterattack was planned for the following day, with the French on the left of the American line and the Marine Brigade attacking Hill 142 to prevent flanking German fire.

BLOODIEST DAY IN MARINE HISTORY

On June 6, the 2nd Division went over to the attack, launching an offensive lasting until July 1, 1918. That day, the Marine Brigade captured Hill 142 and Bouresches. Yet June 6 also proved to be the bloodiest day in Marine

Corps history—until Tarawa in World War II—as the 5th Marines began their assault in two phases, on Hill 142 and then Belleau Wood. The 1st Marine Battalion with 49 and 67 Companies led the assault on Hill 142. Despite heavy casualties, the Marines seized and then struggled to hold Hill 142.

The next phase of the operation was to clear Belleau Wood. Disastrous French intelligence reported that the Wood was lightly defended when, in fact, the Germans were there in force and heavily dug in. The 3rd Battalion, 5th Marines, lead the attack against Belleau Wood, with the 6th Marines on its right. Bad battlefield preparation, erroneous tactics and poor communications set the stage for a shockingly frightful day.

The 5th Marines were stopped cold, while the 6th had to move through an open wheat field. In the words of a lieutenant from 96 Company, 6th Marines: "We charged across an open field for eight hundred yards and there were eleven machine guns playing on us—honest, the bullets hitting the ground were as thick as rain drops."

With devastating losses, the ill-fated attack was called off at 9:15 p.m. On this "longest day," the brigade lost 31 officers and 1,056 men. It would take six assaults over the next month before the Germans finally could be driven from Belleau Wood.

These early American successes played an immensely important role in the eventual Allied victory as the increasing stream of fresh American troops began to destroy German morale and capabilities.[56]

One of the first Marine casualties at Château-Thierry was young Montanan Harold McLennan Mady of Great Falls. Serving with 17 Company, 5th Marines, Corporal Mady was wounded in action on June 2. He was awarded the French Croix de Guerre (BS) and cited in General Order 40. Just before his Marines and the rest of the 2nd Division were moved up to help the French stop the massive new German offense, Corporal Mady wrote to his mother and sisters in Great Falls:

Somewhere in France May 26, 1918

Dear Mother & Sisters
…The last time we came out of the trenches for a rest I was called up before the Captain and recommended for a commission as 2nd Lieutenant. In order to qualify a person had to have a High School education in Mathematics, geometry and trigonometry which I did not have so I guess I will have to sit steady in the boat for a while. If the order changes, I will

have a chance for a commission. I may have to wait 6 months or a year but it is nice to know I have been appreciated in doing my duty in this big war. The Captain recommended me and if it goes through I probably will go to school for a while.[57]

After Corporal Mady had been wounded on June 2, he wrote to his mother within the constraints of the ever-present censor:

June 15, 1918

Dear Mother & Sisters:
I am feeling a lot better and think I will be O.K. soon. Our last move was a great one. No doubt the papers back home have told of the Marines doings in our last battle.

Corporal Harold Mady, a Marine of Great Falls, wounded at Chateau Thierry. *The History Museum.*

... Then after getting our stomachs filled, up to the front we went. Each man willing and ready to do his part. Then with a yell and singing "Hail, Hail the gangs all here and [in the] midst of a rain of bullets and heavy shelling we sure gave them hell."
The Boche could not see why we did not stop. They were surrendering so fast for a while we could not handle them. We did not want to take prisoners but they took themselves. They were glad to be captured and finished with the war...
P.S. Just heard some news. Marines made another charge through heaps of German dead.
I am in Base Hospital No. 8. Please excuse writing, [I'm] a little nervous yet.[58]

At Base Hospital No. 8 in Savenay in the Loire-Atlantique department, perhaps treating Corporal Harold Mady, was Nurse Lucy Walters of Glasgow. Nurse Walters arrived at the hospital in early June and served there until February 1919. Upon her return home, she was appointed superintendent of the Valley County Detention Hospital.[59]

THROUGH THE EYES OF CORRESPONDENT GIBBON

Sixteen years after the end of the war, Fort Benton Woman's Club members gave their impressions of leading newspaper columnists. They talked about Will Rogers, Walter Lippmann and others. Mrs. Joel R. Overholser, wife of the *River Press* editor, talked about *Chicago Tribune* war correspondent Floyd Gibbons, who won prominence through war service as well as newspaper work. In fact, Floyd Gibbons was in the field on Bloody Thursday, June 6, when the U.S. Marine Brigade first assaulted the seemingly impregnable Belleau Wood—and Gibbons almost died that day with many of the Marines he accompanied.

Two days later, as the fight for the Wood still raged on, Floyd Gibbons, though badly wounded, survived operations on his arm and head and the loss of his left eye. As he lay in his hospital bed, he listened to the latest reports from the battlefield and wove them into his experiences on the field of battle at Belleau Wood. Gibbons began his story with words that would raise Marine heroism into legend—the day the "Devil Dogs" were born:

> *But I have a new ideal today. I found it in the Bois de Belleau. A small platoon line of Marines lay on their faces and bellies under the trees at the edge of a wheat field. Two hundred yards across that flat field the enemy was located in the trees. I peered into the trees but could see nothing, yet I knew that every leaf in the foliage screened scores of German machine guns that swept the field with lead. The bullets nipped the tops of the young wheat and ripped the bark from the trunks of the trees three feet from the ground on which the Marines lay. The minute for the Marine advance was approaching. An old gunnery sergeant commanded the platoon in the absence of the lieutenant, who had been shot and was out of the fight. This old sergeant was a Marine veteran. His cheeks were bronzed with the wind and sun of the seven seas. The service bar across his left breast showed that he had fought in the Philippines, in Santa Domingo, at the walls of Pekin, and in the streets of Vera Cruz.*
>
> *As the minute for the advance arrived, he arose from the trees first and jumped out onto the exposed edge of that field that ran with lead, across which he and his men were to charge. Then he turned to give the charge order to the men of his platoon—his mates—the men he loved. He said:*
>
> *"COME ON, YOU SONS-O'-BITCHES! DO YOU WANT TO LIVE FOR EVER!"*[60]

Right: *Chicago Tribune*'s daring young war correspondent, Floyd Gibbons, was awarded France's greatest honor, the Croix de Guerre with Palm, for his valor on the field of battle. "And they thought we wouldn't fight."

Below: Georges Scott illustration, *American Marines in Belleau Wood (1918)*— originally published in the French magazine *Illustrations*. Wikipedia, "*Battle of Belleau Wood.*"

Marine Gunnery Sergeant Daniel Daly, who challenged his men as he led them forward, survived the first assault on Belleau Wood on Bloody Thursday, June 6—but more than one thousand Marines did not. Master Sergeant Daniel Daly, an Irish American, had already earned two Medals of Honor, the first during the Boxer Rebellion in China and the second during the Haiti Occupation. For his repeated deeds of heroism at Belleau Wood, Sergeant Daly was awarded the Navy Cross and the Médaille militaire, the second-highest French military decoration.[61]

Image of then gunnery sergeant Daniel Daly, a double recipient of the Medal of Honor. *From the Dan Daly Collection (COLL/3334), Marine Corps Archives and Special Collections.*

Overall, American casualties at Belleau Wood totaled a devastating 9,777 before it was taken at last on June 26. At least 14 Montanans, including 11 Marines, were among the known casualties after the first week of June in the Aisne Defensive at Château-Thierry and Belleau Wood. Private Douglas Gerald Marsh of Missoula, serving in 74 Company, 6th Marines, was killed in action on June 10 a few yards from the frontline trenches by concussion from the explosion of a shell. Private William John Kehoe of Great Falls, serving in 47 Company, 5th Regiment Marines, was killed in action on June 25.

Private Elwood Harrison Best, residing in Missoula and serving in 83 Company, 6th Marines, was wounded on June 17. Best was one of 10 survivors of the 250 men originally in 83 Company. He was medically discharged and returned to Montana to enter university. The *Missoulian* of February 9, 1919, carried his story:

> E.H. BEST TELLS STORIES OF WAR. WITNESSED SINKING OF SUBMARINE WHILE ENROUTE TO FRANCE.
>
> *E.H. Best of the 83rd company, 6th Marines, is not only a fighter, but a poet, as evidenced by the following verse. Best is now a student in the forestry department at the university. He enlisted in the Marines in September, 1917. Gassed twice and wounded thrice, he returned to Montana to continue his education.*

...*In Belleau Wood, machine guns cleverly hidden beneath crags and rocks poured forth leaden hail and from the tops of the large trees of the forests machine guns camouflaged swept the ranks of the Marines, "who fell like autumn leaves."*

A well-placed shot picked off the gunner, who fell to the ground. He was silenced, but not the gun, for it floated off through the air to the top of another tree, where was hidden another machine gun crew, the gun being mounted on a cable so it could be moved from tree-top to tree-top, another proof of Hun cleverness. Best has seen it all. He is reticent and does not care to talk, least of all about the part he played in aiding in the winning of the great war. But of the Marines he will tell great stories, if urged to do so.

His poem follows [in part]:

> *I enlisted in Missoula,*
> *'Twas on an autumn day,*
> *To go to fight the Teutons,*
> *In the land so far away*
> *And granting God is willing,*
> *Before the first of May,*
> *I will be chasing Germans,*
> *In the thickest of the fray.*
>
> *So, farewell to old Montana,*
> *And the girl that I adore,*
> *For I am on my way,*
> *To a far and distant shore;*
> *We will hit 'em hot and heavy,*
> *Break the Hun's defending line,*
> *Double quick down Wilhelmstrasse,*
> *And chuck the Kaiser in the Rhine.*
>
> *...We were ordered to the front,*
> *On the seventh night of June,*
> *We were told what was coming*
> *By the battle's roar and boom,*
> *Bullets fell like rain drops,*
> *And men like autumn leaves,*
> *But they failed to break the line*
> *Of the United States Marines.*

The blood it flowed in torrents,
In the streets of old Borchay,
And may it be remembered
That was our Victory day.
For they chased the Huns across the hills
And through the bloody streams,
Today they are in Germany,
The United States Marines.[62]

Navy Corpsman McGee in Action

Henry Eugene McGee of Fort Benton enlisted in the Naval Hospital Corps on June 5, 1917. After training, he moved on to Quantico Marine Barracks and was promoted to HM 2-Class. In April 1918, he deployed to France with the 6th U.S. Marines, 4th Brigade, 2nd Division, AEF. The Marine Brigade was ordered to shore up crumbling French lines near Château-Thierry in late May. The 6th Marine was ordered to clear the southern half of Belleau Wood on June 6. These attacks were the beginning of a monthlong battle that would become a landmark battle for the U.S. Marine Corps. Displaying uncommon bravery, the 6th Marine lost 2,143 over forty days in this sector. In recognition of the "brilliant courage, vigor, spirit, and tenacity of the Marines," the French government awarded the 6th and other Marine units at Belleau Wood the Croix de Guerre with Palm and renamed Belleau Wood "Bois de la Brigade de Marine."

During this combat assignment, HM McGee was promoted to HM-1 and was cited three times for heroic conduct during the fighting. The letter accompanying the third citation read, in part, "Attached to the 16 company during the action of June 23–25, 1918, Mr. McGee was one of three men who established a first aid station directly in the rear of the firing line, making several trips to the firing line to remove wounded. They worked continually from 7 p.m. June 23 to 3 p.m. June 24 caring for and removing wounded."

In a later battle, HM-1 McGee was wounded in the thigh by nineteen pieces of shrapnel from a German shell that burst about three hundred yards from him. His parents received a letter in mid-November 1918 advising that he was in a base hospital "somewhere in France" being treated for wounds sustained in combat but was making good progress. Returning to the United States in a partially disabled condition, HM-1 McGee was discharged in June 1919.[63]

UNCLE SAM'S ROUNDUP

The *River Press* of June 19 carried news of the war effort of famed Montana cowboy and poet Wallace D. Coburn:

MONTANA COWBOY POET HAS BECOME WRITER OF WAR SONGS
Our oldtime friend, Wallace D. Coburn, who punched cows in this part of Montana in early days and is now engaged in the production of films for moving picture shows, has turned his attention to composing war songs. Coburn is a versatile kind of genius and tried his hand at the poetry mill several years ago, when he published a little volume entitled "Rhymes of a Roundup Camp," which enjoyed brief popularity among the cowboy fraternity. He was later engaged in the sheep business near Malta, but there was not sufficient excitement in that occupation to awaken his poetic proclivities and cause him to express his sentiments in verse.

The war news, however, has started the machinery in Coburn's poetry mill, and the first grist is a song, with musical accompaniment by Homer Tourjee, entitled "Uncle Sam's Roundup." It runs this way:

> *Oh, we like our "boss," old Uncle Sam,*
> *Whose brand is the U.S.A.,*
> *And we're starting out on a grand round-up*
> *Of the range over Berlin way:*
> *Where the outlaw chief is running free,*
> *Called "Bill of the Kaiser-bung,"*
> *Who's the meanest rustler ever known*
> *Or ever was left unhung.*

> *Chorus:*
> *So it's on to Berlin, brave "Sammies,"*
> *Where the devil has made his nest,*
> *And we'll tan the hide of that Teuton pride,*
> *We boys of the Golden West.*
> *And when we're through the world will know*
> *When the smoke has cleared away,*
> *That the wildest maverick ever burnt*
> *Wears a trawl called the U.S.A.*

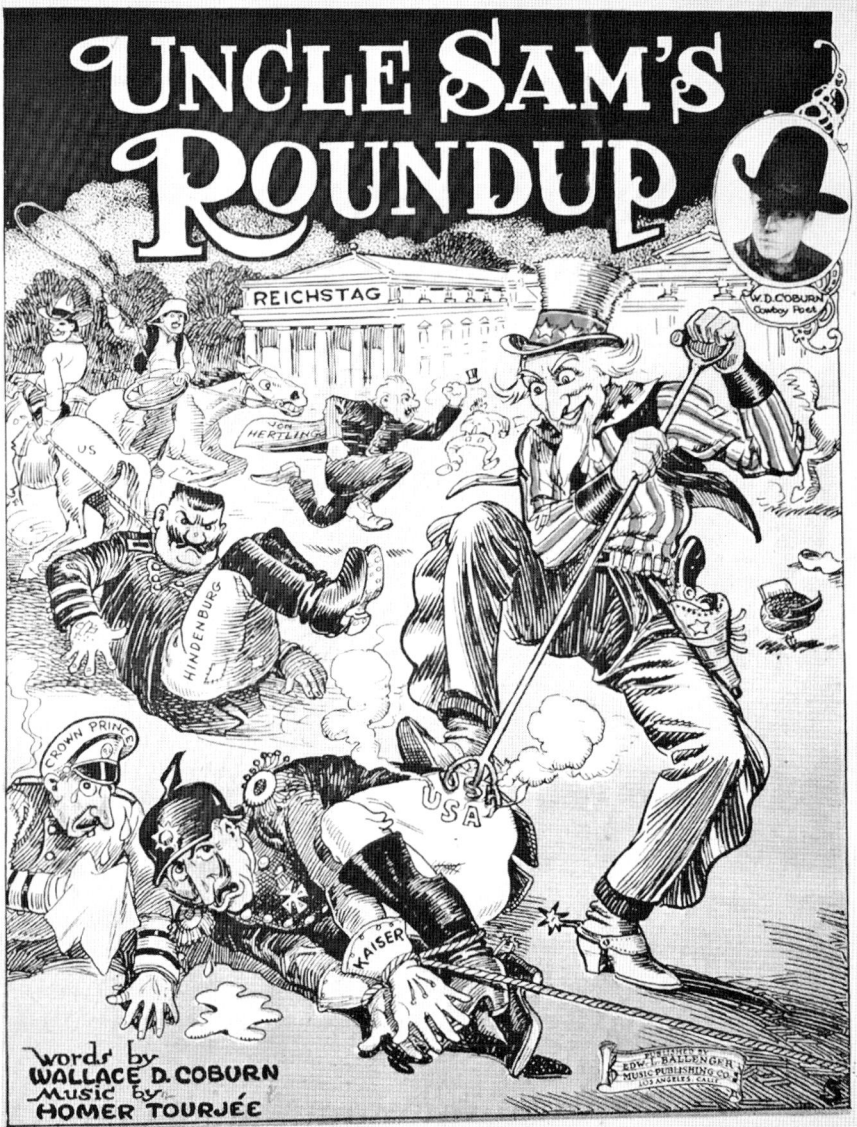

"Uncle Sam's Roundup," with words by Wallace D. Coburn and music by Homer Tourjee, published by Ballenger in 1918. *Library of Congress.*

When our wild stampede is over
We'll rope old Kaiser Bill
And we'll trim, his horns and we'll mark his ears.
Just to conquer his stubborn will;
And we'll brand him on his scaly hide
'Till he bawls like a lonesome stray,
'Till he begs for mercy never shown,
In frenzy to rend and slay.

The title page of the song consists of a design in colors showing Uncle Sam applying his branding iron to the left flank of the Kaiser, while the crown prince is mopping up the tears that stream from the eyes of his anguish-stricken parent. Another figure in the sketch is that of Von Hindenburg, who has been roped by a soldier cowboy and is awaiting his turn, while Von Hertling is being pursued by another member of the roundup. A portrait of Mr. Coburn appears in the upper right hand corner of the title page.[64]

WHERE "HORROR AND HUMOR WALK ARM IN ARM"

In striking and colorful terms, a visitor to Missoula in the late spring of 1918 brought home to Montanans the war in France as tens of thousands of Yanks were beginning to move into the frontline trenches. William Allen White—one of the nation's greatest authors, editors and war correspondents—came to Missoula to speak at the commencement of Montana State University on June 12. "A New Heaven and a New Earth" was the title of White's commencement address, presented to fifty-six graduates of the university—of the fifty-six, but fifteen were men, "all that the war had left." His optimistic theme centered on "now that we are in, and that we are in to win, whatever victory we may have shall be a victory for world democracy!"

While in Missoula, editor White met with journalists to share some of his experiences as a member of the Red Cross mission to the French front the previous year. In the words of the *Missoulian* of July 28:

In a quiet corner of a local inn, [William Allen White] met with the newspaper folks of the city and gave to them one of his celebrated "essays set to voice." Mr. White entertained them royally for more than an hour with

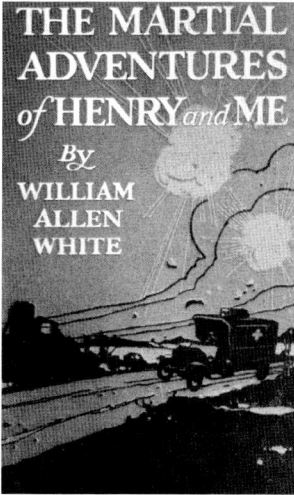

Left: William Allen White's *The Martial Adventures of Henry and Me* brought the horrors and humor of the Great War to the American people. *Author photo.*

Below: Charlie Russell and his guest, William Allen White, spend an afternoon together swapping stories in Great Falls. *From the* Great Falls Tribune, *June 23, 1918.*

KANSAS AND MONTANA IN FRIENDLY BATTLE FOR SUPREMACY IN WITS

Charles M. Russell (left), William Allen White (right)

William Allen White, editor and lecturer of Emporia, Kansas, delivered the flag day oration in Great Falls under the auspices of the Elks and women's convention then in session. In the afternoon Mr. White was entertained about the city by Charley Russell and a bunch of the local newspaper men. Some stories were told. It was Kansas vs. Montana. The picture apparently indicates a big one for Kansas, and "Charley" with a countenance indicating much incredulity is preparing to put one over that will close the series.

stories of the things which he and his co-Kansan, Henry J. Allen, passed through in the process of serving as members of the [Red Cross] *committee.*

But this essay set to voice, as he so capitally terms it, included, of course, only a very small part of the things he and Mr. Allen saw and did in France. And so, now, Mr. White has written a book about it, and he has called the book "The Martial Adventures of Henry and Me."

In this book he has set down the horror of the war and the humor of it in a way which could be done by none other than he. And the result is an enormously interesting war book, brimming over with observation, insight and wisdom, and flavored with a racy irony suggestive of Mark Twain. "Henry and Me" finds new things to see and say about Americans at the front, German atrocities, the French spirit in war, the Italian struggle, the new European woman, and what is going to happen after the tumult and the shouting dies. But perhaps the most absorbing chapter in the book is the telling how the soldiers of the allies—including our own—are taught the lesson of hate and what is the fruit of the teaching. Here, indeed, horror and humor walk arm in arm.[65]

Prior to his visit to Missoula, William Allen White gave a stirring commencement address at Montana State College in Bozeman. By Friday of that same week, White had moved on to Great Falls, where he gave a patriotic flag day address for the Great Falls Elks Club and the delegates to the state convention of Federated Women's Clubs. Displayed at the event was an Elk's service flag, newly containing thirty-five stars, one for each member serving in the armed forces. During his visit, humorist White met his match in Charles M. Russell as the two spent the afternoon swapping stories about Kansas and Montana.[66]

Charlie's No Hoarder

Charles M. Russell's support to the war effort took many forms. In a gracious gesture, smoker Charlie passed up an opportunity to "hoard" a supply of Bull Durham tobacco from Goodman Cigar Store to let it go to the troops. The *Hardin Tribune* covered the story:

Charlie Russell, cowboy artist, has smoked nothing but Bull Durham for 40 years. He started rolling his own when he hit Montana at the tender age of 14 [actually sixteen], *and he has been doing it ever since.*

Some weeks ago announcement was made that the government had taken the entire product of the American Tobacco Company's plant that is making Bull Durham, and that no more Durham "makin's" would be forthcoming for the trade after the supply in the hands of the jobbers had been exhausted. Russell was informed of this condition by the tobacconist from whom he buys his Durham and cigarette papers.

"You'd better lay in a supply of Durham," suggested the tobacco man. "Get enough fer a year, anyway."

"No," said Russell, in his slow way of talking. "I guess I'll just take a couple of packages, as usual."

"What's the idea?" inquired the tobacconist. "You don't smoke anything else, and we won't be able to get any more after what we have on hand is gone."

"Well," replied Russell, "they say they can't get enough Durham for the boys over in France. I wouldn't feel just right with a big bunch of it in the cellar and knowing that the fellows in the trenches were hungry for a 'Bull' smoke. No, I'll just take my two packages, and when that runs out I guess I'll have to learn to smoke something else."

Russell couldn't help smiling to himself, however, at the thought of the roar some of the old time cowpunchers would put up if they couldn't get Durham for their makings. "If a puncher couldn't get but two sacks of

GO EASY ON "BULL;" THE SOLDIERS NEED IT
WORSE THAN I DO, SAYS CHARLIE RUSSELL

A Load of Durham "Makin's"

Charlie Russell's gracious gesture, giving his Bull Durham to the troops. *From the* Hardin Tribune, *July 19, 1918.*

'Bull,'" he remarked, "I'll bet I know what size sacks he'd like to have put up for him," and to illustrate, he made the above group in clay.

"That's about the way that puncher would look leaving McNamara & Marlow's trading post at Big Sandy," he said.[67]

A BLACKFEET PRAYER

Browning, May 16.—Mountain Chief, an oldtimer of the reservation, who has been delegated to Washington upon several occasions, appeared at the agency office Monday in full war regalia. He sang a couple of war songs for Superintendent [Fred] Campbell, one of which included a prayer for the success of the allies. The old man claimed the singing of these songs would surely put the jinx on the Kaiser.[68]

AVIATION ADVANCES

When the Great War began in 1914, aircraft performed valuable observation and reconnaissance service. As the war progressed, the role of aircraft broadened greatly to air-to-air combat, bombing, strafing, observation and photographic reconnaissance. With expanded roles, the need for new aviation technology continued to advance. The *River Press* reported on the latest developments:

EQUIPMENT FOR AIRPLANES

Before an airplane can be put into military service it must be equipped with at least nine delicate aeronautic instruments, some of which are absolutely essential to exact flying, and all contribute to the successful operation of a plane. One gives the pilot his location as to height and direction; others tell his speed through the air, the speed of his propeller, the amount of gasoline carried, water temperature, operation of the oiling system, and guide his "banking" on turns. Another necessary article is the oxygen-supplying apparatus, without which an aviator could not climb to any great height.

For operation of actual combat planes, such as observing, photographing, bombing, and fighting planes, other complicated and expensive instruments and sets of apparatus are necessary. Among them are machine guns, gun mounts, bomb racks, bomb-dropping devices, bomb sights, radio and photographic apparatus, electrically heated clothing, lights and flares. These bring the total cost of equipment for an airplane to several thousand dollars each, depending upon the type of plane.[69]

A Bold Aviation Innovator

In February 1915, more than two years before the United States entered the war, Clifford B. Prodger of Fife, Cascade County, arrived in England to teach aviation students of the British Royal Naval Air Service and the Royal Flying Corps. Pilot Prodger proved so talented that after nine months he was assigned to perform the official testing of aircraft before acceptance from the manufacturer for the Royal Naval Air Service. This led to his selection to become a "test pilot," testing experimental aircraft before they were selected for production for service at the front. Prodger's testing of almost two hundred new aircraft designs, both land aircraft and flying boats, proved a major factor in ending the war with the Allies in command of the air.[70]

Montana Politics

As Montana entered the 1918 political season, Representative John M. Evans and Senator Thomas J. Walsh, both Democrats, announced their intention to run for reelection. The situation for Republican representative Jeannette Rankin, the nation's first and only woman in Congress, was far more difficult. While she had voted against declaration of war in April 1917, she accepted that the voice of democracy had spoken and voted for war effort measures, including the selective draft to provide men and the Liberty bond program to finance the war. She had also voted against the War Espionage Act of 1917, an act that led to prosecution of aliens and suppressing dissent. Both of these votes were red flags for her political future in Montana. Her vote against the Espionage Act was tempered by her vote for the even more draconian Sedition Act of 1918.

Despite her antiwar vote, Representative Rankin was compiling a strong reputation nationally. She received extensive coverage in national publications, and she had led the effort that brought narrow passage of the Woman's Suffrage Amendment in the House of Representatives in January 1918. In mid-May 1918, Representative Rankin spoke to the largest audience that had assembled in Knoxville, Tennessee, since Theodore Roosevelt's address there on behalf of his candidacy for president as a Progressive in 1912. Speaking in the auditorium filled to overflowing, with almost as many more turned away, Representative Rankin spoke on behalf of the Red Cross war fund drive. In the words of the *Great Falls Tribune*:

She thrilled her audience by a petition of the duty of women of America in the world crisis, the great part they are playing and opportunities they are seizing to help win the war. The appeal for the Red Cross was as eloquent as it was earnest. She told of what the west, particularly her own state, has done for the cause. Following the address Miss Rankin was given an ovation, many hundreds mounting the stage to meet her personally.[71]

On June 8, Congress held its annual baseball game, and Representative Rankin even became a factor in that nonpartisan sports break from politics:

REPUBLICANS WIN SOLONS' BALL GAME
Washington, June 8.—President Wilson laid aside the duties of state today to see the Democrats and Republicans of the house of representatives struggle through their annual baseball game, which went for six and one-half innings and was staged for the benefit of the American Red Cross. For once there was no debate as to the winner. The official scorer said the minority representatives [Republicans] *had 19 runs to 5 for the majority party* [Democrat] *players and nobody disputed him.*

The Republicans lay much of their success to the fact that they had selected Miss Jeannette Rankin, representative from Montana, as their mascot.[72]

Aside from her contentious votes in Congress, Representative Rankin faced a powerful political opponent in Montana, the Anaconda Copper Company, as a result of the dramatic speech she had given at Columbia Garden in August 1917, in support of Butte miners. So, just what was to be Jeannette Rankin's political fate during the primary and general elections of 1918?[73]

★

PART II

THE YANKS MOVE FROM DEFENSE TO OFFENSE

Chapter 4

JULY 1918

Powder River, Let 'Er Buck!; Sowing Seeds of Victory;
Rock of the Marne; On to Soissons; Turn of the Tide

As the American army built steadily from the first draft contingent in September 1917, the men from the Northwest trained at Camp Lewis, Washington, near Tacoma. Massive Camp Lewis was one of the sixteen draftee training camps spread around the United States, each designed for fifty-five thousand soldiers. From the first contingent, Camp Lewis continued to be the hub of training activity.

One of the key components of Camp Lewis was the Remount Station, where horses were received and trained for wartime use. The *Flathead Courier* of June 27, 1918, reported on the men and the range of their activities at Camp Lewis Remount Station:

MONTANA COWBOYS "LET HER BUCK"
They have a wild west show out at Camp Lewis that is a continuous performance. It is the great remount station of the national army at the western cantonment. The cowboys are soldiers in the service of the United States army, picked because of their training on the stock ranges of Montana and other western states. The slogan of the camp is the age-old slogan of the Montana cowboy, indicating the devil-may-care spirit of the range rider of the Treasure State, "Powder River, let 'er buck."

Here the horses that go to supply the thousands of cavalrymen who are called into the service are trained for the hard duties that are before them on Flanders' fields. Immediately after the arrival of the horse at the remount station, he is inoculated against glanders. After that nothing but a German

Charles M. Russell painting *Smoking 'Em Out*, which hangs over the mantel of the fireplace in the Assembly Hall at the Remount Station in Camp Lewis. *From Alice Palmer Henderson's* The Ninety-First, the First at Camp Lewis *(2016)*.

bullet can stop him. As the life of the average horse in action at the front is only 21 fighting days, it will be seen that our equine friends are doing their part in the war. And in the great struggle he served two purposes. Alive, he smells the battle afar off, like the war horses of old Israel, and rides into the thick of the fray with his head up and snorting defiance. Dead, if death comes to him quickly from shrapnel or rifle bullet, and the savage butchers of the French commissary department get to his quivering carcass in time to make good most of what is left, he goes into the pot and cheers and sustains our allies of beloved France.

Guy Wedick's Riders. As a rule these animals come to the remount station fresh from the ranges of Montana and other western states, and they are put through their paces by Montana cowboys, who have learned the art of riding hell for leather before the days of dry land farming. The muster rolls of the companies of busters read like a program of one of Guy Wedick's [Calgary] stampedes, and all of the old time champions are there, except Fannie Sperry, who is barred from being a horse soldier by reason of her sex, but who could do the work as well as any man in the service. Tom Three Persons, the Canadian…champion of the world is there riding better than he has ever ridden before in his life, and among the other busters are men who have won fame at Calgary, Pendleton, Cheyenne, Missoula, Billings and Havre in the Wild West shows and rodeos.[74]

CAMP LEWIS REMOUNT "RODEO"

Most cowboys were assigned to the 91st "Wild West" Division forming at Camp Lewis. Rather than marching drills and shooting, the cowhands broke wild horses and taught draftees blacksmithing, mule packing and how to handle and care for horses and mules.

Captain Joseph W. Jackson proved the perfect leader for the Remount Station. Jackson, a graduate of Harvard and the owner of a large ranch in Williston, North Dakota, was respected by both cowboys and professional military men. He arranged for construction of the "Assembly Hall," equipped with an extensive library for use of the soldiers of the Remount Station.

The cowboys from Montana and the Northwest were not content just to do their jobs at the Remount Station. They also organized exceptional rodeos to demonstrate the military skills of the soldiers involved.

The largest of the Camp Lewis Rodeos was held on Sunday, July 4, on a clear and sunny day before an estimated crowd of more than thirty thousand cheering spectators. The rodeo began with a military parade, martial music and drill. Remount Station students demonstrated their skills in mule packing, blacksmithing, horseshoeing and working with wagon teams.

The second half of the rodeo presented a "rip-snorting, crowd pleasing, Wild West Show." Here the champion cowboys could show off their exceptional talents as western horsemen and cow punchers. Final events included Cossack riding and a Roman race, where standing riders straddled two horses, riding full speed around the arena.

Just two days after the July 4 rodeo, the soldiers of the 91st "Wild West" Division boarded transport ships for deployment to France to join the AEF. The division went on to fierce battles in the final Meuse-Argonne

Wild West Show in Remount Station at Camp Lewis Stadium. *Library of Congress.*

"Montana Day" at Camp Lewis, July 23, 1918. *Author's collection.*

Campaign. The soldiers of the 91st, who had trained on the fields and Remount Station of Camp Lewis, brought great credit to their frontier heritage, and they went into battle shouting their stirring war cry, "Powder River, Let 'Er Buck!"

Captain Jackson also deployed to France and was assigned to command the Remount Depot at Gievres, patterned after Camp Lewis. At war's end, the promoted Lieutenant Colonel Jackson was cited by General Pershing "for exceptionally meritorious and conspicuous services as Commanding Officer at Gievres."[75]

VETERINARY CORPS

When the United States entered the war, it was woefully prepared on many fronts, none more so than for the care of animals, yet other than men, horses and mules were one of the largest assets. The result was immense suffering on the part of the animals, a consequence of army bureaucracy and mismanagement. Estimates run as high as 76 percent of mule casualties in the AEF occurred from inadequate veterinary care, not from battle injuries. The advice of veterinarians was routinely ignored, and in the words of the chief veterinarian of the AEF, "more horses and mules in the U.S. Army in 1918 did not mean more transportation in France for the Army but it meant more waste of animals, time of men and money." Finally, in the summer of 1918, the Veterinary Corps was established at last as a medical branch with one commissioned officer and sixteen enlisted men per four hundred animals in service.

PFC Herman Kulage of Shonkin was one of many Montanans assigned to the new Veterinary Corps. He embarked the SS *Oregonian* in late October 1918 with five hundred animals and Veterinary Hospital No. 13 onboard en route to France where he served until June 1919.[76]

"SOW THE SEEDS OF VICTORY!": FOOD ADMINISTRATION DURING WORLD WAR I

The Wilson administration seized the moment as the United States entered the Great War—in lightning fashion, it proposed and implemented an extraordinary series of measures that dramatically broadened the role of the federal government and affected the life of every American.

In August 1917, Congress passed the Food and Fuel Control Act, aka the Lever Act. With the authority granted to him by Congress in this legislation, on August 10, 1917, President Woodrow Wilson issued Executive Order 2679-A, creating the U.S. Food Administration to operate in each state and ensure the supply, distribution and conservation of food during the war; facilitate transportation of food and prevent monopolies and hoarding; and maintain governmental power over foods by using voluntary agreements and a licensing system. Using the same authority, Wilson created two subsidiaries, the U.S. Grain Corporation and the U.S. Sugar Equalization Board. Together these bodies had an extraordinary impact on American lives.

Herbert Hoover, who earlier in the war received acclaim as head of the Belgian Relief Organization, now assumed the job of administrator of the Food Administration. Accepting no pay, Hoover became the "Food Czar." He designed an effort that would appeal to the American sense of volunteerism and avoid coercion, proclaiming, "Food will win the war."

To achieve results, the Food Administration combined an emphasis on patriotism with the power of advertising created by its own Advertising Section. This section produced a wealth of posters for both outdoor and indoor display. Montana's "cowboy artist" rose to the challenge, offering two of his watercolor paintings for use by the Food Administration in its advertising. In a letter of May 27, Charlie Russell wrote:

Dear Sir,
I am sending by todays express, two watercolors which I hope you can use for food conservation purposes.
I never painted soldiers and know little of them. The kinds I met in the old times were calvarymen [sic] and wore the blue. Today, both the horse and the blue are history, so I painted the men I know best. Those who Old Dad Time has barred from the fighting line.

Yours Sincerely
C.M. Russell

Hooverizin'

One of Charlie's watercolors was entitled *Hooverizin'*, and Alfred Atkinson, the Federal Food Administrator for Montana, described this painting in a letter he sent to the Food Administration office in Washington, D.C.:

One of them represents a cowboy cooking his evening meal out on the range, and his horse looking longingly toward the meal, which is made up of oats and barley. Under this is a little verse in which he says he hates to deprive his horse of this feed, but that they are both helping the war.

Hooverizin'
I hate to take your grub, Old Hoss, but then
I'm leavin' meat and wheat to fightin' men;
And by you handin' in your oats to me,
The both of us is Hooverizin'—See?
We're squarin' up with Uncle Sam, Our Friend,
Just kinder helpin' hold the easy end.

Atkinson also described the other Russell watercolor, titled *Meat Makes Fighters*:

> *The other picture is of an old cowboy mounted riding behind a band of cattle and there is a little verse under this expressing his sentiments of helping at home, even though he is too old to go to war.*
>
> *With "Meat Makes Fighters," Charlie sent the following poem:*
> *I ain't a wearin' khaki, 'cause I'm too old a stag,*
> *But I'm a handin' beef and hide to them that holds the flag;*
> *Pie and cake is good when folks just feed for fun,*
> *But beef and leather, plenty, puts men behind the gun.*[77]

HEROISM IN THE GREAT WAR

In an editorial of July 3, the *River Press* addressed heroism, based on words from the *Kansas City Journal*:

> *Just as every Canadian at Vimy Ridge was greater than any Spartan ever born, and every British Tommy in Flanders recorded another Thermopylae and every Frenchman at Verdun enacted a greater Alamo, so the Americans at the Marne are rolling all heroics into a continuous action and true courage has reached its highest pinnacle. The world will never know all its heroes of the great war. Crosses and medals and citations will exalt a few. But in unknown graves sleep men of supreme courage, and far from, the eyes of observers have been performed deeds that have never had a parallel in the struggles of the earth. But if these individual heroes are obscured by the glare of war, their sacrifices will live on to add glory to the name of manhood.*[78]

OVER THERE

By June 26, U.S. Marines had completed the capture of Belleau Wood, and that battle together with the larger Château-Thierry changed the course of the Great War. Fueled by the bravery of the Marines and the fearless reporting of the *Chicago Tribune*'s Floyd Gibbons, Belleau Wood rose to iconic status in the public perception of the Marine Corps. The "public" included the German enemy, who quickly learned at Belleau Wood that they were facing a foe with the discipline and bravery to match their own. America's allies, Britain and France, were learning that the AEF was a valuable force to be admired and reckoned with, coming of fighting age just in time. The French, military and civilian alike, were buoyed by Bois de la Brigade de Marine.

Just a week later, massive crowds attended a Fourth of July parade through Paris featuring U.S. Marines. In the words of correspondent Gibbons, "The bravery of that Marine brigade in the Bois de Belleau fight will ever remain a bright chapter in the records of the American Army. There is no bugle call, no sword waving, no dramatic enunciation of catchy commands, no theatricalism— it's just plain get up and go over."

For George Seldes, special war correspondence for the *Buffalo (NY) Sunday Express*, young Private Elmer G. Groves of Billings, Montana, exemplified the U.S. Marines in action. Seldes was with the stretcher bearers who went out over the newly won ground at Château-Thierry, retrieving the dead and wounded. There he talked with the exhausted Marines and from them obtained stories that bid fair to go down in history, among them Groves's.

U.S. Marines marching through the streets of Paris on July 4, 1918.

The Marines had swept over the hills and valley from Villers-Cotterets Forest to Vierzy and beyond, fighting four days practically without rest. The Germans were driven in disorderly flight. Private Groves was in the fourth "wave" of "Devil Dogs" that went over the top and, in the fog of battle, was separated from his company. While wandering about on the battlefield, he heard machine gun fire over a knoll, and one of the bullets struck the Billings boy in the left hand. He started after the nest, as related in the *Conrad Independent* of September 19:

> *When Seldes found Groves, the Billings boy was seated under a tree digging listlessly into a can of stew with his fork. It was his first meal in three and a half days. He answered the questions of the correspondent in a tired voice, meanwhile running his fork through the stew and holding up morsels of the beef for epicurean inspection. The fiction monger who pictures half-starved men tearing at their bread and meat after some fortunate rescue, has strayed from fact, Seldes says. Starved soldiers are the most leisurely eaters, according to the Buffalo writer.*
>
> *Groves had lost his company in the confusion of attack and wandering about the battlefield he heard a gunner firing over a knoll. Wearily he approached the enemy position, and gaining a point of vantage, plugged his man through the hand. The German could no longer work the machine gun, so he got out his revolver and was about to shoot, when Groves shot him through the head.*
>
> *The noise of the duel disturbed 35 other Germans who were weathering the American artillery showers in a dugout. Groves approached the nest, and, bombs in hand, called upon the Boches to surrender. One by one they stumbled up the dugout steps, hands over their heads. Groves asked one of them to bandage his* [own] *bleeding hand, then, not knowing where his company was, marched the 35 prisoners into regimental headquarters, and got a receipt for them. He was told to stay to have his wound treated.*[79]

Private Elmer Groves had lived in Billings about eight years, attending public schools and business college. After college, Groves joined the Northwestern Auto Supply Company and was transferred to the Great Falls branch. He joined the Marine Corps in November 1917 and spent two months at Mare Island, California, before being sent overseas. Private Groves served in 17 Company, 2nd Battalion, 5th Marine Regiment in the 2nd Division. Commanding 2nd Battalion, 5th Marine, was Colonel Frederick M. Wise, who remarked when ordered to retreat at a time when the French were falling back on both his flanks, "To hell with retreating. Let the Germans do the retreating!" His battalion captured 580 Germans and many machine guns at a cost of 75 percent casualties during June 2–5.

Coming home from France, Groves had another close call with death. His transport, the USS *Pocahontas*, encountered heavy storms coming across, sprang a leak and slowly proceeded on. A fire broke out in the hold the same day the ship sprang the leak, but the crew extinguished the blaze and managed to keep the transport afloat, with the lower deck awash, as it limped into Newport News on February 13.[80]

MONTANA AVIATOR KILLED

In mid-July, the *Great Falls Tribune* brought news of the death of First Lieutenant Charles L. Watkins, one of Montana's early combat aviators killed in France. At this time, the life expectancy of an aviator in combat in France was just twenty days. Lieutenant Watkins was killed on June 23 near the 3rd Aviation Institute Center, and he rests today at St. Mihiel American Cemetery, Thiacourt, France:

Grave marker for First Lieutenant Charles L. Watkins, St. Mihiel American Cemetery, France. *Find a Grave.*

GREAT FALLS BOY MAKING HIS SECOND SOLO FLIGHT WHEN MACHINE SUDDENLY TAKES NOSE DIVE OF 125 METERS—BURIED WITH MILITARY HONORS

Lieut. Charles Lloyd Watkins, son of Mr. and Mrs. Jared Watkins of 212 Twelfth street north, sleeps in a grave in France as one of the American boys who gave his life in his efforts to help turn the Hun hordes back toward Germany. Lieut. Watkins was killed at the flying field in Issodun, France, at 9 Sunday morning, June 23, when the airplane which he was driving took a sudden nose dive when at an altitude of 125 meters, or about 400 feet. He was instantly killed and the machine he was driving was a complete wreck.

…Lieut Watkins is survived by his father and mother and one brother, Robert Lowell Watkins, a paying teller in the United States Navy, now with a cruiser in the waters of the Bering Sea.[81]

Lieutenant Watkins's brother, Ensign Robert L. Watkins, served as chief storekeeper onboard the USS *Explorer*. The *Explorer*, built in 1904, served as a survey ship in the U.S. Coast and Geodetic Survey until it was transferred to the U.S. Navy in May 1918 and commissioned as the USS *Explorer* to patrol Prince William Sound in the Gulf of Alaska.

AN UNDERAGE DESERTER

In June, Seaman 2nd Class Arthur De Grazia suddenly returned to his East Helena home. He was charged with being a deserter from the navy who quit his ship, the battleship USS *Georgia*, in Southern California, to return home because he was homesick. De Grazia was surrendered by his father, M. De Grazia, a storekeeper in East Helena, and returned to the U.S. Navy at the receiving ship at Puget Sound, Washington. While his navy enlistment record recorded his age in 1917 as eighteen years and ten months, Seaman De Grazia declared that he was only sixteen years of age, under the age

USS *Georgia* (Battleship no. 15) shown on its trials, June 13, 1906. *National Archives.*

prescribed as minimum for recruits to the navy. This proved to be the case, and young Arthur was discharged from the navy on July 30, facing no further disciplinary action.[82]

WAR ANGELUS MOVEMENT

Billings Mausoleum window honoring veterans who lost their lives in World War I. *Author photo.*

In March 1918, the Billings Rotary Club started what would become the national "War Angelus" movement. Two months later, the International Association of Rotary Clubs at its national convention adopted the idea, urging all member organizations to arrange for the observation of the War Angelus for one minute, at the hour of 11:00 a.m., in an "appeal to the Supreme Being for inspiration, strength and guidance." An Angelus came from a Roman Catholic prayer to be said at a set time of day. The War Angelus, adopted by the Rotarians, soon spread widely across the nation.[83]

THE ROCK OF THE MARNE

Ten days after the massive Fourth of July parade through Paris to honor their American allies, the French celebrated their own great national holiday, Bastille Day, in commemoration of the storming of the Bastille in 1789 as a symbol of the French Revolution. With Bastille Day in mind, the German High Command planned a final ultimate offensive code-named *Friedensturm*, or "Peace Offensive," to commence early July 15 to take advantage of known French excessive celebration the previous day.

Unbeknownst to the Germans was the fact that the Allies had learned details of the attack plan from captured German prisoners, including the exact time that an artillery barrage would launch the offensive. With this crucial intelligence, the Allies prepared their own surprise: deployment of several new American divisions to reinforce French lines, withdrawal of many of the French troops to secondary trenches minimizing the effect of the initial German barrage and a massive allied artillery barrage timed for two hours before the planned German attack.

Although rocked by the Allied preemptive measures, the scale of the German assault was so great that it came close to breaking through the French lines at the Marne River approaches on the road to Paris. After initial successes, by Tuesday, July 16, the German offensive began to stall as a result of combined French-American forces, especially by heroic action from the AEF 3rd Division that would lead to their honored designation as the "Rock of the Marne."

The *River Press* reported on the all-out German offensive, under the constraints of wartime censorship that precluded mention of specific AEF military units:

> *KNOCKED OUT BY AMERICAN PUNCH*
> *Fierce German Attack in Marne District Repulsed by Smashing Blows from Yankee Boys*
> *Paris, July 15.—In the desperate fighting which is reported in the official communication from the war office tonight the American troops are given the credit for driving back the Germans who had succeeded in crossing the Marne southwest of Fossoy.*
>
> *With the American Army on the Marne, July 15.—A strong American counter attack south of the river bend completely upset the Germans, who broke in retreat. The American troops drove the enemy back all the way to the railway skirting the Marne in the region southwest of Jaulgonne. This position now is being held.*
>
> *The German prisoners captured in the counterattack by the Americans at the bend of the Marne number 1,000 and 1,500. They include a complete brigade staff.*
>
> *The fighting continues with fierce intensity in this district while the battle rages with equal ferocity on the right, where the French are reported to have delivered a smashing blow against the enemy. From this section of the battle front it appears that the German offensive, at least for the time being, has been badly shattered.*
>
> *The Americans now command the river front at the bend. At the left of the bend the famous German tenth division has made repeated attempts all day to cross, but all assaults have been smashed by the well-directed fire of the American gunners, and not a single German had succeeded in getting over at this point up to 9 o'clock tonight.*
>
> *The French general commanding the group of armies on this sector sent a congratulatory message this afternoon to the American general commanding the forces which beat back the enemy.*[84]

"Like Hell Turned Loose"

The *Great Falls Tribune* of March 2, 1919, carried gunner Daniel J. Griffin's thrilling letter to his aunt describing his own experience during the Battle of the Marne. Gunner Griffin of Williams, Teton County, served in Company D, 9th Machine Gun Battalion, 3rd Division:

> *Niedermendig, Germany.*
> *December 25, 1918.*
>
> *My Dear Aunt*
> *You must excuse me for not writing sooner. Well, thank God, the war is over, for nobody knows what war is only we poor boys who had to face the shot and shell.*
>
> *We took over the front line from the French on June 1 on the Marne river. Everything was very quiet until July 14, when old Fritz made a drive for Paris, but he got badly fooled. We were getting relieved by another division that night but old Fritz spoiled the game and cut loose at midnight with the worst bombardment that has ever been thrown over by the Germans in the war history. The night was as dark as pitch, the heavens lit up by the gun fire. Our artillery opened up on them and then it was like hell turned loose. The infantry in front of us were nearly all killed by the shell fire but there were enough of us left to stop the Hun. They tried to come across the river at the break of day; 1,700 of them got across, but they never got back. We opened on them with machine guns. All my squad were killed but two of us. I was gunner and when the Germans started to come over I cut loose. I had 2,000 rounds of bullets and I let them have it. I mowed them down like corn. I would have got more of them but their artillery got my range; the first shell hit 100 yards in front of me, the second 50 yards, but I did not wait for the third. The loader and myself had just moved when the third shell hit our gun and blew it to pieces. The 3rd battalion of the 38th infantry came up to help us….*
>
> *P.S.—As I forgot to tell you in the other part of my letter this will give you an idea of what the Americans can do. Six hundred of us fought two divisions of Germans and drove them over the Marne River. That was 600 fighting 80,000.*[85]

THE MIRACLE

The best-detailed account of the Battle of the Marne appears in Colonel R. Kelton's article, "The Miracle of Chateau-Thierry," in *The Century* of May 1919. In his account, Colonel Kelton extolled the performance of the 30th and 38th Infantry Regiments and the 9th Machine Gun Battalion as they effectively denied the crucial German crossing of the Marne:

> *The defeat of the Germans had been complete. True, they had gained a few kilometers at some points, but though parts of the Allied line had sagged a little it did not break. No troop operations were needed anywhere to stop a gap, and when Marshal Foch was assured of this fact on the night of July 15, the anxiously waited opportunity was at hand.*
>
> *The German high command was bewildered; they had counted it an easy step in their operations toward Paris and ultimate victory. Hertling, the German chancellor, three days before his death stated that he was convinced on July 1, 1918, that the Allies would propose peace before September. He said: "We expected grave events in Paris before the fifteenth of July. But on the eighteenth even the most optimistic among us knew that all was lost. The history of the world was played out in those three days."*
>
> *…If unseasoned American troops could fight like that, then when twenty-five divisions were available instead of only five, and the hope of victory and the will to conquer burned again with an unquenchable flame, the war could still be won.*[86]

"WILD WEST" DIVISION DEPLOYS

The 91st "Wild West" Infantry Division was formed at Camp Lewis of draftees from eight western states, including Montana. The 361st Regiment was composed largely of Oregon and Washington men. The spirit of Montana dominated the 362nd Regiment, while the 363rd and 364th featured California men. Yet there were Montana men in all four regiments of the "Wild West" Division. These were men from the forests, farms and mines of the West. However, tragedy struck on July 25 shortly after arrival in France:

> *On the afternoon of June 23, 1918, the 362nd Infantry began its seven thousand mile trip to the trenches. At Camp Mills some men of Company E*

broke out with the measles so were left behind. The 91ˢᵗ Division sailed from New York July 6 in the largest convoy that up to that time had crossed the Atlantic. Escorted by destroyers, the fourteen-ship convoy, carefully made its way across the Atlantic. About noon on July 17ᵗʰ the convoy continued down through the Irish Sea to the Mersey River, and on to the Liverpool docks.

After a short period in English rest camps and travel across England, the 362ⁿᵈ arrived at Le Havre on July 22ⁿᵈ. The first train to leave Le Havre carrying 362ⁿᵈ men left about three o'clock on the afternoon of July 23ʳᵈ. Little, toy-looking cars, with dinky, little engines, compared to the iron monsters of America, made up the French train. The term "Hommes 40— Chevaux 8" was forever engraved upon the memory of the Yanks, "Men 40—Horses 8" were the capacity of the French box cars.

It was in these little cars that American soldiers were transported, forty big western men with their packs were uncomfortably crowded. If lucky, the men had straw on the floor to sprawl or sit, taking turns at sleeping as room permitted.

Tragedy soon struck. While the train was standing on the main line near the station in the village of Bonnieres a short time before midnight there came a terrible crash. A heavy loaded, fast moving train plowed into the rear end of our troop train, piling many of the cars one on top of another, and breaking some of them into kindling wood.

On each side of the track, as far as sixty feet, lay the wreck of the box cars, the dead and dying in grotesque positions. As the engine plowed through the last seven cars, it scrambled tracks, wood, iron, bodies and rifles in a tangled mass. Feet and arms peeped forth from the wreckage. Blood and brains and dismembered legs and arms were spattered and scattered everywhere. One body rested under the rear wheels of the engines.

The noise brought from the village some old peasants, who in turn called doctors and nurses from a French hospital nearby.

Sufficient men were called from the other cars to rescue the wounded. They were dug from the debris with care and placed side by side along the country road. There, by a flickering lantern, the village Cure administered last rites while Red Cross nurses from the hospital busied themselves with those in whom the light of life burned stronger.

…It is of such stuff that American soldiers are made.

Those poor fellows, traveling across the ocean to fight for their country, had their lives crushed out in a miserable train wreck, with never the chance to hear a shot fired. But they died bravely and are as much heroes as those who gave their lives on the battlefield.

But war is war. And at half-past three the remainder of the train moved on, leaving the wounded in care of two of the regimental doctors, with ambulances from a nearby town taking them to a hospital there.

Later investigation showed that a French engineer in the other train ran through danger lights at sixty miles an hour and ignored the frantic signaling of the brakeman, causing the tragic accident. Three officers and twenty-one men from the 362nd remained to care for the wounded and bury the dead. The funeral was held three days later, with an estimated five thousand French paying respects to the dead Yanks. Train wreck casualties suffered by the 362nd included thirty-two killed and sixty-three injured. Among the known Montana casualties were eight killed, two wounded, one severely and one slightly, all from the Machine Gun Company. Most are today interred at Suresnes American Cemetery in France:

- PFC Edward Dalman, of Zurich, Montana; born in Russia.
- Private George E. Dean, of Conrad; born in Choteau.
- Private Laurence E. Fleming, of Creston; born in Lynden, Kansas.
- PFC John M. MacLeod, of Harlowton.
- PFC Elbert Robinson, of Forsyth; born in Juett, Illinois.
- Private Nils A. Sanderson, of Forest Grove, Fergus County; born in Cokedale, Montana.
- Private Angus Stone, of Winnett; born in Boston, Massachusetts.
- Mechanic Wayne Hubert Westcott, of Ismay, Montana; born in Bertrand, Nebraska.
- Private Oscar Rasmussen, of Miles City, severely wounded; born in Nevada, Iowa.
- Horseshoer John Watson, of Noxon, slightly wounded; born in Red Lodge.[87]

With this, the "Wild West" Division went into intensive training for the following six weeks.

THE BATTLE OF SOISSONS

The massive German *Friedensturm* offense of July 15 came perilously close to overrunning the approaches to Paris before it stalled because of staunch resistance by combined French-American forces. The heroic action of the

AEF 3rd Infantry Division stopped the German assault cold at the Marne River, halting the German drive and saving Paris. For this, the 3rd Division would forever bear the honored name the "Rock of the Marne."

After initial success, by Tuesday, July 16, the German offensive was stalling, and Allied commander general Foch saw an opening to launch his own planned offensive. H-hour was set for 4:35 a.m. on the morning of July 18, with the main objective to cut the primary German supply route in the Marne region. For the first time, this would be led by an AEF Corps–level operation composed of the combined 1st Division and 2nd Division, including the 4th Marine Brigade, fresh from its costly victory at Belleau Wood just two weeks earlier. III Corps, supported by the French Foreign Legion, quietly moved into position on the rainy, overcast night of the seventeenth before launching its offensive to cut the highway between Soissons and Château-Thierry.

In a letter to his aunt, Gunner Daniel J. Griffin of the 9th Machine Gun Battalion, 3rd Division, reported on the action:

We went over the top on the morning of July 17 [sic]. We took 1,000 prisoners and killed the rest of the Huns who had come across. The 6th engineers built a bridge that night under heavy shell fire and we got across to the other side under machine gun fire. That morning at daybreak we went

"The Rock of the Marne" combat poster. *U.S. Army.*

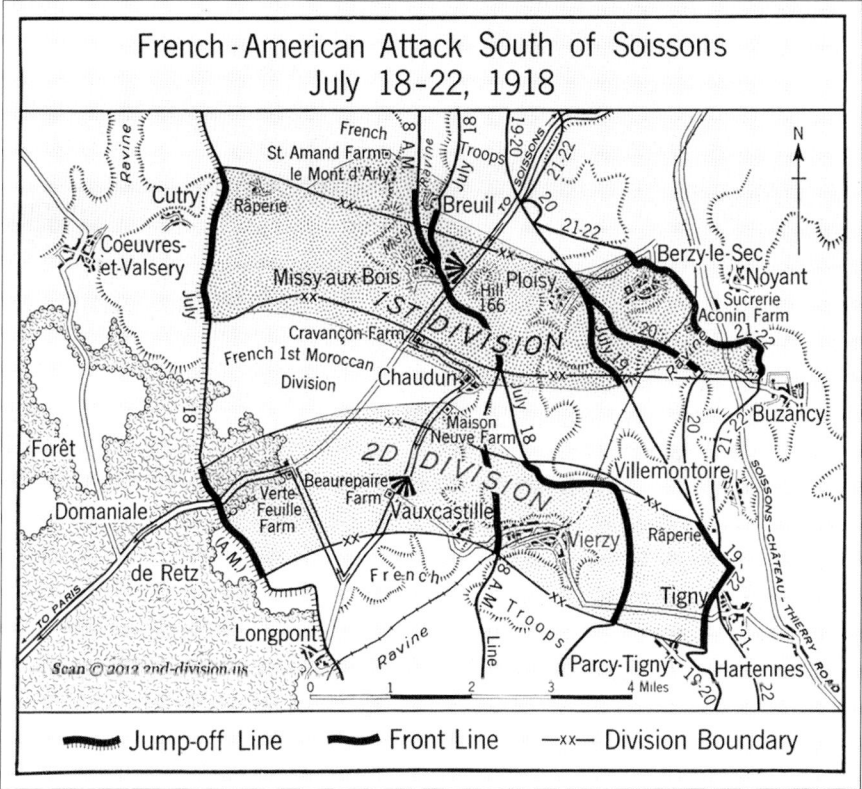

Map of the Battle of Soissons, known also as the Battle of Vierzy.

over the top again. The battle lasted for seven days and we drove them 11 miles to the Vesel river. We had taken 15,000 prisoners, a lot of field guns and ammunition.

It was on this river that I was wounded, a 6-inch shell burst near 15 of us, killing six and wounding nine. The force of it threw me to the ground. I was half dead for three hours and when I came to, I was lying in a Red Cross station. A piece of the shell went into my side. The next day I was taken to the base hospital in Paris, 300 of us were on the Red Cross train. The French women along the line at every station were cheering us and some of them came into the cars and kissed us, saying, "you boys have saved Paris."

When we got to Paris the people nearly pulled us off the stretchers. I enjoyed the fun but I could not see for I was blinded by the gas that the Hun threw over while I was lying on the ground. I am now in the best of health, thank God, a few days [later] I was able to see again.[88]

Gibbons Again in Action:
"The Turn of the Tide"

American war correspondent Floyd Gibbons accompanied the troops throughout the Battle of Soissons despite serious wounds, including the loss of sight in his left eye, suffered at Belleau Wood just five weeks earlier. Gibbons captured the essence of the battle as it launched early on July 18:

> *There was some suspense. We knew that if the Germans has the slightest advance knowledge about that mobilization of Foch's reserves that night, they would have responded with a downpour of gas shells, which spreading their poisonous fumes under the wet roof of the forest, might have spelt slaughter for 70,000 men.*
>
> *But the enemy never knew. They never even suspected. And at the tick of 4:35 a.m., the heavens seemed to crash asunder, as tons and tons of hot metal sailed over the forest, bound for the German line…*
>
> *All through that glorious day of the 18th, our lines swept forward victoriously. The 1st Division fought it out on the left, the Foreign Legion in the centre and the 2nd Division with the Marines pushed forward to the right. Village after village fell into our hands. We captured batteries of guns and thousands of prisoners.*
>
> *On through the night the Allied assault continued. Our men fought without water or food.…By morning of the 19th, we had so far penetrated the enemy's lines that we had crossed the road running southward from Soissons to Chateau-Thierry, thereby disrupting the enemy's communications between his newly established base and the peak of his salient. Thus exposed to an enveloping movement that might have surrounded large numbers, there was nothing left for the Germans to do but to withdraw.*

The eloquent correspondent concluded, "The Germans began backing off the Marne. From that day on, their movement to date has continued backward. It began July 18th. Two American Divisions played glorious parts in the crisis. It was their day. It was America's day. It was the turn of the tide."[89]

German frontline troops, taken by surprise, initially gave ground, although resistance soon stiffened. Meanwhile, the French armies in the offensive also made important gains, and the German commander ordered a general retreat from the Marne salient. Before the 1st and 2nd Divisions were relieved (on July 19 and July 22, respectively), they and the Foreign Legion had advanced about seven miles, making Soissons untenable for the enemy and capturing 6,500 prisoners.

Gibbons's stirring coverage masked the immense cost in casualties among the twenty-four French, two British and two American divisions. The Allies suffered 107,000 casualties (95,000 French and 12,000 American), while the Germans suffered 168,000 casualties. Montana casualties in the Battle of Soissons totaled at least 160, including 96 killed. Many Montanans served in the 1st Division's 16th Infantry Regiment, and at least 39 of them lost their lives in the battle.

MEANWHILE AT HOME

On July 5 in Washington, D.C., Representative Jeannette Rankin announced that she would be a candidate for the U.S. Senate to succeed Senator Thomas J. Walsh. In her declaration, Representative Rankin stated:

> *If nominated and elected, I will, during my term of office support the president and a vigorous prosecution of the war to a victorious conclusion and, as heretofore, vote for every measure he may recommend to more efficiently prosecute the war.*
>
> *I will stand for legislation to prevent profiteering and thus protect people from unnecessarily high prices; to prohibit the consumption of grain for the manufacture of liquor; to secure adequate compensation for farmers' products; national prohibition; to give administration power to fix food prices and necessities of life including farm implements, etc.; for national equal suffrage. I shall endeavor to faithfully care for the interests of Montana and her people in Washington.*[90]

The critical question for Representative Rankin was whether she could overcome staunch opposition from the Anaconda Company. The "Company" cast a wide net across the state's politics in wartime Montana.

DEVASTATING DROUGHT

America's capacity to raise grain and produce food to feed the Allies and the homeland was a critical factor in winning the war. Yet a severe drought in 1917 had cut Montana's cereal grain production by half. As Montana neared the 1918 harvest season in late July, reports began to come in from northern, eastern and central Montana—and the news was not good.

Joseph T. Berthelote, chairman of Hill County commissioners, reported that conditions in the Sweet Grass Hills were not good. He believed this was one of the driest seasons during his twenty-five years living in that part of northern Montana. O.C. Ihmsen of Big Sandy reported that this was one of the driest seasons ever known in the Bear's Paw country, resulting in a serious shortage of feed and forage as well as almost a total failure in grain crops. U.S. Weather Bureau meteorologist William A. Mitchell reported in early July that the winter wheat had been ruined by the drought and that rain was badly needed to save the spring wheat in the northern half of Montana. George Streit arrived in Fort Benton from his ranch about six miles east of town with the first load of wheat brought to this market in mid-July. His winter wheat was harvested with a combine, the crop averaging just twelve bushels per acre. The farm bureaus of Chouteau, Valley, Phillips, Blaine, Toole and Teton Counties began holding meetings to organize efforts to secure federal aid for drought-stricken farmers.[91]

Montana's War on Words

By mid-1918, the iron fist of wartime limits on free speech was descending on Montana and the nation. Among the rash of new prosecutions were the following.

Herman Heimann of Carter was charged with sedition for words to the effect that he would as soon see President Wilson killed as the kaiser, adding, "We will have enough fighting to do here without going over there; and we should not condemn the Kaiser, he may be right, we don't know."

The three-day trial of Heimann concluded in the district court in Fort Benton with the jury returning a verdict of guilty and fixing the penalty at a $500 fine under the Montana anti-sedition law. In passing sentence on Heimann, Judge John Tattan remarked:

> *I agree with the verdict of the jury that you are guilty, but a fine of $500 is not enough for a man like you, who, came to this country because you could not live in Germany. You came to this country as the country of your choice. After you became 21 years of age you voluntarily went into court and took a solemn oath that you would renounce the emperor of Germany forever, and*

swore positive allegiance to be true to the United States of America. You have committed perjury. The verdict of the jury says when you took that oath and acted as you did that you committed perjury, and it is a question whether you should continue to be a citizen of the United States.[92]

John Harrington, a miner in Fergus County, was charged with uttering disloyal, profane language. Found guilty, Harrington was sentenced to prison and served twelve months from April 19, 1918.[93]

In Lewistown, Edward A. Foster, who served in the Spanish-American War as a lieutenant in the Montana regiment, was charged with having said, "Because I don't carry the goddam flag they call me pro-German; because I don't buy Liberty Bonds and don't carry the flag they call me a pro-German." At Foster's trial, the jury, after having been out more than twenty-four hours, returned a verdict of guilty and fixed the penalty as a fine of $500.[94]

On July 23, the Montana Council of Defense endorsed formation of a Montana Loyalty League with hyper-patriot Will A. Campbell, of Helena, as secretary-treasurer. The league proclaimed that there was only "one qualification for membership—pure, unadulterated Americanism without reservations, mental or otherwise." Campbell quoted General Pershing as saying, "I will smash the German line in France if you will smash that damnable Hun propaganda at home." The league's two principal targets were the Non-Partisan League, then growing in strength in the Dakotas and Montana, and the IWW.[95]

FEMININE SEDITION

Application of the tough Montana Sedition Law even began to affect women. In June, Mrs. Florence E. Miller of Columbia Falls was charged with sedition, the first such charge brought against a woman in Montana. According to witnesses at her trial in Kalispell, Mrs. Miller said, "I hope the Germans get every American who goes over there. Germany will win the war." On June 22, after the jury deliberated for twenty-four hours, she was found guilty of sedition and fined $350.

Mrs. Miller was Colorado-born, the wife of Bohemia-born immigrant Joseph E. Miller, and the mother of two children. Her father had served in cavalry in the Indian Wars, stationed at Fort Custer.[96]

Chapter 5

AUGUST 1918

War at Sea; Battle of Montdidier; Aisne-Marne Offensive

OVER THERE

The Allied offensive begun at the Marne on July 18 continued into early August. The French Sixth Army—including the American 3rd, 4th, 28th and 42nd Divisions—reached the Vesle River on August 3. The 4th and 42nd Divisions were under command of I Corps, the first AEF corps headquarters to participate in combat. On August 4, the AEF III Corps headquarters entered combat, assuming command of the 28th and 32nd Divisions, the latter relieving the 3rd Division on the line on July 29. By August 5, the entire Sixth Army front was held by the two AEF corps. The French Fifth and Ninth Armies advanced with the Americans as the Germans retired across the Aisne and Vesle Rivers, stoutly defending each strongpoint as they retreated.

By August 6, the German Aisne-Marne Offensive was over, ending the threat to Paris. Now, the initiative was held by the Allies, ending further German offensives for the duration of the war. The dramatic successes of these three weeks confirmed the new unity of Allied command and the fighting qualities of the American soldiers. Eight AEF divisions (1st, 2nd, 3rd, 4th, 26th, 28th, 32nd and 42nd), with 270,000 men, spearheaded much of the Allied offensive advance.

From the arrival of General Pershing in France in June 1917 and the formation of the AEF, the general steadfastly worked to organize separate American military units, to avoid having his men simply become replacements

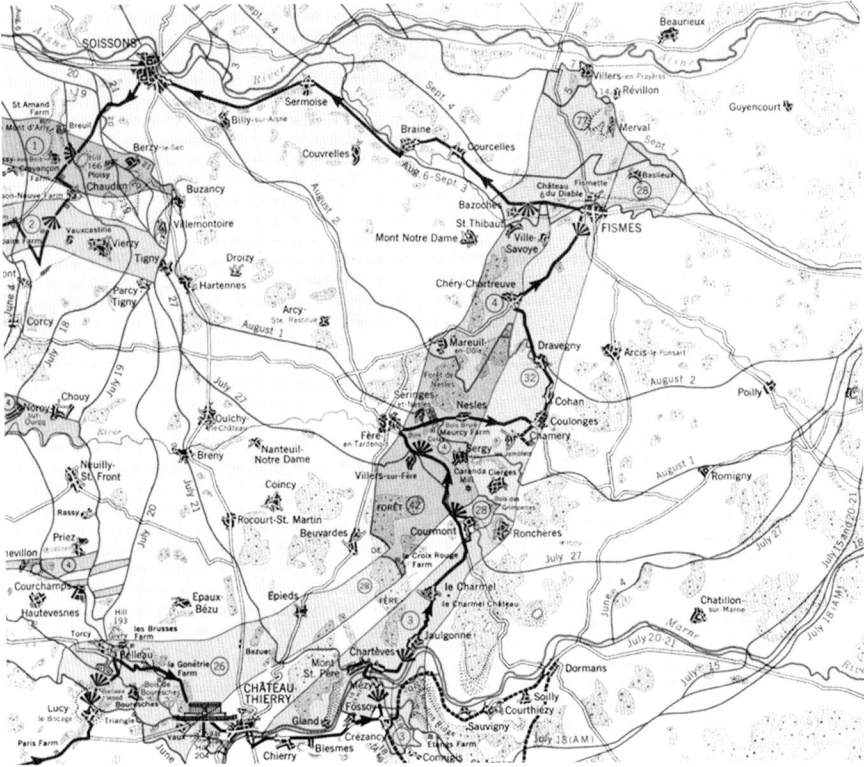

Aisne-Marne battle map, July–August 1918. *American Battle Monuments Commission.*

for the French and British military. With the massive buildup of the AEF by the summer of 1918, General Pershing was finally able to implement his plan to organize AEF corps and armies.

As the Allies captured Château-Thierry before the end of July and pressed on to force the Germans back to the Hindenburg Line, the experience of one Montanan reminds us that each battle and each mile gained came at a cost. That young man was Vester Andrews.

CAPTURED AT CHÂTEAU-THIERRY

Vester L. Andrews came to Montana in 1912 from Piney Creek, North Carolina, and filed on a claim at Colony Bay, a homestead community in Chouteau County. He proved up his 160 acres in April 1917, before entering the draft. Andrews was assigned to the 163rd Infantry, which sailed for France on the transport USS *Plattsburg* in December 1917. In France, the 163rd served as a replacement regiment in the 41st Sunset Division, and Private Andrews with many other Montanans was assigned to the showcase 16th Regiment, 1st Infantry Division. Serving in Company B, PFC Andrews spent several months on the front lines until he was captured July 21, on the fourth day of the fighting near Château-Thierry, after he had been wounded in the shoulder by a machine gun bullet.

Private Andrews survived his ordeal and related his story to a *Billings Gazette* reporter after his return to freedom in 1919:

> *My regiment was one of those thrown into the breach at Chateau Thierry with orders to halt the Germans at any cost. The world knows what we did there during those eventful days in July, 1918.*
>
> *I fought through three days without receiving a scratch, with a muggy haze stifling the breath and partially obscuring the view. The smoke of battle clung to the blood soaked earth and the nauseating stench of the unburied dead smote our nostrils on every hand.*
>
> *Early in the morning our barrage lifted and at the zero hour we resumed our advance. There was no artificial shelter, excepting scattered entrenchments deserted by the Germans in their slow retreat. The country is dotted with woods and underbrush, which offered a modicum of protection from the devastating machine gun and rifle fire of the foe.*
>
> *I was on scout duty* [to gather information], *advancing through a field, when I became aware of a machine gun nest not far away. Bullets were whizzing in my direction, I dropped to the ground, too late.*
>
> *I had had a morbid sort of curiosity as to what it feels like to be shot. I learned then. I can remember hearing a wicked, wasp-like whiz-z-z. Then I felt a sting in my right shoulder. That was all. I knew I was hit. There was no particular pain—not at first. I glanced down at my tunic. I had to look carefully before I discerned the bullet hole. I was not bleeding yet. A little later, when I felt of my shoulder over the hole in my tunic I could feel the warm blood soaking my under clothing. I started for a first-aid station in the rear, crawling on my stomach until I thought I was out of range of the machine gun. My right arm was useless.*
>
> *Whether I lost my direction, or whether the Germans had closed in behind me I am not certain. I was quite a distance in advance of the main body of our troops, and I believe the Germans had outflanked me. A few hundred yards to the rear I ran plump into a company of about*

seventy Prussian guards. No Americans were near. I realized that to resist was hopeless.

The Germans stripped me of all weapons and sent me back toward their lines, heavily guarded. The next day I was placed with other allied prisoners and my wound was dressed hurriedly. We were sent to the rear.

Private Vester Andrews lived through his captivity and returned to the United States aboard the USS *Leviathan*, landing in New York Harbor on January 30, 1919. After spending most of February at Camp Funston, Kansas, where he was discharged from service, Private Andrews stopped over in Billings between trains en route to Fort Benton. His only concern was about his homestead, as he remarked, "It's been a year and a half since I saw my homestead, but I guess Uncle Sam won't let anyone take it away from me." The reporter assured Andrews that he had nothing to fear on this score.[97]

Marshal of France

The *River Press* reported news from France as the Aisne-Marne Offensive ended:

French President Announces Success of Recent Allied Drive
Paris, Aug. 6.—The council of ministers has elevated General Ferdinand Foch, commander in chief of the allied forces on the western front, to a marshal of France. The ministers also have conferred the military medal on General Petain, commander in chief of the French armies on the western front.

President Poincare presided at the meeting of the council. In presenting the name of General Foch, Premier Clemenceau said: "At the hour when the enemy, by a formidable offensive on a front of 100 kilometers, counted on snatching the decision and imposing a German peace upon us, General Foch and his admirable troops vanquished him.

"Paris is not in danger, Soissons and Chateau-Thierry have been reconquered and more than 200 villages have been delivered. Thirty-five thousand prisoners and 700 cannons have been captured, and the enemy's high hopes before the allies' drive began have been crushed. The glorious allied armies have thrown him from the banks of the Marne to the Aisne. Such are the results of high command's strategy, superbly executed by incomparable commanders."[98]

OVER HERE

Representative Jeannette Rankin campaigned through northern Montana to secure the Republican nomination for U.S. senator, arriving in Fort Benton to address an audience of about seventy-five people who had assembled on the lawn at the Arthur and Dorothy McLeish residence along the levee. Representative Rankin talked about her work in Washington and included in her remarks her personal views on labor conditions in the Montana mining industry.[99]

A continuation of the dry spell in the Havre district was announced in the report of the weather bureau station at Havre for the month of July. The total precipitation for that month was only 0.75 inch, while the normal rainfall for July during the period since 1880 has been 1.92 inches. The deficiency in precipitation during the seven months of this year had been 5.70 inches, compared with the average of former seasons.[100]

SECOND COLORED CONTINGENT

On July 18, Montana adjutant general Phil Greenan announced that 101 African American registrants in Montana would be called up for service in early August. Among these was one black resident of Chouteau County, Emmett McGee, who registered for the draft in June 1917 while working as a section track laborer at Pownal, near Square Butte, on the Chicago, Milwaukee, St. Paul & Pacific Railroad. From the smallest to Montana's largest black contingent, Cascade County sent nineteen young men: Franklin Orme, James Parker, Eddie Welsh, Bennie Bell, Charles Thomas, William Lovings, Anton Williams, William A. Anthony, Will Harris, Edward G. Simms, John Porter Connell, Johnny Bukey, James Allen Jr., Ernest J. Penn, William Knott, Lawrence Jones, Fred S. Boston, George L. Hagen and Claude McGuire.

As this contingent left for Camp Lewis, the men marched down Central Avenue following the Black Eagle Band, police and fire companies. Crowds lined the avenue, and in the words of the *Great Falls Leader*, "[T]he men received as great an ovation as their white brothers-in-arms who left the week before.…The contingent carried a banner on which was inscribed 'Fast Black Won't Run,' and the record made by our colored soldiers in action so far demonstrates that this is no idle boast."[101]

African American soldiers fighting German soldiers in World War I, with portrait of Abraham Lincoln above. *Library of Congress.*

DEATH OF A FLYING CADET

On July 27, a promising young aviator died in a training accident at the Fort Worth, Texas Aviation Service airfield. Fred C. Campbell, a solo flier within a few days of his commission, died when his airplane dropped into a tailspin at low altitude, hurtling him to his death. He was excelling in flight training before his tragic death.

Cadet Campbell had grown up in Montana at the Fort Peck Indian Agency and Fort Shaw Indian Industrial School, where his father served as superintendent before assuming his present position as special supervisor of the Blackfeet Indian Reservation. After two years at Great Falls High School, young Campbell graduated from the high school course in a military school at Tonkawa, Oklahoma. He then took a three-year engineering course at Kansas University and completed college on scholarship at Montana State College of Agriculture and Mechanic Arts in Bozeman.

Campbell owned a sheep ranch with his father on Freeman Creek. He enlisted in the aviation service while serving as assistant manager for the Diamond A Cattle company, with headquarters at Eagle Butte, South Dakota.[102]

THE SUN NEVER SETS

A useful reminder of the new global reach of America during the Great War came from the *Indianapolis News*:

> *Once it was stated that the sun never sets on the British flag.*
>
> *One year after America is in the war the sun cannot set upon the American soldiers. They are in France and they are in Germany, across the border in Alsace. They are in Italy. American soldiers are in Archangel, Russia, up under the Arctic circle. They are also in Vladivostok.*
>
> *American soldiers are in the Philippines, Hawaii and Samoa. American soldiers are in Panama and one of the Central American republics. They are in Haiti and San Domingo.*
>
> *When the American soldiers landed in Vladivostok and Archangel they were in the same empire, but they were 8,000 miles apart.*
>
> *This gives you some idea of the colossal size of Russia....*[103]

Homesteader and First Class Chauffeur Frank O. McNaughton serving in France with the 172nd Aero Squadron. *Jean Spurgeon.*

THE WAR AT SEA

While American participation in the ground war in France was accelerating, it is useful to remember that the first shots fired by America in World War I were in the Atlantic Ocean on April 19, 1917, when the merchant ship *Mongolia*, newly armed with six-inch guns and manned by trained navy gunners, fired on and sank a German submarine. From that day forward, the war at sea continued with intensity as the U.S. Navy and the Royal Navy fought every day around the clock to protect the massive flow of shipping that was providing "beans and bullets and soldiers" to the AEF and our European allies.

USS Covington *Sunk*

On the evening of July 1, the U.S. Army transport *Covington*, homeward bound after landing several thousand soldiers in France, was torpedoed and sunk in the war zone while proceeding with a convoy of transports and destroyers. Six members of the crew were lost, but all the other officers and men were landed at a French port.

On board were at least two Montana crewmen who survived, Machinist Mate 1st Class Joseph Johnson Pickett, Crow Nation of Pompey's Pillar, and Hospital Apprentice 1st Class Albert Edward Griffith of Great Falls, who was injured. Petty Officer Pickett later commented, "I was a member of the crew on the USS *Covington* and was on board same when it was torpedoed and sunk by a German submarine July 1, 1918. Was picked up, transferred to the USS *Wainwright* of the Destroyer Flotilla."[104]

On July 25, the cargo ship SS *Tippecanoe*, 6,187 tons, was torpedoed and sunk by German submarine *U-91* 550 miles from Brest, France, with one death. Onboard was young Machinist Mate 2nd Class Edmund Lee from a ranch on the Marias River, then serving as a naval gunner.[105]

By the summer of 1918, the German U-boat threat remained daunting. During August, American ships and boats were being sunk at a rate of more than one per day by torpedoes or gunfire by German submarines. That month, a total of thirty-three U.S. ships were lost, including the cargo ship *Montanan*, 6,659 gross tons, torpedoed and sunk by German submarine *U-90* on August 15. Three civilian crewmen and two members of the naval armed guard were lost, while eighty-one survivors were rescued. The American-Hawaiian line owned the *Montanan*, which was requisitioned in

1917 along with many other merchant ships by the U.S. Shipping Board and assigned to the army quartermaster's department.[106]

BATTLE OF AMIENS-MONTDIDIER

By August 2, the French had captured Soissons, and two days later, AEF troops took Fismes. By now, much French soil captured during the German Spring Offensive had been retaken. On August 8, a British-led Allied force launched the Amiens Offensive, the first in a series of continuing offensive operations over the next one hundred days that would result in German losses that would end the war. Significantly, this battle, also known as Amiens-Montdidier, marked the end of trench warfare on the Western Front—the speed of Allied advance overran German trenches, opening a new era of open warfare and effecting a systematic retreat, with German forces fighting delaying tactics all the way. Over time, it became clear to both sides that Allied numbers, equipment and morale would first force the Germans onto defense and then simply overwhelm their ability to resist—but this would come at a tragic cost in lives lost on both sides. The "Hundred Days Offensive" of open warfare was underway.

THE "FIGHTING EDGE"

As more AEF divisions moved into the front lines, our French and British allies began to discern the boundless energy and spirit the Yanks brought with them. The *River Press* reported this important factor:

THE "FIGHTING EDGE"
The story of American achievement at various points on the battle front supports the view of a high official of the French army who declared that the huskies from the United States brought with them a vigorous, enthusiastic and youthful spirit that meant misfortune for the Huns. He spoke of the war weariness of the French and British veterans who had sustained the brunt of battle for four years. These men are still excellent fighting troops, but they are no longer buoyant and responsive to the stimulation of combat.

They fight with wonderful effectiveness, but to some extent they lack a certain eager alertness that is essential in victorious troops.

…After all the Americans have what is called in this country the "fighting edge." It is what the French and British and many of the Germans had in the early stages of the war, but it has worn off. The same physical and mental condition is wonderful in battle and it is counting now wherever the Americans are sent against the Boches. The French and British do not lack for bravery, but the Americans are furnishing the dash, the impetuosity, the elastic physical and mental faculties and the splendid youthful strength that is called the "fighting edge." It is little wonder that they sing and laugh in the face of death. These boys have consciences as vigorous and clean as their bodies. They know what they are fighting for and they take joy in their work. It is part of the "fighting edge."[107]

MONTANA AVIATOR

Montanan Willis Bradley Haviland was the sixteenth American volunteer in the Lafayette Escadrille and among the first air combat pilots to fight the Germans in World War I, before the United States entered the war. Born in Minneapolis in 1890, the only son of Dr. Willis Henry Haviland, five-year-old Willis moved with his family to Butte in 1895. He enlisted in the U.S. Navy in 1907 and served until 1911. When war broke out in Europe, Willis joined the American Field Service American Ambulance Corps in 1915, driving ambulances on the Alsace front until the summer of 1916. After receiving a pilot's license, Lieutenant Haviland joined the Lafayette Escadrille.

In the Escadrille, Haviland flew primarily as an escort and reconnaissance pilot. Since he was permitted to engage only in air combat with the enemy in defense, he earned just two confirmed "kills." During his time in France, his mother, Mrs. Grace King Haviland, served in Red Cross work there to be nearer her son. After the United States entered the war, Haviland returned to U.S. Navy duty. The *Butte Miner* provided the latest news of Lieutenant Haviland:

Further honor has come to Aviator Willis B. Haviland, formerly of Butte, and son of Dr. W.H. Haviland of [Butte], *according to advices which have reached Butte and this intrepid warrior of the skies now is a senior lieutenant of the American naval aviation unit in European waters. Lieutenant Haviland was an adjutant for two years in the French escadrille and he became prominent in the war news from the front when he and another aviator engaged a fleet of the Kaiser's sky cruisers. Haviland, at a height of 4,000 feet, downing one adversary, after the other Boches had refused to fight and had taken flight in the clouds and two of Haviland's fighting mates had been lost. At the time the Associated Press painted the dare-devil feat of the former Butte boy in fighting at odds of three to one, as one of the striking features of the combat raging along the Verdun front.*

Lieutenant Willis Bradley Haviland, an early Montanan volunteer in the Lafayette Escadrille and among the first American air combat pilots to fight the Germans. Lieutenant Haviland is holding the lion cub mascot of the French Escadrille. *From the* St. Louis (MO) Star and Times, *February 22, 1930.*

This was when the aerial fighters of Germany were menacing Paris and the routing of the Hun airplane fleet won for Lieutenant Haviland signal honor from the French government. At the critical period in the war, when it was feared that the Germans would reach Paris, the American flyer drove the members of the French cabinet and the president of the republic to Bordeaux.

Lieutenant Haviland, 28 years old, is every inch of the type of the soldier ready to take any chance and to whom the love of adventure carries those characteristics which go to make up the ideal trooper of high-air battle fame. He is six feet one inch tall stripped and weighs 204 pounds and is an athlete in every sense of the word, being largely interested in sports and before the opening of the war a national figure in tennis…

At the beginning of the war he laid everything aside and voluntarily joined the first unit of doctors and nurses which left this city for the front under the direction of Mrs. W.K. Vanderbilt and other well-known women of the nation, forming what was known as the American ambulance and hospital corps in France.

The spirit of adventure early asserted itself and Haviland after a year's service as an ambulance driver associated himself with the escadrille when a call was issued by the French government for air men, and he rapidly was promoted to an adjutancy. When the United States entered the war he was transferred December 28, 1917, to the American [naval] aviation unit.[108]

With Lieutenant Haviland's return to the U.S. Navy, he became executive officer of the Naval Air Station at Dunkirk, France, with one month of special duty in the British 13th Squadron flying a Sopwith Dolphin single-seater biplane. He then was sent to Porto Corsini, Italy, where he assumed command of the naval air station. He was called back to the United States in January 1919 by Admiral Henry T. Mayo, commander U.S. Atlantic Fleet, and assigned as the only pilot on the battleship USS *Texas*. Lieutenant Haviland became engaged to Miss Mary Lucile Satterthwait, a socialite and dramatic vocalist who had volunteered the previous year to go overseas with the YMCA entertainment branch. Just before sailing for France, she was recalled as the war ended.[109]

"OVER THERE" THEATER LEAGUE

Blanche Savoie and Lillian Pearce were two performers from Montana who were selected to entertain the troops overseas. They joined the "Over There" Theater League, organized in early 1918 to provide entertainment for the troops with the famed George M. Cohan as president and Winthrop Ames as executive director. The first party of 44 league volunteers sailed on July 31, 1918, and over the course of the war and postwar occupation of Germany, some 1,470 men and women entertainers were sent overseas.

The *Anaconda Standard* covered the experiences of Blanche Savoie and Lillian Pearce:

> *Would it cheer a soldier's heart to have a pretty, vivacious American girl sing the latest song from Broadway after he has heard nothing but French patois for months? It would—he would shed tears of joy even if she sang "The Girl I Left Behind Me," and his burdens would be comparatively light for many a day.*
>
> *That was Miss Blanche Savoie's task—making lighter the burdens of United States soldiers who might be called on within a few days to die. On October 27, 1918, she sailed for France as a member of the "Over There Theater League" to play a role entirely different from that of her other Butte sisters, cast for parts at Red Cross hospitals and military telephone exchanges. She went over to heal men's souls of wounds as deep as shrapnel pierces the flesh.*

LILLIAN PEARCE
TWO YEARS OVERSEAS
SINGING FOR
SOLDIERS

Left: Popular entertainer Lillian Pearce of Butte, the "Montana Sunbeam." *From the* Anaconda Standard, *October 26, 1919.*

Below: Tribute to YMCA Over There Theater League entertainer Blanche Savoie of Butte, Montana. *From the* Anaconda Standard, *December 14, 1919.*

THE ANACONDA STANDARD, SUNDAY, DECEMBER 14, 1919.

MONTANA GIRL
DID HER BIT ~

WINS·HIGHEST·PRAISE·
OF·PERSHING·AS·AN·
ENTERTAINER" OVER THERE"

MISS SAVOIE IN THE VERDUN TRENCHES

Barcelona

Blanche Savoie

BLANCHE SAVOIE GLAD
SHE HAD OPPORTUNITY
TO SERVE MEN OVERSEA

CAPT BRUCE BAIRNSFATHER
FAMOUS BRITISH WAR ARTIST

PENCIL SKETCH of MISS SAVOIE BY BAIRNSFATHER

ONE Butte girl has returned home from service overseas with about all the honors, except the war cross, that it is possible for a young woman to have attained. Also this young person has

When hostilities ceased there following a strange lull and a period of inaction; and men's nerves, trained to resist to the breaking point, became poignantly aware of a great depression. Then they had to be brought from the morass of despondency and relieved of a yearning for home, to which all could not return at once. Again, it was Miss Savoie who would do just that—with a song from Broadway and a cheering word from the very home they longed for.

Washington had realized that the winning of the war hinged upon army morale, and Miss Savoie was one of many assigned to keep up that morale.[110]

Draft News

Reports in the *River Press* serve to remind that Montana's population estimate for 1917–18 was greatly overstated. While the U.S. Census Bureau continued to estimate that Montana's population was nearly 1 million residents, in reality it was just half that, around 500,000. This resulted in a significantly inflated draft quota for Montana, demonstrated by the fact that Montana was sending more draftees than the State of Washington yet had half of Washington's actual population.

> *Entrain for Camp Lewis. Camp Lewis, Aug. 19.—Ten thousand draft men will entrain for this camp from nine states during the period of August 22–30, according to advices received here today, when preparations were begun for receiving the new soldiers into service.*
>
> *New Mexico will furnish 160 men, North Dakota 1,000; California 2,157; Colorado 800; Idaho 500; Montana 1,650; Oregon 1,000; Utah 1,125, and Washington 1,400.*[111]

All young men between twenty-one and thirty-one years of age originally registered for the draft on June 5, 1917. A Second Draft registration was held on June 5, 1918, and a third registration was planned for August 24, 1918; all males who had reached their twenty-first birthday since June 5, 1918, and on or before August 24, 1918, had to register on August 24, 1918.[112]

Student Army Training Corps

Twenty-one-year-old Frank F. Morger was among six Chouteau County men called up in August for service in the Student Army Training Corps (SATC) at the Montana State University. The SATC program was designed for colleges to train draftees in trades needed for the war effort and develop a pool of potential officers for the army. It was jointly administered by the military and the university, and the students took part in an academic learning environment while also training to become soldiers—an early version of the Reserve Officer Training Program on college campuses. Morger served there until mid-October, when he was sent to Fort Worden, at Port Townsend, Washington, to the 40th Company Coast Artillery Division, where he trained until discharge in January 1919. Coast Artillery units were trained on heavy artillery, railway artillery and, later, on antiaircraft artillery before deployment to the AEF in France.

Frank's elder brother, Earl R. Morger, was drafted in May 1918. After training at Camp Lewis, Earl was assigned to Company G, 306th Infantry, 77th "Statue of Liberty" Division. The 77th Infantry Division, composed largely of men from the streets of inner New York City, was the first American division composed of draftees to arrive in France in World War I. Throughout its service in France, the 77th Division sustained a stunning 10,194 casualties: 1,486 killed and 8,708 wounded—among whom were many Montanans.

Earl Morger and his 306th Infantry landed in France on August 8. Hundreds of Montanans were transferred to join the 77th in September. In a letter to his father, Fort Benton mayor Frank Morger, dated November 10, Earl mentioned five local men serving in the 77th with him, including Private Rudolph Larkin (Company L, wounded in his leg by shrapnel); Private Leo Voeller (Company H, wounded in the hand); Private Boyle (Company I) and Sergeant Joseph E. Zimmerman (Company F), the latter two both wounded and in the hospital; and Private Knute Fosen, "a runner in Company F" from Loma.[113]

Private Morger's 306th Infantry Regiment earned four campaign ribbons over the course of the war, for service at Oise-Aisne, Meuse-Argonne, Champagne and Lorraine. The famed "Lost Battalion," occurring later in the war, was composed of six companies of the 308th Regiment and one from the 307th.

The 306th Infantry Regiment was involved in a great battle on October 14, when it took the northern French town of St. Juvin on the Aire River from the Germans. From the history of the 306th Infantry:

> *Some idea of the desperate fighting at St. Juvin is given by the casualty list for the period from the morning of the 14th to the late evening of the 15th. The Regiment lost 7 officers and 37 men killed, 4 officers and 213 men wounded.* [A regiment had about 3,800 men.]
>
> *A tiresome and leg-weary march of the exhausted troops of the 306th Infantry from St. Juvin to Cornay, and thence to Camp Buzon, then began. The men had had little to eat for nearly two days and had been through a severe engagement, sustaining numerous losses and casualties.*[114]

Remarkably, ten men of the 306th received the Distinguished Service Cross for their performances at St. Juvin. Later, in World War II, the 306th recognized this battle on its unit insignia, which featured a shepherd's crook—the town's namesake, Saint Juvin, had been a shepherd.

RUSSIA'S BLOODY CIVIL WAR

While the Bolsheviks seized power in Petrograd and Moscow in the fall of 1917 and ended Russian participation in World War I with the Treaty of Brest-Litovsk, they faced multifactional counterrevolutions in many parts of Russia, from Far Eastern Siberia to North Russia to the Caucasus. The Red Army of the Bolsheviks battled the fragmented White Army on many fronts.

In secrecy on the night of July 16–17, 1918, the Russian Romanov family—Tsar Nicholas II, Tsarina Alexandra and their five children—were executed by Bolshevik troops on orders from Lenin and other Bolshevik leaders. The bodies were buried in unmarked graves.

President Wilson decided that the United States would join Allies to intervene in the Russian Civil War, and the 339th Infantry Regiment and

Nicholas II of Russia with the family (*left to right*): Olga, Maria, Nicholas II, Alexandra Fyodorovna, Anastasia, Alexei and Tatiana, Livadiya, 1913. Portrait by the Levitsky Studio, Livadiya. Today, the original photograph is held at the Hermitage Museum, St. Petersburg, Russia.

American supply depot Archangel. *Bain News Service, publisher, circa 1918–20, https://www.loc. gov/item/2014708486.*

support units of the 85th Infantry Division were designated to form the North Russian Expeditionary Force, or the Polar Bear Expedition. On August 27, the expedition sailed from Newcastle upon Tyne, England, and landed on September 4 at Archangel on the far northern coast of Russia to join Allied forces already there. On the ground, American troops deployed along a front 450 miles long, operating with Allies to cover the main avenues of Archangel from the south opposing the Soviet Sixth Army.

Less than a month later, the first Montanan fell mortally wounded in North Russia. Matti I. Niemi, a thirty-one-year-old Finnish immigrant from Butte serving in Company M, 339th Infantry, died on September 30 of wounds received in action. Captain Joel R. Moore of Detroit, who had coached football and taught at Great Falls High School in 1910–11, served with the 339th Infantry and wrote two books about the Polar Bear Expedition.[115]

Under the headline "American Troops in Russia" the *River Press* reported on the sequence of events leading to this drastic reaction to the state of affairs in Russia:

Washington, Sept. 11.—American troops have landed at Archangel to assist the other allied forces there in their campaign for the re-establishment

137

of order in northern Russia. This announcement was authorized tonight by General March, army chief of staff.

For military reasons the number of soldiers landing was not revealed, nor was it made clear from whence they had embarked. It was assumed, however that the soldiers had been sent from English camps, where Americans are training.

The purpose of the allied campaign in northern Russia is to keep open the railroad from Archangel to Vologda and to protect the government of the north which has been set up at Archangel and through which it is hoped to re-establish order in Russia and overcome German influence.[116]

MONTANANS IN SIBERIA AEF

World War I Montana: The Treasure State Prepares provided the background for the deployment of American railway men and soldiers to Siberia in 1917–18. Montanans, including Lieutenant Ed Shields of Great Falls and others, serving in the Railway Service Corps in Siberia—originally charged to help the Russian Provisional Government in 1917 return neglected Russian railways to operation—by late 1918 found themselves in an untenable position in the midst of the civil war following the Bolshevik Revolution. Lieutenant Shields and other railway men departed Vladivostok in early 1919 to return to their homes and jobs with the Great Northern Railroad. Soldiers of American Expeditionary Force Siberia consisting of several regiments of the 8th Infantry Division continued to serve in Siberia until June 1920, although Montanan Lieutenant Colonel Albert Galen, the division's judge advocate general, resigned from the army to return to Montana one year earlier, in July 1919.[117]

MASTERLIEST AERIAL RETREAT

Montanans found many paths to serve during the war. Young Ben Harwood's path was among the most unique. Born in Helena in 1891, Benjamin F. Harwood graduated from Butte High School and then entered Yale, graduating in 1913 and going on to Harvard Law School. By this time, Ben's family had relocated to Billings, where his father, a former Montana Supreme

Court justice, opened an active legal practice. Ben, ever the Montana boy, made Billings his "hometown," yet he joined the Massachusetts National Guard and served on the Mexican border in 1916 before returning to complete his law degree at Harvard in 1917.

On September 21, 1917, Lieutenant Ben Harwood arrived at Saint-Nazaire, France, with the 102nd Field Artillery Regiment, 26th Infantry "Yankee" Division, making this the second division to join the AEF. There Lieutenant Harwood volunteered as an aerial observer and gunner and received training with the French. He was assigned to 12th Aero Squadron, flying the French Salmson two-seat biplane configuration reconnaissance aircraft.

American "Aces" Return on Mauretania

—Copyright by International Film Service.

Lower a group of American "Aces" home on Mauretania. They are left to right: Captain Roscoe Fawcett of Portland, Oregon; Captain James Norman Hall of Colfax, Iowa; Major Kenneth P. Littauer of Washington; Lieutenant Colonel H. E. Hartney of Washington; and Captain Benjamin P. Harwood of Billings, Montana.

Captain Ben Harwood and other American "aces" returning to United States after the war. *From the* Buffalo Evening News, *March 8, 1919.*

Lieutenant Harwood received citations including Croix de Guerre, War Medal of the Aero Club of America, Purple Heart and Distinguished Service Cross with a Citation:

The Distinguished Service Cross is presented to Benjamin P. Harwood, First Lieutenant (Air Service), U.S. Army Air Service, for extraordinary heroism in action while serving with 12th Aero Squadron, U.S. Army Air Service, AEF, near Chateau-Thierry, France, July 5, 1918. Lieutenant Harwood volunteered with another plane to protect a photograph plane. In the course of their mission they were attacked by seven planes (Fokker type). Lieutenant Harwood accepted the combat and kept the enemy engaged while the photographic plane completed its mission. His guns jammed and he himself was seriously wounded. After skillfully clearing his guns, with his plane badly damaged, he fought off the hostile planes and enabled the photographic plane to return to our lines with valuable information. General Orders 7, War Department, 1919.

Ben Harwood was assigned to the staff of the chief of air service, General Headquarters AEF. He later served in the Division of Military Aeronautics, Washington, D.C., under the direction of the famed Brigadier General Billy Mitchell. After discharge in 1919, he returned to Billings for an illustrious legal career, remaining a staunch advocate for military aviation.[118]

From Mean Streets to Legend, Montana's Little Sailor

Michael Joseph Mansfield, almost an orphan, arrived in Great Falls in 1910 from the mean streets of New York, a seven-year-old tough guy, hard to control and quick with his fists. For seven tempestuous years, young Mike was in and out of Great Falls public and parochial schools and an orphans' home. As the United States entered World War I, Mike rode the rails and altered his birth certificate to join the army at age fourteen, one month shy of his fifteenth birthday.

Yet Mike Mansfield overcame his boyhood obstacles to become in succession a miner, a revered university professor, a U.S. congressman, a U.S. senator, the longest-serving Senate Majority Leader and an ambassador to Japan. Young Mike, of southside Great Falls, achieved legendary status as both politician and diplomat.

Mike Mansfield was born on March 16, 1903, in New York of Irish immigrant parents. His father, Patrick Mansfield, was severely injured in a construction accident with long-term disability, and his mother, Josephine, died in 1910, leaving three small children. Unable to care for the children, Patrick asked the help of his brother, and this brought seven-year-old Mike and his siblings to Great Falls.

Richard and Margaret Mansfield operated a neighborhood grocery on the lower south side in Great Falls, a multiethnic working-class neighborhood. The Mansfield Grocery was the front room of a one-story frame building. It was a community convenience store with no indoor plumbing or electricity. The children slept in the attic, and Richard and his wife lived in a tiny house in back. Mike entered school and helped deliver groceries on a horse-drawn wagon or two-wheeled cart.

Uncle Richard died two years later, and trouble began. Aunt Margaret had no children and, without her husband, could not handle those she inherited. In the years that followed, Mike bounced from school to school, ran away from home, spent a night in city jail, was committed to the state home for wayward and orphaned children at Twin Bridges and returned to Great Falls. As the United States entered World War I, Mike left home for good. Walking and riding the rails to the West Coast, he got a job in a lumber camp. Along the way, he befriended soldiers of the Oregon National Guard, then protecting bridges and tunnels, and managed to attach himself to a squad. When his Guard friends were ordered to the East Coast, they smuggled Mike aboard their troop train.

Reaching New York, Mike visited his father before trying to enlist in the army. Turned down because of his age, in February 1918, Mike altered the 1903 in his birth certificate to read "1900" and got his father to write a false statement. Enlisting in the navy on February 23, 1918, Mike Mansfield reported to Naval Training Station Newport, Rhode Island. After basic training, Seaman Mansfield reported in May to the USS *Minneapolis* (C-13). For the next six months, that armored cruiser joined three convoy cruises across the Atlantic before the end of the war. During these voyages, the

Fourteen-year-old sailor and later famed U.S. senator Michael Joseph Mansfield, portrait oil on canvas by Aaron Shikler. *Library of Congress.*

Minneapolis, with its convoy, would depart New York and sail to an ocean rendezvous off the Irish coast danger zone, where the convoy was turned over to British destroyers.

Seaman 2nd Class Mansfield was placed on inactive duty on Armistice Day and finally discharged from the navy at Salt Lake in August 1919. He likely spent some of those nine months of inactive navy duty in Great Falls, but after his discharge, he joined the army and was assigned to Fort McDowell, Angel Island, San Francisco. After this one-year enlistment, he was honorably discharged and joined the Marine Corps, finally attaining age seventeen. During these two years, he served at Subic Bay in the Philippine Islands. While there, he was among 150 Marines to board the USS *Huron* and land at Taku on the Chinese coast. This service in the Far East sparked a lifelong fascination in him for the region. Returning to Montana, Mike Mansfield moved steadily upward to achieve greatness.[119]

Nurse Virginia Flanagan

Nurse Virginia Flanagan, born in Fort Benton and educated at the Columbus Hospital, Great Falls, was called to service in the Army Nurse Corps on June 28, 1917, along with four other Montana nurses: Elizabeth Messner of Utica, Marga Slater of Glendive, Alta Melott of Alton and Elizabeth Sterling of Missoula. Nurses Flanagan and Sterling were assigned to Letterman General Hospital at the Presidio, San Francisco. Six months later, Nurse Flanagan moved on to Camp Kearney, near San Diego.

After six months, Nurse Flanagan was ordered to overseas duty. On June 11, 1918, she boarded the transport *Magenta* and sailed in a seventeen-ship convoy to Liverpool. Arriving at Le Havre, France, on June 28, she wrote in her diary:

> *We stayed* [at Le Havre] *that night, and slept in a very damp room with no running water. From there we went to Paris where we marched from the train to the station for Blois. We were the first ones on the train, and were given our rations for the day, consisting of a can of salmon, a can of tomatoes, and some hard tack. When we got hungry, we decided to open the cans, but no one had an opener. While the train made a short stop, I hailed a soldier and asked him if he had a can opener; he replied that he had, but that he needed it. When I told him of our plight, he gave it to me and said he guessed we needed it more than he did.*

Left: Fort Benton–born nurse Virginia Flanagan serving in France *Author photo*.

Below: Tribute to World War I nurses at the Montana State Agricultural Museum, Fort Benton. *Author photo*.

…We went on to Blois which was a division front at the time. We were billeted in a ward in an old convent which was being used for a hospital. The water supply was very inadequate. We had bought rubber basins and proceeded to try to do the family washing with inadequate water, and a little string to hang the clothes on to dry. The building was very old and run down with plaster falling off the walls; it had a deserted look.

We saw our first wounded soldiers there, not the worst of the wounded, but even at that it gave us a strange feeling of realization of where we were. All they wanted was water. Blois is a very interesting old town, and we saw Joan of Arc's banners in an old Church in the town. We did not go on duty at this hospital, but waited orders, and had to report at headquarters every two or three hours, while we were there.

We stayed at Blois for the Fourth of July, and had a celebration in an old building where Napoleon and his soldiers had headquartered. There still was writing on the walls which had been written at that time. The soldiers moved provisions stored in the building, so we could have a dance. They found musicians, and we had refreshments consisting of lemonade and doughnuts. It was a great treat, we had a very good time, and I also had the pleasant surprise of meeting Dr. Vidal from Great Falls. He was also waiting for orders, also Dr. Johnson, a Dentist from Great Falls. Naturally, we talked about Great Falls, and Dr. Vidal left for the Front from there.

…We had air raids every moonlit night, and the "Big Berthas" boomed constantly. Some nights all the lights would have to be put out, and on such nights we carried lanterns with petticoats on them, so we could visit the most seriously injured patients and check for bleeding.

The night nurses dining room was in the basement down a long stairway, and sometime the lights would go out while we were on our way down; often by the time the lights came on, the horse meat would be cold.

We had French ladies who were volunteers, and they came to help at night. At about 10:30, they would make themselves comfortable with blankets in wheel chairs, and if there was an air raid, they would get up and hold the hands of the best looking French soldiers. But, they really were very nice ladies, and after all volunteers.

One night I was awakened by what sounded like cannon, and looked out of the window, and all the sky was red. I woke up my roommates, and told them that there must be a big battle close by, but they only laughed at me. However, when we got up in the morning, the court yard was full of stretchers of wounded from a fierce battle at Chateau Thierry.[120]

FOCH, THE MASTER STRATEGIST

While the Allies' offensive continued through August, the *River Press* featured Supreme Allied Commander Marshal Ferdinand Foch:

> *The strategy of Marshal Foch is believed to be well understood by both sides. He is endeavoring to reach the lines of communication established by the Germans and pinch off the salient of which Montdidier is the apex. By pushing forward from the west and at the same time exerting pressure along the Soissons-Rheims front, the German armies under the crown prince will be forced to make a great retirement and it is not without the bounds of probability that the Germans will go back as far as the old Hindenburg line of 1916.*
>
> *…Several things have been definitely established by the events of the past few weeks. The greatest of these is the fact that the initiative has passed definitely into the hands of Foch. For months he waited silently and patiently for his great opportunity. The Germans swept down over the vast area between Soissons and Rheims to the Marne and beyond it. Those were days of deep and undisguised anxiety for the allies. But Foch said nothing. Grim and determined he watched and waited, while the mutterings of fear grew louder and louder. Paris was in danger and the allied troops moved back day after day. But there came a time when Foch looked at the map and gave an order. That was the turning point of the war. With astonishing quickness and stealth Foch assembled an army upon the western flank of the enemy. Day after day this army advanced, while a similar army upon the Rheims side pushed toward the common center. It was a remarkable feat and was properly characterized by Lloyd George as the "most magnificent achievement in the annals of war."*
>
> *Foch's great plan is still unknown. But his armies are advancing everywhere, and every day the Germans are more demolished and their defeat is made more sure. It is a magnificent panorama of war that is unfolding under the magic touch of Foch's supreme military skill. It is comforting to know that he has the men to perform these miracles, and it is more comforting yet to know that in America there is an unlimited reservoir of man power upon which he may depend. The world may rightly rejoice over what has been done, and it may look forward with entire confidence to what will be done in the future. Foch has already justified his reputation as the "master strategist of Europe," a title conceded to him even by the Germans.*[121]

A Dramatic Sea Change

With the failure of Germany's desperate Spring Offensive and the striking increase in number and experience in AEF Yanks on the front lines, momentum was building. The Aisne-Marne operation, a Franco-American offensive, hailed the beginning of the German army's retreat from France. Participating in this offense from July 18 to August 6 were the new AEF I and III Corps with the 1st, 2nd, 3rd, 4th, 26th, 28th, 32nd and 42nd Divisions.

From August 7, the Allies kept the pressure on, launching the Oisne-Aise operation with the AEF III Corps, 28th, 32nd Infantry Divisions and the 70th Infantry Regiment (Colored) attached to the French, contributing to the Allied counterattacks. In mid-August, the French with U.S. Buffalo Soldiers of the 92nd Infantry Division (Colored) (under the AEF) and 93rd Infantry Division (Colored) (integrated under French command) started a series of drives on their front, extending about ninety miles from Reims westward through Soissons to Ribecourt on the Oise River. These operations continued on into late September, when they merged into Marshal Foch's great final offensive in October–November.

The AEF 32nd Red Arrow Division spearheaded the drive to take Fismes, and then, as part of the French Tenth Army, it led an operation to penetrate the main German line on August 22. The 32nd was instrumental in capturing and holding Fismes and then Juvigny on August 30, which secured tactically vital high ground. Through the exceptional performance of the 32nd, the German front was so badly breached that they were forced to abandon the Vesle River line.

The eight AEF divisions that participated in breaking through the Aisne-Marne salient suffered a staggering fifty thousand casualties in the fighting between July 18 and August 6. This continued the transformational change from the years of "trench warfare" into Pershing's concept of "open warfare." General Pershing directed his staff to plan on improved tactics to lower casualties. This plan concluded that where strong resistance is encountered, rather than continuing frontal assaults, every effort must be made to push through gaps on the flanks or rear. The Aisne-Marne operations dramatically changed this whole aspect of the war. The Germans were now in a fighting retreat. The Marne salient had ceased to exist, and the Germans were never again able to undertake major offensive action.

Headline featuring new Allied offensive during early August. *From the* Great Falls Leader, *August 8, 1918.*

In Flanders on August 19, the British-led Ypres-Lys operation commenced with the AEF 27th, 30th, 37th and 91st Divisions eventually attached to the Belgium, French Sixth and British Second Armies. This commenced Allied offensive operations in Flanders that would continue to the end of the war, forcing the German army from Flanders.[122]

With eight AEF divisions in action through the month of August, and more like the 91st "Wild West" Division coming on-line late in the month, Montana casualties rose dramatically. During August, twelve divisions suffered at least 62 Montanans killed and 58 wounded, with 5 more accidental deaths for an overall total of at least 125. Two divisions, the 32nd Red Arrow Division and the 4th Ivy Division, had over 90 percent of Montana's casualties, two-thirds being in the 32nd Division, which spearheaded two important assaults, first to capture and hold Fismes and then Juvigny.

Captain Charles L. Sheridan of Bozeman deployed to France with the 163rd Infantry before transferring to command Company A, 128th Infantry, as it went into the trenches in Alsace on May 26, 1918. The regiment remained there until July 10, when it moved to Château-Thierry on the Marne. Captain Sheridan was commissioned major and placed in command of the First Battalion of the 128th on the day the regiment went into the fight in this sector. In Major Sheridan's own words:

On July 10, we were taken out by train to Point St Maxime, south of Champagne, and on the way we passed through Paris, where we were given quite an ovation, as the people knew we were on our way to a big battle. At Point St. Maxine we were loaded into motortrucks and taken to Chateau Thierry.

We got into the fight July 29 and drove the Germans back across the Oureq river, pushing them until we had taken the village of Fismes. It was on the Oureq river July 30 that Captain [Orville] Anderson [of Company C, 128th Infantry] was killed. On August 4, near Fismes, I received my first wound but was not incapacitated. After we had taken the village we were relieved by the 28th Division and marched back 10 miles for rest.

Aug. 12 we were again taken in motor trucks, this time to St. Gauden forest, and went into battle with the Tenth French army and had two weeks of the hardest fighting there that we saw in the war. I was wounded Sept. 1 and was sent back to the hospital at Paris. I returned Sept. 30, joined the battalion as they were moving up to the front. We made an attack Oct. 1, relieving the 91st division in that fight which was between the Argonne forest and the Meuse river near Verdun. We made an attack every morning at 5:30.

My division was in the front line for 31 days without relief. I was wounded October 14 in the right arm and was sent back to the hospital at Bordeaux, where I was classified "D" and ordered to be sent home. I was granted permission to go back to my regiment to get my baggage before leaving for home and arrived the day after the armistice was signed. I found my regiment considerably reduced, only three of the officers being there that I knew. From there I was sent to St. Nassir and sailed for home Dec. 14, 1918, on the steamship Zealandia.[123]

Major Charles L. Sheridan of Bozeman, the only Montanan in the Great War nominated for the Medal of Honor, shown here wearing the Belgium Croix de Guerre and the U.S. Distinguished Service Cross. *Gallatin County Museum, 452.*

Major Sheridan was the only Montanan nominated for the Medal of Honor in World War I—he did not receive it, but he was awarded the Belgium Croix de Guerre and the Distinguished Service Cross, with the citation reading: "For extraordinary heroism in action while serving with 128th Infantry Regiment, 32d Division, AEF, on Hill No. 230, near Cierges, France, 31 July and 1 August 1918. Captain Sheridan demonstrated notable courage and leadership by taking command of the remnants of two companies and leading them up the hill and into the woods against violent fire from the enemy. His grit and leadership inspired his men to force the enemy back. He personally shot and killed three of the enemy and under his direction six machines were put out of action and the hill captured."

Captain Sheridan's friend Captain Orville L. Anderson of Kalispell, commanding Company C, 128th Infantry, was killed in this offensive. In the action that cost his life, he commanded a picked detachment of twelve men, who were sent against a menacing machine gun nest. Details of the story of how Captain Orville Anderson and twelve men met death came from an officer in his regiment:

> *Machine guns had been doing considerable damage to the Americans. Captain Anderson called for volunteers and 12 men stepped out. Placing himself at their head the detail attacked with spirit and dash. Every man was killed before the guns were reached but the machine gun nest was later wiped out.*
>
> *The night after the battle had died down, Captain Charles Sheridan, returning from another part of the battle line, learned of the death of his chum, Captain Anderson, from whom he had parted in the morning before going into action. Calling a squad of his men he went onto the battlefield and after a search discovered the body of Captain Anderson, which he brought to the little village of Roncheres, where a brief service was held that night and burial took place. The bodies of the men who gallantly went to their deaths with their captain, were recovered and buried near the village.*[124]

LES TERRIBLES

The action and casualties for the 32nd Division went on throughout the month of August as the troops successfully captured Fismes at great cost from extremely heavy street fighting and fended off constant German counterattacks before moving on to overrun Juvigny. Sergeant Arthur Aamot, of Saco, Company D, 126th Infantry, received the Distinguished

Service Cross at Juvigny: "For extraordinary heroism in action near Juvigny, France, August 29, 1918. Sergeant Aamot had sought cover in a shell hole, after a difficult advance in the face of heavy machine-gun fire, when he observed distress signals from a tank nearby on which concentrated artillery and machine-gun fire was being directed by the enemy. Leaving his shelter, Sergeant Aamot proceeded through the fire to the tank where he found a wounded man, whom he courageously carried to safety."[125]

During the month of August, the 32nd Division rose to greatness—and "Les Terribles" were born. On the drive to capture Fismes, the men successfully attacked over open ground at great cost against intense artillery and machine gun fire. The 127th Infantry captured Fismes but lost many men. The 3rd Battalion was reduced from twenty officers and one thousand men to just two officers and ninety-four men. In the words of the division history:

> *This operation tested the ability of the Division in almost every phase of warfare. The men demonstrated that they could outfight the Germans in hand to hand encounters; that they could take his positions by assault; that they could outmaneuver the enemy when maneuver tactics were desirable; and that they would go without food and sleep when it became necessary to leave their supplies behind and relentlessly pursue a retreating foe.*[126]

General de Mondesir, the French 38th Corps commander, under which the 32nd served, went to the front to observe the fighting at Fismes. When he observed how the 32nd cleared the Germans out of their reinforced positions with unrelenting and successful attacks, he exclaimed, "*Oui, Oui, Les soldats terrible, tres bien, tres bien!*" French general Charles Mangin heard of it and referred to the 32nd Division as "Les Terribles" when he asked for the division to join the shock troops of his French Tenth Army north of Soissons. He later made the nickname official when he incorporated it in his citation for its attack on Juvigny.

Thus, the Red Arrow Division became the only American unit in the famed French Tenth Army, positioned between the Colonial Moroccans and the Foreign Legion, two of the elite divisions in the French army. In the five-day battle against five German divisions at Juvigny, the 32nd suffered 2,848 casualties, including many Montanans. Overall during its month of combat, the Red Arrow Division had more than 4,100 casualties.

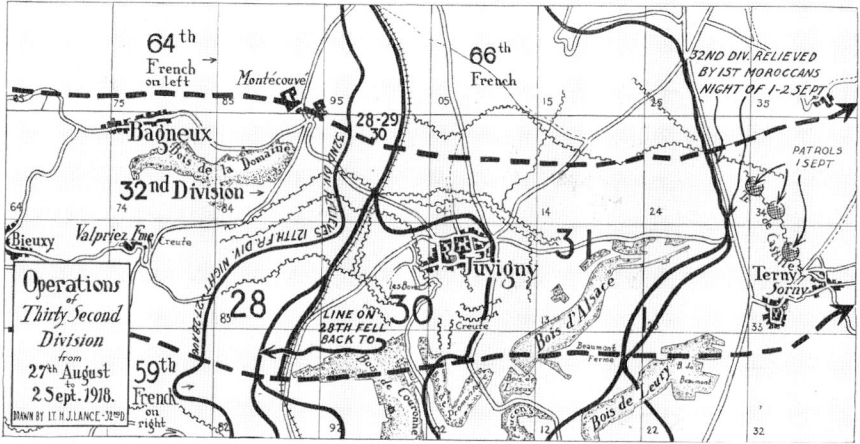

Map of 32nd Red Arrow Division capturing Juvigny. *From* The 32nd Division in the World War, 1917–1919.

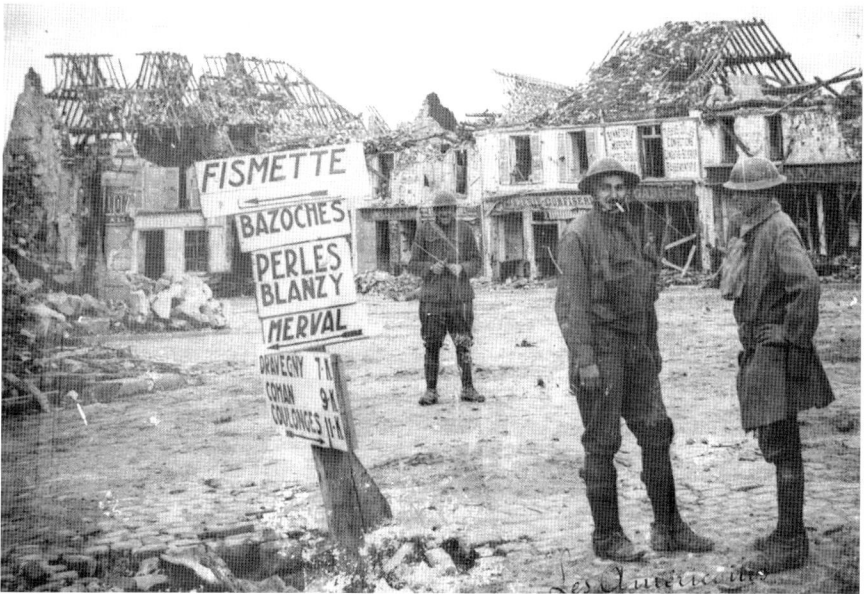

Yanks after the 32nd Division captured the vital town of Fismes, France. *Ville de Fismes.*

On September 5, the 32nd was relieved on the line and withdrawn to a rest area. There, it received five thousand replacements and underwent intensive training to integrate the new men into its regiments before returning to the front line at the end of September.[127]

Chapter 6

SEPTEMBER 1918

*The Naval War; Battle of St. Mihiel; Nurses at War;
Native and Black Warriors*

THE NAVAL WAR

During the Great War, U.S. Navy ships were deployed both to the Atlantic and Mediterranean, with their primary mission to escort Allied convoys and attack German submarines. Throughout the summer of 1918, the war at sea continued as German U-boats sank an average of 250,000 tons of Allied and neutral shipping every month.

American and British ships from the United States steamed across the Atlantic in the face of submarine attacks, underwater mines and aerial bombardment. As the war progressed, new technologies and techniques became operational, such as submarine and anti-submarine warfare, improved convoys and camouflaged hulls. Yet many sailors, soldiers, passengers and crew members were sent to the bottom of the sea.

USS *DORA* LOST

The small seven-thousand-ton American cargo ship *Dora* was torpedoed and sunk on September 4, about four hundred miles off France, as the result of an attack on a cargo convoy. The crew was saved. One crewman, Montanan seaman Ellis Grant Hardesty, age eighteen from Bozeman, received a commendation by the secretary of the navy for gallant conduct during this attack. As reported in the *Great Falls Tribune*:

London, Sept. 10.—…The steamship [Dora] was struck at 6:20 o'clock in the morning. Calm sea enabled all the crew of 85 to escape. They were picked up by destroyers.

The submarine daringly took up a position about 150 yards from the starboard side of the convoy column and about an equal distance from the nearest destroyer, and fired at the Dora, which was heading a column of three vessels.

The torpedo struck aft, throwing the cargo of army supplies as high as the mast tops, but only one member of the crew was hurt.

The escorting ships immediately dropped depth charges where the torpedo came from. It is thot the submarine was destroyed or badly damaged.

The attack is somewhat different from the recent methods of U-boats in firing on lone vessels and giving no attention to protected convoys, and it shows more reckless daring in an effort to sink convoyed boats than has been usual during the past few months.[128]

USS MOUNT VERNON TORPEDOED

The *Mount Vernon*, formerly the German passenger ship *Kronprinzessen Cecilie* and converted to a troop carrier, began sailing to the war zone in October 1917. On its ninth eastbound voyage, it was torpedoed by the German submarine *U-82*.

Thirty-five members of the crew of the *Mount Vernon* were killed by the explosion as a torpedo struck the ship when it was two hundred miles from the French coast, homeward bound. The passengers included two congressmen, Senator James H. Lewis of Illinois and Representative Thomas D. Schall of Minnesota, who were among those safely landed when the transport returned to a French port under its own steam.

The torpedo struck on the starboard side, flooding the no. 4 fireroom. The crewmen killed were firemen, enginemen and water tenders on duty in the flooded fireroom. The *Mount Vernon* underwent repairs at Brest and rejoined the fleet in early 1919 to bring Yanks home from Europe.[129]

Seven Montanans served as crewmen onboard the *Mount Vernon*. All seven received commendations from the secretary of the navy for the manner in which they performed their duties and remained at station following the torpedoing of the ship:

- Fireman 1ˢᵗ Class John Thomas Chandler of Bozeman
- Fireman 1ˢᵗ Class Chester Ward Howe of Troy
- Fireman 1ˢᵗ Class George Dewey Martin of Deer Lodge
- Fireman 2ⁿᵈ Class Edward Henry Kindall of Coalwood, Powder River County
- Fireman 2ⁿᵈ Class Joseph Warren Mitchell of Butte
- Seaman 2ⁿᵈ Class Henry Koeber of Kalispell
- Seaman John Baier Jr., first from Great Falls to enlist in the navy after war was declared[130]

Many young naval officers gained valuable experience in the hostile combat waters of the Atlantic during the war. Through rapid wartime promotions, Lieutenant John Howard Hoover of Fort Benton found himself a temporary commander and in command of the USS *Cushing*, where he received the Navy Cross for distinguished service escorting and protecting convoys of troops and supplies to European ports. Remaining on active duty after the war, Admiral Hoover assumed important commands during World War II, including deputy commander of the Pacific Fleet under Fleet Admiral Chester Nimitz. Today, Admiral Hoover's exceptional career is honored at the Montana State Agricultural Museum as one of four navy flag officers graduating from Fort Benton, the world's innermost port in steamboat days.[131]

USS *Mount Vernon* steaming toward Brest, France, after it was torpedoed on September 5, 1918. An escorting destroyer is laying a smoke screen in the background. *Naval History and Heritage Command.*

CHARLIE'S ILLUSTRATED WAR LETTER

Charles M. Russell rarely illustrated his letters with World War I battle scenes since he felt far more comfortable depicting American Indians, frontier army soldiers and cowboys. In a letter to his "Friend Bumsky" (*sic*) (Abe L. "Bumpsky" Goodman), Charlie drew a dramatic colorful battle scene of the Great War:

Rare Charles M. Russell letter to Bumpsky Goodman, dated September 6, 1918, with World War I battle scene. *Private collection (anonymous).*

Sept. 6 1918

Friend Bumsky [sic], *I got the smoking all right and am much obliged. Will square for it when I get home.*

I see that Uncle Sams raised the age limit on the draft and I have a hunch som brothers that I know whos four Fathers came from Jerusilam will go not to Hel In A but Hell in France to help make those that kicked the lid of[f] *put it back are take the hell they turned loos home with them. If you do go Bumsky it may be a comfort to you to know that I will be with Burt Patrick working for an honest farmer. They say any body can get work since the bulls started a slave market for the benifet of dry landers.*

Give my regards to the bunch
Your friend
C.M. Russell[132]

THE BATTLE OF ST. MIHIEL

LIEUT. FORREST LONGEWAY
Great Falls aviator who, in bullet-scarred airplane soars over Hun lines several times a day dropping tons of explosive shells on retreatnig Boches.

Lieutenant Forrest Longeway, son of Dr. A.F. Longeway of Great Falls, served as a bomber pilot in France. *From the* Great Falls Tribune, *October 27, 1918.*

Captain Dr. Charles E.K. Vidal, member of the fourteenth Montana legislature from Great Falls, enlisted in the Medical Corps Reserve and was assigned duty with a heavy artillery unit in France. On the front line, he found himself "sleeping with my gas mask on my chest and to the music of the heavy guns—which is some orchestra, believe me."

His son, Lieutenant Lawrence E. Vidal, was made adjutant in his 327th Battalion, 1st Brigade, Tank Corps, in the recent fighting in the Montdidier sector. In a letter home, Captain Vidal told of meeting his son on the battlefront lines "somewhere in France" and of himself taking a ride in one of the new fighting tanks "over rocks, holes, brush, trees, trenches and nearly everything else." This experience led Captain Vidal "to believe most anything I am told of the fighting qualities of the tank service."[133]

The late summer of 1918 found Captain Vidal and his son, Lieutenant Lawrence E. Vidal, preparing for a major offensive. They had recently spent time with a young friend, First Lieutenant

Forrest Longeway of Great Falls, an aviator flying bombers with the French Air Service. Captain Vidal frequently corresponded with Dr. A.F. Longeway, Forrest's father, and in this gem of a letter, he provided rare insight into the early stage of the most significant American battle to date: the Battle of St. Mihiel, an all-American operation, with Yanks leading and fighting on their own, smashing through a key German salient that had previously proven impregnable to French forces. For the first time, Yanks were in command with French forces supporting. (A salient is a battlefield feature that projects into enemy territory, surrounded on several sides.) In Captain Vidal's words:

Five days ago I was surprised to run across one of the officers of Lawrence's battalion; and two days after, who comes in as we were finishing dinner but the boy [Lawrence]. *Looking well and very busy. For three days he is to be located at this very village. On the way up he stopped at ____, and while in the officers' YMCA whom does he run across but Forrest. He says that he is looking very fit and is doing splendidly.*

The reason that I said early in the letter that [Forrest] *might be flying overhead tonight is because he is directly tributary to this front and will almost certainly be used in this push. I see Lawrence about twice a day. Now everything is up and ready and we get our orders. Everyone at his battle station at midnight.*

Zero hour, 1 a.m. The evening is spent writing and getting the dugout ready. One hospital corps man to every two guns. The sergeant is helping me at the station.

12 o'clock. The office force and orderlies report as litter bearers and are assigned to an adjoining dugout.

12:30. An engineer doctor, named Kreiger, of the fighting 42nd division, comes in and says he has 200 men in a trench in an adjoining field; so he makes good company and a nice addition to the staff.

12:45. Outside inky black, and a drizzle of rain.

12:55–6–7–8–9 and 1 a.m. Wang-Waand. The dugout trembles and the gas doors bulge as old No. 2, fifty yards away, lets go, and now the steady roar sets in. No individual notes except our own guns. Just a deep-throated roar. Outside to look. The night, before so black, is aflame. Within four kilometers we have 400 heavy guns at work—155s up to naval 14-inch. The roar fairly jars you.

2 a.m. Fritz has been surprised. Return fire is feeble. Quite a bit of 77's busting overhead, but nothing to embarrass.

3 a.m. We are shelling villages and cross roads now. Gun crews changed. One man in with shrapnel wound of face.

3:30 Casualty at No. 3. Shell carrier killed. Two French artillerymen in—shrapnel wounds.

4:00 Change gun crews.

4:30–4:45. A suspicion of daylight. Planes are out.

5 a.m. The 75's open fire with a creeping barrage. The tanks are off. The doughboys go over the top. Our fire slackens up.

5:15 Daylight. The air is alive with our planes.

5:30. The fast-moving, low-lying clouds make our planes fly low. There goes one down. The poor fellow flew so low that he was hit by one of our own 75's....[134]

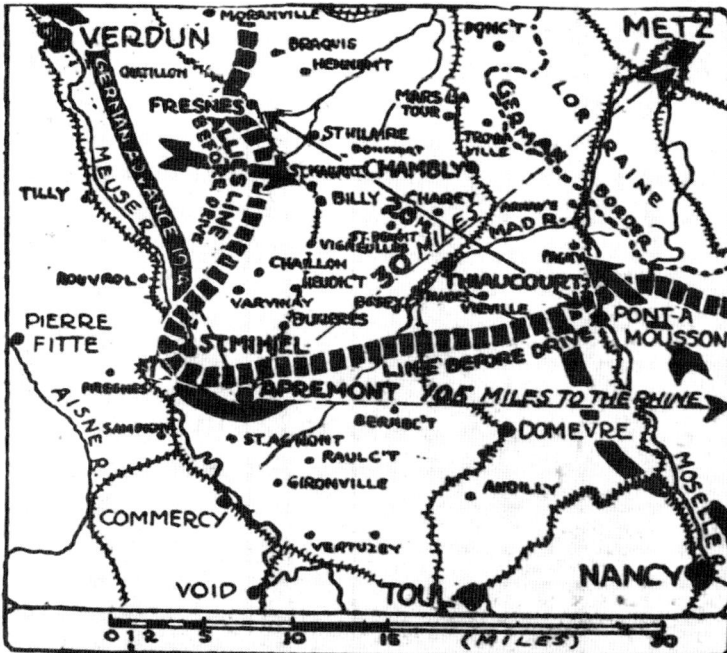

Map, *How the Yanks Smashed in the St. Mihiel Salient. From the* Great Falls Tribune, *September 17, 1918.*

"Open Attack at St. Mihiel." *Library of Congress.*

The smashing American victory on September 12–13 at St. Mihiel was hailed by America's allies and on the homefront. At dawn, September 12, the first all-American major offensive of the war began reducing in forty-eight hours the wedge held by the Germans since 1914. In the operation, the Americans took sixteen thousand prisoners, 443 guns and vast quantities of material and established the Allied line in a position to threaten Metz. Many of the prisoners proved to be Austrians, none too keen on the war to begin with. The assaulting Yanks suffered seven thousand casualties.

The divisions participating in battle were the 1st; 2nd; 4th, "Ivy," regulars, from all states; 5th, "Red Devils," regulars, from all states; 26th, "Yankee," New England National Guard; 42nd, "Rainbow," National Guard from twenty-seven states; 82nd, "All American," Georgia, Alabama and Tennessee national army troops; 89th, "The Rolling W," Kansas, Missouri, South Dakota and Nebraska national army troops; and 90th, "Tough 'Ombres,'" Texas and Oklahoma national army troops. Montanans served in every division.

In tribute, Brigadier General Douglas MacArthur, who had been with the 42nd Division Rainbow Division since its formation, said, "We cannot forget, blue-lipped, smudged with sludge, chilled by the wind and rain of the foxhole, forming grimly and without emotion in the muck which the ground was throwing up as heavy as that which the skies were letting down, they drove through to their objective and to the judgment seat of God. We will not say they have died. They have but passed beyond the mists that blind us here—and come to the end of the Rainbow."

While eight divisions of the AEF participated in the battle, a ninth was positioned nearby in reserves. That division was the 91st "Wild West" Division, composed of Montanans and other men from the Northwest and California. The "Wild West" Division trained intensively throughout August—its time to go "over the top" would soon come.

In a letter to Montana governor Stewart, First Lieutenant Lawrence Vidal wrote a snappy account of his 327th Tank Battalion, equipped with French Renault light tanks, driving back the Germans at St. Mihiel. His battalion

Lieutenant Colonel George S. Patton, commanding the tanks at St. Mihiel, with a Renault FT light tank. *World War I Signal Corps Photograph Collection.*

was later renamed the 344th and 345th and organized into the 304th Tank Brigade, commanded in its first battle by Lieutenant Colonel George Patton. Lieutenant Vidal wrote in part:

We trained, waited, prayed, etc., and at 1 a.m. September 12 the fireworks started. At 5 a.m. the tanks went rollicking after the fleeing Boche. Once or twice I wished I hadn't lied about my weight to get in this man's army. But this vermin ran so fast and surrendered in such mobs that it turned from a battle into a tea party. Naturally those whiz-bangs make you a temporary pacifist, but toward the end of the day you couldn't tell you were in a battle.

…The tanks are shock troops, so we do our bit here then "partee" and do our bit there until so many tanks are put out, then we go back and get re-equipped and journey forth again until a certain race of barbarian is exterminated.

…I know you are very busy, but I just wanted to let you know I haven't forgotten that I owe you everything for being so luckily situated and to assure you that I won't do anything to make you regret giving me my appointment. I'll write from Metz. Respectfully.

Lawrence Vidal.
327 Battalion, First Brigade, Tank Corps.[135]

Native Nurse Lafournaise

One of the first American nurses to serve on the front lines during the Great War was Louise Lafournaise (or La Fournaise), one of two known Montana Native American nurses in the war. While Regina McIntyre was a member of the Salish-Kootenai tribe, Louise was a mixed-race Métis, from a Chippewa tribe not recognized at the time—today she would be a member of the Little Shell tribe. Louise Lafournaise was one remarkable young woman. Born in August 1889 at Willow Bunch, Saskatchewan, Canada, she was raised just south of the border near Opheim, Montana.

Louise graduated from St. Ignatius Training School for Nurses in Colfax, Washington, in 1914. The following year, she filed on a homestead north of Opheim and received patent to her 320 acres in 1918. During this time, she worked also as a nurse at Columbus Hospital in Great Falls and the Fort Benton Sanitarium. In the fall of 1917, she received a Montana

Remarkable Métis and Little Shell nurse and homesteader Louise Lafournaise, one of two Montana native nurses to serve in World War I. *Nicholas Vrooman.*

State Nurses' Certificate to work at the Sacred Heart Hospital in Havre. In March 1918, Louise enlisted with the U.S. Army Nurse Corps and was assigned to Evacuation Hospital No. 1, just behind the front lines in France. For her World War I service, Louise was authorized two chevrons for service with the AEF, the victory service ribbon and one Bronze Star for her part in the St. Mihiel Offense at Evacuation Hospital No. 16. In August 1919, Nurse Lafournaise returned to the United States, where she continued her extraordinary life, surviving spinal meningitis, to live to age ninety-four. She rests today at the Presidio Veteran's Cemetery, San Francisco.[136]

POLITICS OVER HERE

During Representative Jeannette Rankin's term in office, the Montana legislature reapportioned from two at-large Congressional seats to two districts, western and eastern. Representative Rankin was faced with running against her fellow incumbent, Representative John M. Evans, in an overwhelmingly democratic western district or running for the Senate, which she opted to do. On primary election day, August 27, she ran second

Portrait of Senator Henry Cabot Lodge of Massachusetts, painted by John Singer Sargent. *Library of Congress.*

of four Republican candidates, losing by 2,800 votes of about 40,000 cast. Her defeat likely came from having to run a statewide race and from the Anaconda Company doing its all to defeat her.

Rankin made more history in the fall of 1918 when she accepted the nomination of the National (Independent) Party for the U.S. Senate, joining Anne Martin of Nevada in third-party bids that fall. Under the slogan "Win the War First," Representative Rankin sought to appeal to a coalition of labor, agriculture and women, running against incumbent Senator Thomas Walsh and Republican nominee Oscar M. Lanstrum of Helena. The campaign was on.

On August 17, Jacob H. Gallinger of New Hampshire, Senate president pro tempore during the Sixty-Second Congress and Republican Conference chairman, passed away. Picking up the mantle as Republican Senate leader was Senator Henry Cabot Lodge of Massachusetts, who would emerge as a powerful national figure. In late August, Senator Lodge proclaimed his party's policy for ending the war and winning the peace. This declaration, while similar to President Wilson's Fourteen Points program for peace, announced on January 9, 1918, strikingly omitted Wilson's call for a League of Nations. The *River Press* carried the story of Senator Lodge's peace terms on September 4:

WILL DICTATE PEACE TERMS

One of the most ringing declarations of American war ideals and aims which have been made by any American since the country entered the war is that of Senator Henry Cabot Lodge, ranking republican member of the senate foreign relations committee and generally conceded successor to the late Senator Gallinger as the minority leader in the senate. Senator Lodge declared that no peace satisfactory to Germany would be satisfactory to America and her allies. In the senator's own words:

"No peace that satisfies Germany can ever satisfy us. It cannot be a negotiated peace. It must be a dictated peace and we and our allies must dictate it."

He outlined his views as to the chief terms which must be forced upon Germany as follows:

Complete restoration of Belgium.

Unconditional return of Alsace and Lorraine to France.

Unconditional return to Italy of that country's "lost provinces."

Safety for Greece.

Independence for Serbia and Rumania.

An independent Poland.

Independence of the Slav peoples.

Freedom of Russia from German domination, including return to Russia of territory wrested from her by the so-called Brest-Litovsk "treaty."

Constantinople must be made a free port.

Palestine must never be returned to Turkey... [137]

BASE HOSPITAL COMMAND

While the summer of 1918 saw the men of the AEF entering combat in dramatically increasing numbers, the buildup of medical doctors, nurses, ambulance drivers and facilities kept pace. Dr. Thomas C. Witherspoon, long the chief surgeon at Murray Hospital in Butte, personified this buildup. Almost fifty years old, Dr. Witherspoon, a former president of both Montana and Silver Bow County medical associations and an early member of the National College of Surgeons, was called to active service as a lieutenant on November 14, 1917, at Camp Dodge, Iowa. After other assignments at Camp Wadsworth, South Carolina, and Camp Merritt, New Jersey, and promotion to major, Dr. Witherspoon was sent to France in early September 1918. There he was promoted to lieutenant colonel and given command of the massive Base Hospital No. 56 in the small town of Allerey, Saone-et-Loire, a medical complex with ten 1,000-bed barracks. As the fighting and resulting casualties escalated in the fall of 1918, the hospital had 10,728 beds occupied.

The *Butte Miner* of September 29 brought news of his new assignment and summarized Butte's other medical personnel in the army:

> [Dr. Witherspoon] *was commissioned lieutenant colonel just before leaving for France, where he arrived two weeks ago. Dr. Rodes* [at Murray Hospital in Butte] *received word of Dr. Witherspoon's latest promotion from Lieut. C.T. Pigot at Camp Dodge, formerly a physician of Butte.*
>
> *Four other physicians formerly of the Murray Hospital staff are in the army. Dr. Harold Schwartz and Dr. Theo. W. O'Brien are in France with the rank of lieutenant; Dr. Joseph C. Storken is stationed at Douglas, Ariz., and Dr. Lee Smith is at Camp Greenleaf, Ga.*
>
> *One of the former nurses of the hospital, Mrs. Henrietta Vineyard, is in France and Miss Eunice Collins and Miss Irene Howard are in New York awaiting orders to go overseas. Others in the service are Miss Minnie Tippett, Miss Lillian Noeth and Miss Amy Dowling at Camp Lewis; Miss Nellie Ouldhouse, Miss Kate Boles and Miss Anna Britz at Camp Dodge and Mrs. Isabelle Gage at Philadelphia. Miss Hazel Young, Miss Sara Alexander and Mrs. Oliver LaGue are on duty, while Miss Louise Nelson, formerly one of the supervisors at Murray hospital; Miss Theo Coffee, now living at Bozeman; Miss June Daily, now at Wicks; Miss McCullan, Miss Emily Jackson and Miss Frances Sewell are among the present or former nurses of the hospital who are waiting to be called.*[138]

Two Montana nurses serving under Dr. Witherspoon at Base Hospital No. 56 were Elizabeth Ellen Sterling of Missoula, who had been one of the first Montana nurses called to duty in 1917, and Cecilia Brackett Snyder of Butte.[139]

Nurse Snyder's service at the Allerey Base Hospital was featured with her eloquent commentary in the *Anaconda Standard*: "Picture a pretty young woman clad in regulation Red Cross uniform, wearing high rubber boots, and sipping from a can of tomatoes because there was no water, and you have a vivid conjuration of Mrs. Cecilia B. Snyder, born and reared in Butte and trained at St. James Hospital to take her part when war's alarm sounded."

Occasionally, the nurses at Allerey got a bucket of water to do washing, which was ironed by being flattened out against a window. Oftentimes there was scarcely enough water for the needs of the thirty thousand wounded cared for at the newly and hastily constructed hospital. Mrs. Snyder would ask:

> *And who wouldn't do everything that could be done for those poor, brave chaps? There were times when the juice of a can of tomatoes proved a gratifying drink. Sometimes we had no water for two or three days. Our tongues were parched, but we poured lavish portions for the fevered mouths of the wounded, who came in on convoys of 200 or 300 at a time.*
>
> *Those certainly were the sad days, the whole world drenched with rains that seemed never to cease—and yet those gritty boys came in endless streams, dripping water and blood, and actually smiling.*

From Allerey, Mrs. Snyder was transferred to Hyers, a sunny French port on the Mediterranean, where she waited three months for transportation home. On May 16, 1919, her birthday, she arrived in Butte and resumed her work as a nurse. Mrs. Snyder concluded:

> *"Those scenes at Allerey can never fade from the memories of 200 nurses who were there when I was," Mrs. Snyder declared in retrospection. "Some tell us that it must have taken an unbounded courage and bravery to have undertaken the work of a nurse at such a hospital, but it must have required tenfold that courage to have faced, unflinchingly, the terrible rain of bullets, shrapnel and gas that causes such horrible wounds."*[140]

Montana Native Warriors in Action

From the U.S. declaration of war, many native tribal leaders proclaimed the support of indigenous people for the war effort. Remarkably, this came just over one generation after the end of the western Indian Wars. Early in the Great War, the War Department distinguished between "fullblood" and "halfbreed," requiring the former to serve in the segregated army's colored units. At the time, Montana's native population stood at about 12,000, with only four states having more native residents, led by Oklahoma with more than one-third of the nation's

Montana native warriors, including Private Bird Above and several Métis from Lewistown, served in the 148th Field Artillery in France. *Author's collection.*

330,000. Many more were among the large mixed-race population in Montana and other western states, descended from early white robe traders and pioneers.

During the course of the war, about 12,000 Native Americans served, and in Montana just over 170 have been identified, although more likely served. Natives who served in combat compiled a sterling record, including the first "code talkers," and this proved a major factor in the decision of Congress in 1924 to grant U.S. citizenship to all Native Americans.[141]

On Independence Day 1917, Secretary of War Newton D. Baker addressed a large audience at the stadium of the College of the City of New York:

"We must fight for democracy here at home as our armies will fight for democracy abroad."

...I can see the day when this harbor of yours will be filled with ships bringing back our soldiers. They will come, it may be, with their ranks somewhat thinned by sacrifice, but with themselves glorified by accomplishment. And when these heroes step ashore and tell us what they have won for democracy in Europe, we must be able to tell them in return that we have kept the faith of democracy at home, and won battles here for that cause while they were fighting there.

On the platform with Secretary Baker that day was a young multiracial Blackfoot man, Red Fox St. James, who roused the audience when he pleaded that his race be given a place in the war:

"My own people, the North American Indian, has heard the call to arms," he said, *"but you will not let us answer. Do you not need us in this terrible conflict? Are we to remain inactive when 50,000 Indians are ready to serve as cavalry?*

From all over the west we stand ready to spring to the saddle. We stand ready to protect the 1,400 miles of border between the United States and Mexico; 50,000 men who know a horse as no white man ever knew it; 50,000 men who can live where no white man has ever lived, 50,000 Indians, who when their hearts are in a cause, as our hearts are in this cause, would die for it as no other nation.

Turning to Secretary Baker, St. James concluded, saying, "Mr. Secretary, call us to arms. Let us guard and fight for our country." In response to his challenge, St. James was told that he and his fighters must come into the army the regular way.[142]

By early 1918, the War Department was welcoming all Native American warriors into the midst of the rapidly growing national army. Among Montana's 174 natives known to have served were:

- Nurses: Regina McIntyre of Flathead Reservation, and Louise Lafournaise of Opheim served in France;
- Marines: PFC David F. Pease, of Lodge Grass, 22nd Company, 1st Regiment, served in Cuba.

- Sailors: Musician 1st Class Charles J. Eder, of Poplar, enlisted on April 12, 1917, served aboard the USS *Cheyenne* and at Submarine Base San Pedro, California; Thomas Jennings Flynn, Chippewa-Cree, and Harry Simons served in the navy.
- Army: About 160 native soldiers, including one death. Stephen C. Knight (Stephen Chief at Night), Crow, entered service at Salem Indian Training School, Oregon. He served in Headquarters Company, 44th Infantry. He died of tuberculosis at the Letterman General Hospital, San Francisco, in May 1919, and was buried at Custer Battlefield.

Seven other known casualties:

- Irvin Bird Above, St. Xavier, Crow, served in Battery C, 148th Field Artillery Regiment, 41st Division. PFC Bird Above fought in the Champagne-Marne Defense, Aisne-Marne, St. Mihiel and Meuse-Argonne Offenses, receiving four wounds in four engagements.
- Joseph Gardipe, Malta, served in Company H, 127th Infantry, 32nd Red Arrow Division; slightly wounded August 30 in the attack on Juvigny.
- James Kallowat, Dayton, served in Battery A, 12th Field Artillery Regiment, 2nd Division; slightly wounded on June 18 at Château-Thierry.
- Benton Rowland, Cheyenne, served in Company M, 167th Regiment, 42nd Division; fought at Château-Thierry and Meuse-Argonne Offensive, wounded twice.
- Joseph Schenderline, Lodge Grass, Crow, served in Company H, 308th Infantry, 77th Division; wounded in Argonne Offensive.
- Louis J. Tellier, St. Ignatius, Flathead Agency, enlisted on March 26, 1917, served in Company E, 127th Infantry, 32nd Division; slightly wounded in action July 31 during the battle of the Marne.
- Jerome Kennerly, Browning, Blackfeet, was among at least one hundred Montanans onboard the ill-fated troop transport *Tuscania*, which was torpedoed and sunk on February 5, 1918. Private Kennerly served with the 158th Aero Squadron and was among the ninety Montanans who survived this tragedy that cost the lives of ten Montanans killed in action.[143]

MONTANA'S BLACK WARRIORS

Montana's Africans Americans were drafted and served at a disproportionately high rate—more served (198) than from Washington State (173), yet Montana's black population was less than one-third that of Washington's. In addition, Montana's black soldiers served at three times the combat rate of the national average—30 percent versus 10 percent.

More than half of Montana African Americans were in noncombat service battalions, with many of them in stevedore and labor battalions. These battalions did the critical heavy lifting as the AEF grew to almost 2 million in France by the end of the war. There were more labor battalions composed of white soldiers, some 207 in France, the difference being that the majority of African Americans were in service battalions, while the majority of white soldiers were on the line in combat units.

The tasks of service battalion soldiers were many and important. Upon arriving at French ports, they handled bags of mail and freight sent to supply the AEF. The army had to be furnished with horses and mules, which meant feed for forage and saddles and harnesses. The men needed bullets, meat, bacon, flour, lard, ice, shoes, clothes, gasoline and much more. When the AEF was in full swing in France, the supply system had to keep up with shipments of millions of rounds of ammunition and large supplies of blankets, rubber boots, hay and medicines to support combat operations.

In a tribute to the AEF's Colored Stevedores, Reverend D. Leroy Ferguson of Louisville, Kentucky, stated:

> *On the same day that the American Infantry, trekking in the wake of the retreating Germans, gained the outskirts of Fismes, colored stevedores unloading a ship at one of the base ports unostentatiously won an important victory by discharging 1,200 tons of flour in 9½ hours, setting a record for the AEF and a pace which is rarely excelled on the best-equipped docks in the United States The same group of stevedores over a period of five days discharged an average of 2,000 tons of cargo a day from one ship, a record more notable still.*

Most of these stevedores had never seen a ship until they started for France, but they proved their worth as cargo handlers.[144]

Montanans assigned to combat units served with either the 92nd Infantry Division or the 93rd Division (Provisional). Twenty-one black Montanans served in the 92nd Division, which was the only black division of the AEF in

France. The 92nd Division had only white officers. Throughout its time in France, the 92nd Division fought two enemies: the Germans and pervasive white racism. Composed of about twenty-eight thousand black soldiers, it fought in two sectors of the great battle of the Meuse-Argonne in October, the largest and most costly battle in all American history.

The four black regiments of the 93rd Infantry (Provisional) were proof that the U.S. War Department simply didn't know what to do with black combat troops. Its first plan was to deploy them as the 93rd Division under the AEF. Fortunately for the four regiments, soon after their arrival in France, they became an American Foreign Legion brigaded to the French. All American equipment was turned in except uniforms, and the men were given French rifles, bayonets, helmets, packs and other equipment of the French soldier.

The regiments, after just a few weeks instruction on the new equipment and French tactics, went into the trenches as part of the manpower-strapped French divisions—long before the 92nd Division under the AEF. The French were used to integrating black soldiers into their operations, as with French colonial troops from Africa.

The outcome of this combination, American black regiments embedded in French divisions, proved successful. All four regiments performed well, and three regiments earned the signal honor of being awarded the regimental Croix de Guerre: the 369th, 371st and 372nd. The 369th (the old 15th New York National Guard) was especially honored for its record of 191 days on the firing line, exceeding by 5 days the term of service at the front of any other American regiment.

Remarkably, three Montana African Americans served as commissioned officers—Captain Horace Bivins on duty in the United States, while Second Lieutenant Charles H. Conley and First Lieutenant Charles Holmes served in the 93rd Division. Montana had an officer for every 66 enlisted men, while nationally there was just 1 black officer for every 400 enlisted—overall 1,000 black officers served in the almost 400,000-strong African American army.

The 370th Regiment, formed from the highly respected 8th Illinois National Guard, was the only regiment in the U.S. Army with an almost complete complement of black officers, from the highest rank of colonel on down. Three Montanans served with the 370th: Lieutenant Conley of Havre; forty-one-year-old Charles Tully of Fort Assinniboine, band leader of the famed 8th Illinois Band; and Private Fenton Campbell of Lodge Grass.

In France, the 370th was brigaded with French troops and given every opportunity to get into the heaviest fighting. The men quickly established a reputation, called by the Germans "the Black Devils" and by the French

American black military jazz bands were a hit throughout France in the Great War. *U.S. Signal Corps, Library of Congress.*

"the Partridges" for their proud bearing. The 370th served with distinction with the French 34th, 36th and 59th Infantry Divisions, earning streamers for the battles of Lorraine and Oise-Aisne.

On September 11, 1918, the 370th began a fifty-nine-day drive with continuous fighting until the day of the Armistice, November 11. As the war ended, the 370th won distinction on the battlefield as the last regiment pursuing the retreating German forces in the Aisne-Marne region of France.

Lieutenant Conley was born at Fort Bayard, New Mexico, where his father, Sergeant Pasqual Conley, was serving. In France, Conley quickly worked his way up the ranks to sergeant major of the 350th Machine Gun Battalion in the 370th Regiment. Shortly after, he was appointed second lieutenant, commanding Company C. After the war, Lieutenant Conley returned to Montana, moved to Great Falls, earned a good job working for the Great Northern postal service and rests today in Veterans Plot at Highland Cemetery.[145]

Trouble in Butte

The copper mines of Butte and the smelters of Anaconda and Great Falls were vital to the war effort. A combination of the worst mining disaster in Montana history (Granite Mountain), labor strife fostered by the IWW ("Wobblies"), the perceived threat of sabotage and antiwar sentiment among several ethnic groups and socialists led to deployment of the U.S. 14th Infantry Regiment to Butte during 1918 to augment police presence in the tense, war-critical environment. Captain Omar N. Bradley, of later World War II army fame, arrived with Company F on January 26 in temperatures forty degrees below zero.

Dozens of Montanan draftees, including Irish from Butte, served with the 14th Infantry, including at least two Montana native soldiers: PFC Albert C. Courville, age eighteen, from St. Ignatius, serving in Company M, and Corporal Charles H. Renz, age twenty-three of Poplar, serving in Company F.[146]

The *River Press* of September 18 reported the latest labor strife under the headline "Striking Miners Arrested":

> *Butte, Sept. 13.—An unsuccessful attempt to stop the production of copper and other metals essential to the prosecution of the war was made in the Butte district this morning by the I.W.W.*
>
> *The movement, said to be national in scope, it was stated by local labor leaders, was calculated to paralyze industry through the course of sympathy strikes for Haywood and Debs, imprisoned as the I.W.W. and socialist leaders.*

U.S. 14th Infantry Regiment, under Captain Omar Bradley, organized a baseball team while keeping order in Butte during 1918. *U.S. Army Heritage and Education Center.*

Eighty arrests were made by the police, practically all the prisoners admitting membership in the I.W.W.

Only a small proportion of the miners, according to the mining officials, abandoned their tasks. In many Butte properties none of the men joined the strike. Leaders of the I.W.W. claim that 2,000 men quit work.

Attempts to create demonstrations were frustrated by the police, aided by federal officials [and the 14th Infantry].

According to mining officials, strike bulletins had been posted at the entrances to all mining properties.

These were signed by the "Worker Committee," and demands similar to those made when John D. Ryan visited Butte recently were made. Those are identical with those employed during the labor troubles of 1917, being $4 a day for eight hours; abolition of the rustling card and authority to inspect the mines monthly.[147]

LAUNCHING THE MEUSE-ARGONNE OFFENSIVE

Through the summer of 1918 and into September, more and more American divisions of the AEF joined in the fighting on the Western Front. One new division was the 91st "Wild West" Division, going into battle shouting, "Powder River, Let 'Er Buck!" It was the drafted men from Montana who gave the cry to the 91st Division. They took it to Camp Lewis with them, and there the cry caught the fancy of the California, Oregon and Washington men with whom they served.

The greatest series of battles along the entire Western Front began to accelerate, and the AEF role was proving pivotal. On September 26, the Allies launched the Meuse-Argonne Offensive, which would become *the* decisive battle series culminating in the end of the Great War. This series would be the largest in American military history, engaging more than 1.2 million American soldiers, costing 28,000 American lives, an equal number of Germans and an unknown number of French lives.

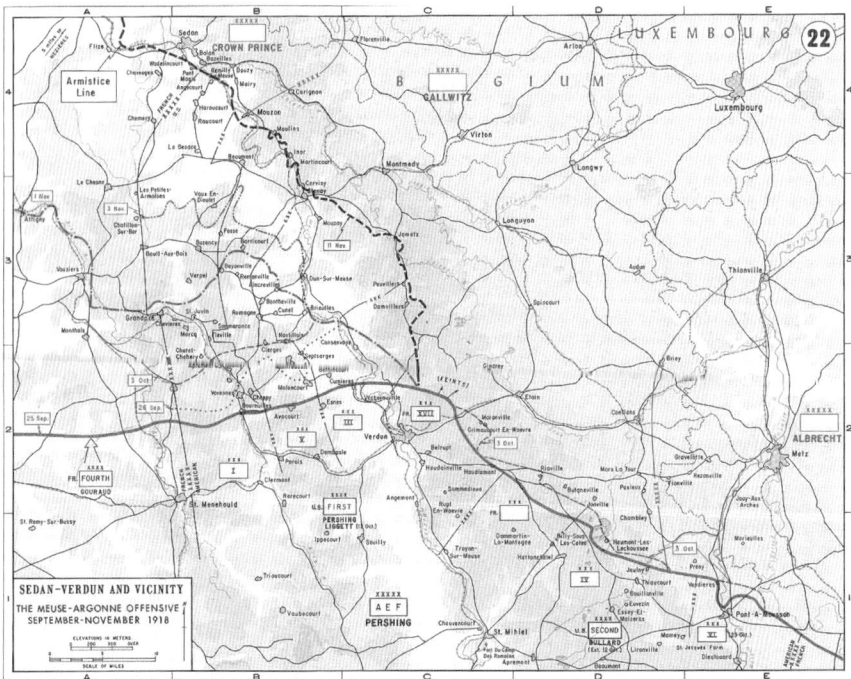

Map, *Meuse-Argonne Offensive, September–November 1918. Wikimedia Commons.*

Sam Caras smiling as he and his company in the "Wild West" Division return to New York after fighting and writing about the bloody Meuse-Argonne Offensive that forced the German surrender. *From the* Missoulian, *February 7, 1965.*

The offensive began with a massive artillery barrage, expending more ammunition than both sides fired over the duration of the American Civil War. It all began at 2:30 a.m. on the morning of September 26, three hours before the launch of H-hour. Sam Caras, veteran of the Greek army in the 1912 and 1913 Balkan wars and an immigrant resident of Missoula serving with the Trench Mortar Battery of the 91st Division, described the action:

The World Was Coming to an End…
It was now 2:25 and in a few moments we would hear the big boys cut loose and they were sure big ones, as I had seen them two days previously. From somewhere behind us there came a single dull boom that sounded like a close blast of dynamite.

"They are off," yelled somebody close to me. I listened intently for a few seconds. "No," I said, "that was only one shot. Listen." There came a long, quivering, murmuring sound, like a swiftly beating pulse that sounded like a thousand faint rolling echoes, of that first, far-sounding boom that we heard. The horizon became fearfully lit with faint flickering flush of pale ghostly light that was like the far distant play of head-lights on a summer night. The murmur of the sound grew to a high rumbling growl, emphasized every few seconds by a deeply thunderous roar. The barrage was on. America was talking to Fritz in close order….I had never experienced in any of the previous wars that I was in such a din. I thought my ears would burst any minute…[148]

It was now 4 o'clock and the barrage going on in full speed. You could see for miles around the flash of the big guns and hear their continual roar. Oh, God! It still rings in my ears. I thought for the minute that the world was coming to an end…

Going Over the Top
Time was passing fast and it was now 5:30; time for us to go "over the top" and put on the finishing touches. We were ordered to "get out" and "go over." Our barrage quieted down somewhat by this time and turned into a rolling barrage, so as to be ahead of us. Our platoon did not get the trench mortars that we were supposed to have had and we had to go "over the top" with our rifles along with the "doughboys."…[The mission of Caras's platoon became a desperate attempt to capture a German *minenwerfer*, or mine launcher, somewhat like their own missing trench mortar, and turn it on the retreating Germans.]

Above: German 7.58cm *minenwerfer* at the Brussels military museum, a trench mortar used in World War I. *Wikimedia Commons.*

Left: Ad for Private Sam K. Caras's "Playing with Death in Three Wars." *From the* Missoulian, *October 17, 1919.*

The dawn was breaking on a day that I shall never forget, a dreadful day and yet a glorious one for the "Wild West" was September 26th. I shall never forget in the years to come this day, although I might forget the long hikes and hardships I underwent while in France and Belgium. It has some bitter and pleasant memories that will never be forgotten. Bitter memories (I don't think that is the word for it) to see the flower of American youth lying in all directions smashed and so cut up as to be unrecognizable. It was a pleasant memory to see the Hun going over the hills in the face of democracy, and to see that autocracy was finally beaten.

It was a foggy morning and one could hardly see further than 10 yards in front of him. Down the hill we went, onto a path not more than three yards wide. Here there was an awful congestion of machine guns, one pounders, "doughboys" and carts of all kinds, jammed up in one mass. A few yards further down was the general and colonel, waving their hands for the men to "double time" and get through a channel as it was a very dangerous place if Fritz cut loose. And he sure did. The first shell that came over hit the top of a tree and on the side of the road there was an awful crash. All the men went down as quickly as they could under the circumstances, but hearing another shell coming, got up and started to double time, except our postoffice sergeant who got a piece of shrapnel in the leg and as I found afterwards, he died in the hospital from blood poisoning.

We did not go over 15 yards when another one came over, this time bursting just across the road, shrapnel flew in all directions, but no one was hurt, except a mule from a machine gun company, went down, shot through the hip. We began to get nervous and although they weren't big shells, they were the first ones to burst as close as they did. We rushed ahead to get out of that trap, you might call it that, and get over in more open ground and spread out. Fritz had our number there and to have stayed there a few minutes longer would have spelled "finish" for most of us.[149]

On the way out, I saw a young fellow sitting by the side of the road with half of his nose cut off. A small piece of shrapnel was going by, and his nose happened to be in the way. We kept on, by this time we were out of the road and in more open ground and there thousands of machine gun bullets greeted us, also the shells were coming over faster, but went over our heads.

As we were advancing, somebody yelled, "Gas." We did not know if there was gas or not. We did not take any chances and put our gas masks on as quickly as we possibly could and flopped down, as we could not advance with those things on, through barbed wire entanglements. Then came the

*word, "No gas; fix bayonets and charge." The order was not quite finished
when there as a whistling and almost at once a terrible roar. A shell had
exploded not more than ten yards away. I closed my eyes and when I opened
them again there were in front of me, six bodies…*

*I tell you folks, I had been in this thing before and I have seen terrible
sights in my experiences, but this thing took my breath away. I was shaking
like a leaf. I was stunned. I couldn't move for the life of me. This was the
worst sight I had ever seen. I don't know how long I stayed there, gazing
away like a big idiot, when our lieutenant came over and patted me on the
back and said: "Caras, isn't this an awful sight; let's get away from here;
I can't stand it."*

*We moved out and then he told me that this shell that had killed these
men was nothing but a* minenwerfer. *Judging by the sound of it, as he
had had a little previous experience at school, and he was able to recognize
it, and it was just the gun that we were after. We moved on through barbed
wire entanglements. They were thick as flies in summer, and one can see
these entanglements for miles around but our pioneers were on the job with
those big shears of theirs, cutting them up and opening the way for us to go
through after Fritz.*

*The 363rd was on the line that day and the 364th was supposed to be
in support. But we didn't care who was on the line or who was in support.
We were after our* minenwerfer *and we were determined to have it that
day. By this time we knew that one was pretty close somewhere. They were
sending shells over at the rate of 25 a minute. We kept on advancing. There
were not only* minenwerfers *pounding away at us now, but thousands
of machine guns and snipers in all directions were firing away at us. But
the morale of the men was high, and all you could hear was jollying and
cursing of troops. And the wild cry still rings in my ears "First aid" or
"Stretcher bearers, forward." And that made us all the wilder to go after
Fritz, with more force than ever before, when we knew that some one of our
comrades paid with his life for democracy.[150]*

The Meuse-Argonne Offensive was underway. Ten AEF divisions of
about 260,000 men began the attack, organized in three corps and arrayed
facing north from Champagne in the west to the River Meuse in the
east. Allied forces from east to west included III Corps, 4th, 80th and 33rd
Divisions; V Corps, 91st, 37th and 79th Divisions; and I Corps, 77th, 28th and
35th Division. Over the next forty-seven days, these divisions would fight
until relieved. Dismounted cavalry served as scouts, and the Light Tank

Brigade under Lieutenant Colonel Patton supported the drive. Landmarks captured on the first day were Butte de Vacquois and historic Varennes.

On September 26, the AEF advanced steadily, except for the 79th Division, which encountered tough resistance in capturing the strong point of Montfaucon. The 91st "Wild West" Division advanced five miles but was compelled to evacuate the village of Epinonville. This delay held up the overall advance for more than twenty-four hours and enabled the Germans to reorganize and hold.[151]

On September 27, the First Army failed to make any gains. By the end of the day, the 79th Division had finally captured Montfaucon, but the thirty-six-hour delay allowed the German forces to escape and regroup, an expensive missed opportunity. The 35th Division captured Baulny village, Hill 218 and Charpentry, moving it forward of adjacent divisions. By the evening of the twenty-eighth, the AEF had achieved a maximum advance of seven miles. The right had made a fine advance into the woods south of Brieulles-sur-Meuse, but the far left of the line was meeting strong resistance in the Argonne. According to General Pershing, "[We] were necessarily committed, generally speaking, to a direct frontal attack against strong, hostile positions fully manned by a determined enemy."

By the twenty-ninth, the Germans had deployed six more divisions to shore up their defenses. The German 5th Guards and 52nd Division counterattacked the AEF 35th Division, which ran out of ammunition and food. Initially, the Germans made significant gains but were repulsed in desperate fighting by the 35th's 110th Engineers, 128th Machine Gun Battalion and Battery D of the 129th Field Artillery, led by future president Captain Harry Truman. In the words of General Pershing:

By nightfall of the 29th the First Army line was approximately at Bois de la Cote Lemont—Nantillois—Apremont—southwest across the Argonne. Many divisions, especially those in the center that were subjected to cross-fire of artillery, had suffered heavily. The severe fighting, and the nature of the terrain over which they attacked, and the fog and darkness sorely tried even our best divisions. On the night of the 29th the 37th and 79th Divisions were relieved by the 32nd and 3rd Divisions, respectively, and on the following night the 1st Division relieved the 35th Division.

The critical problem during the first days of the battle was the restoration of communications over "no man's land." There were but four roads available across this deep zone, and the violent artillery fire of the previous period of the war had virtually destroyed them. The spongy soil and lack of material increased the difficulty. But the splendid work of our engineers and pioneers soon made possible the movement of the troops, artillery, and supplies most needed. By the afternoon of the 27th all the divisional artillery, except a few batteries of heavy guns, had effected a passage and was supporting the infantry action."[152]

Montana Influenza Pandemic

No other natural catastrophe struck the world during the twentieth century quite like the influenza pandemic of 1918–19. The first wave had struck Montana in January 1918. Later that year, an even more virulent form of the virus mutated, and by mid-September, it had struck Montana. The virus caused the flu, and if it wasn't fatal, the ensuing pneumonia often led to death. By June 1919, some five thousand Montanans died, nearly 1 percent of the population.[153]

The first fatality in the second, more virulent, wave was a young Blackfoot boy, Woodrow Lazyboy, who died on Tuesday, September 23, in Browning. Two more deaths occurred on September 25—a fifteen-year-old girl in Scobey and an eighty-six-year-old farmer in Great Falls. Five more deaths occurred September 29–30 in northeastern Montana. In the words of Todd Harwell, Greg Holzman and Steven Helgerson, "These eight mortalities began a tsunami of death across Montana."[154]

This wave included six other cases of influenza in Montana in late September. Dr. E.D. Baker documented one case in Twin Bridges and five cases from Whitehall:

> [The Whitehall cases] *came from the Great Lakes naval station, one of the Whitehall men stricken with the disease having only recently returned from visiting a brother at the naval station who was suffering from the same disease. The patients have been isolated.*
>
> *Because of the importance of checking the ravages of the epidemic, all Montana doctors are asked to report cases at once to local health officers, who will notify the state board, which in turn wires Washington.*[155]

The pandemic struck Montana's soldiers overseas in early September, and during the month, there were at least twelve deaths from influenza and/or pneumonia. SATC students at universities were struck as well as sailors at sea.[156]

THE RED HAND, 157TH FRENCH DIVISION

General Goybet commanded the French 157th Red Hand Division, which consisted of the French 333rd Infantry Regiment and the black American 371st and 372nd Regiments. The two American regiments fought bravely and were awarded the Croix de Guerre, and several men received both the French Legion of Honor and the American Distinguished Service Cross. Freddie Stowers of the 371st was posthumously awarded the Medal of Honor. In addition, General Goybet sent the following commendation: "The 372nd Infantry Regiment under the 157th French Division 'The Red Hand' sign of the Division, thanks to you, became a bloody hand which took the Boche by the throat and made him cry for mercy. You have well avenged our glorious dead. (Signed) GOYBET, General, Commanding 157th Division."

Montanan First Lieutenant Charles L. Holmes of the 372nd, born in Pueblo, Colorado, in 1892, moved to Butte before attending Colorado College. He graduated from college with a major in English after starring in track and football. Holmes registered for the draft while working as a waiter at the Silver Bow Club in Butte. Shortly after, Charles was appointed second lieutenant in the army reserve, together with 638 other black officers at Des Moines, Iowa.

Assigned to the 372nd Infantry in September 1918, Lieutenant Holmes wrote to friends in Butte that he was on the front line with the Red Hand Division for some months and that Boche shells and gas had been everyday affairs to him. He added, "The men are filled with the right spirit and desire to pull off a fast finish." Lieutenant Holmes was wounded toward the end of the war, though not seriously. After the war, he returned to Butte, but he was destined for more achievements than what was available to him in Jim Crow–era Montana. By 1930, he was married and teaching in East Baton Rouge, Louisiana, and a decade later, both Charles and his wife were teaching at a segregated public college in North Carolina.[157]

PERSHING DAY

As General John J. Pershing's birthday approached in September, many newspapers, including the *River Press*, paid tribute to the commander of the American Expeditionary Forces in France:

While it has been deemed incautious to erect monuments to living heroes, the proposal to celebrate September 12, the 51st birthday of the splendid American soldier who commands our troops in France, may be heartily commended, says the Chicago Tribune. From the time when Cadet Pershing graduated at the head of his class at the military academy to the present, when he wears the highest rank in our overseas army, John Pershing has made good. In the Philippines his record was memorable. In the sorely hampered expedition after Villa, he again showed marked ability. But it has been only since his service in France began that he has had opportunity to disclose abilities or command an organization on a large scale.

General John J. Pershing, Commander, American Expeditionary Forces, at General Headquarters in Chaumont, France, October 1918. *Library of Congress.*

We do not like to think what would have happened if the wrong man had been sent to France. The wrong man was not sent. General Pershing had before him a tremendous task in organization alone. We laymen at home will never appreciate what that task was. But we know that it has been achieved in such a manner as to arose the respect and admiration of our allies.

But General Pershing has been more than an organizer. He has represented the American spirit and character His relations with the French and British officers and officials have been maintained on a very high plane. He has begrudged nothing and his tact and judgment have made possible the fullest and most beneficent co-operation.

This is a triumph of character and devotion. The American people will not lack in appreciation of this service. At a historic moment, in a place of great difficulty and critical importance, General Pershing has served his country well and shown qualities of a high and distinguished order. America is proud to be so represented.[158]

PART III

A WAR TO WIN AND AN ELUSIVE PEACE TO BUILD

Chapter 7

OCTOBER 1918

Grand Meuse—Argonne Offensive; Lost Battalion;
Great Influenza Pandemic

MARINE CAPTURED BY GERMANS

Marine private Wayne Colahan, 83 Company, 6th Marines, of Highwood was captured on June 6, 1918, early in the bloody, deadly battle of Belleau Wood. His family first learned of his fate in late September, and his story remained lost in the fog of war until his release shortly after the Armistice. Private Colahan, held at Cassel and Rastatt Camps, was one of eighteen known Montanan POWs during the war. The *River Press* carried this account of his capture and treatment as a German prisoner:

> *A story of privation and suffering while being held in a German war prison camp was related to a Great Falls Leader representative by Wayne J. Colahan, of Highwood, a Chouteau county soldier boy who served with the marines overseas and recently returned from an eastern demobilization camp. Mr. Colahan's story includes his training, trip overseas, and his introduction to the trenches, where he was a dispatch runner. He, with a companion, were victims of a hand grenade, thrown into a shell crater where the two had gone for a moment's safety. In attempting to leave the shell hole, after having been wounded...the two marines were hustled off to a German base where, as prisoners of war, their wounds were dressed.*
>
> *As one of the total of 57 marines who were taken prisoner, Colahan tells a frightful story of an operation for his wounds while being held down by two hospital attaches in order that the operation might be performed without*

anesthetics, according to the Highwood boy, and he said, "I was pretty well fussed about it until I found they were operating upon their own men in the same manner, having no drugs whatsoever to produce sleep. I lost weight because of lack of food and nourishment, going down to 115 pounds when my normal weight is about 165."

Mr. Colahan was turned over to a U.S. Army base hospital shortly after the armistice was signed. Following his recovery from his wounds he was attached to the army of occupation in Germany where he served until his recent sailing for home. Colahan holds a letter written him by the American Red Cross commission in Berne, giving testimonial to his splendid work in assisting the commission towards relief of his fellow prisoners in Germany while he himself was a hospital patient.[159]

An article in the *St. Louis Post-Dispatch* reported on German cruelty toward their prisoners and Colahan's role in revealing German actions:

ST. LOUISAN SHOT WHILE HELPLESS, AFFIDAVITS SAY. EUGENE S. SCHRAUTENMEIER WAS LYING WOUNDED WHEN GERMAN FIRED ON HIM WITH REVOLVER, COMRADES DECLARE…

Affidavits have been received at Marine Corps headquarters in Washington, telling how Eugene S. Schrautenmeier of the 83 Company 6th Marines was shot and presumably killed by a German soldier when he lay wounded and helpless in a shell hole.

…The affidavits…were sworn to by two of Schrautenmeier's comrades, Jules Martin of Detroit and Wayne Colahan.

Colahan relates that he and Schrautenmeier went over the top with their company June 6, having Bouchet as an objective. Both were runners. They dropped down in a shell hole for protection from heavy fire. A Sergeant called out from a clump of trees to them to go to the rear. Colahan heard his companion cry out with pain. "I can't go," he said. "My uncle has got me."

Colahan explains that Schrautenmeier had two German uncles, and that had become a subject of jokes in the company.

Colahan, hugging the ground for protection, did not see all that followed, but he heard a pistol shot, followed by the sound of a fall and saw a German standing over the shell hole.

Martin tells how the company ran into a nest of machine guns that opened fire. He was wounded, and when trying to get back to the rear, fell exhausted and was later taken prisoner. He says he saw a German shoot Schrautenmeier with a revolver.[160]

KNOWN MONTANA PRISONERS OF WAR (POW)[161]

Montana Soldier	Hometown	County in 1918
Andrews, Vester L.	Fort Benton	Chouteau
Colahan, Wayne	Highwood	Chouteau
Hollar, Everett E.	Ovando	Powell
Jensen, Nels K.	Circle	Dawson
Johnson, John W.	Hall	Granite
Larabie, Ned	Deer Lodge/ Bellingham	Powell
McCormick, Everett B.	Chinook	Blaine
Patterson, Lieutenant Robert A.	Havre	Hill
Roberts, Edward M.	Miles City	Custer
Rodin, William V.	Conrad	Teton
Schultz, Otto J.	Somers	Flathead
Skarsten, Robert	Turner	Blaine
Sorensen, Christian	Verona	Chouteau
Sorenson, Lauritis P.	Great Falls	Cascade
Stewart, R.	Findon, MT	Gallatin
Sullivan, Jerry H.	Creston	Flathead
Timmons, Bud	Monida	Beaverhead
Weirick, Arthur Murray	Lewistown	Fergus

THE LOST BATTALION

The Lost Battalion was by no means "lost"—it knew right where it was in its seemingly untenable position, and so did the Germans who had them surrounded. Early in the massive Meuse-Argonne Offensive, on October 2, nine depleted companies of the 308th and 307th Infantry Regiments of the 77th "Statue of Liberty" Division, about 554 men led by Major Charles W.

Whittlesey, broke through German lines and advanced so rapidly into the Argonne Forest that they outpaced French and American forces on their flanks. The Whittlesey battalion found themselves cut off and surrounded, positioned on a steep, heavily wooded slope in the Charlevaux Valley, less than a mile in advance of other 77th Division units. For the following six days, with limited ammunition and supplies but an abundance of courage and a leader who refused to surrender, these Yanks fought valiantly against attacking Germans. Meanwhile other companies from the 307th and 308th Regiments fought desperately to break through German lines to bring relief.

The nine trapped companies—A, B, C, E, G and H of the 308th; K of the 307th Infantry; and C and D of the 306th Machine Gun Battalion and its parent 77th Division—comprised three dozen nationalities from all walks of life in New York. Remarkably, many Montanans were mixed in these melting pot "Lost Battalion" companies—at least 23 Montanans would be among the 197 killed in action, while 1 Montana man, Otto J. Schultz of Somers, was captured and died of his wounds; 18 more Montanans were among the 194 rescued, although 4 more would die of wounds and 1 of pneumonia in the aftermath; 3 of the rescued suffered severe wounds and 1 a slight wound; and just 10 Montana men remained unscathed, while several of them collapsed of exhaustion soon after.

Finally, on October 8, other Yanks broke through German lines to rescue the defiant but desperately weakened survivors of the Lost Battalion. Two Montanans among the survivors, Private James G. Irvin of Billings and Private Marvin B. Long of Glasgow, later related accounts of their ordeal.[162]

The *Great Falls Tribune* carried the dramatic experiences of Private James G. Irvin of Billings, Company D, 308th Infantry, in the Lost Battalion:

> [Private Irvin's] *first hand account of the experiences of the gallant little detachment of the 77th division…reveals some interesting sidelights…*
>
> *Private Irvin was close to Major Whittlesey, commander of the detachment, when the American who had been taken prisoner by the Germans and released to carry the message back to his comrades requesting they surrender, arrived and delivered the message. The widely heralded reply accredited to Major Whittlesey, in which the major is supposed to have told the Germans in stentorian tones to "Go to hell" never was uttered, Private Irvin says, altho the sentiment therein expressed was carried out.*
>
> *"What Major Whittlesey did remark," says Private Irvin, "was addressed to the message bearer and uttered in a low voice. It was: 'I ought to shoot you for bringing this kind of a message.'"*

The pigeon that saved the "Lost Battalion" arrives home. *From the* Anaconda Standard, *April 27, 1919.*

As a matter of fact, the bearer of the message nearly was shot by mistake by Private Irvin, who was stationed several rods away from where the detachment lay partly concealed, by hastily thrown up breastworks and the rank undergrowth. Private Irwin observed the messenger approaching and waited for him to announce himself. The guard had his rifle leveled on a patch of moonlight across a path which

Major Whittlesey (*left*), the Lost Battalion commander, was dubious about pushing ahead, but he was under orders. "You will advance, regardless of flanks," was the command from General Robert Alexander (*right*), the 77th Division commander. *From the* Missoulian, *September 26, 1937.*

the messenger was traveling. If the stranger made no sound before reaching the patch of moonlight, Private Irvin intended to fire. He knew better than to make known his own presence for fear the visitor might be a German, and several enemy raiding parties had already tried to storm the position where the Americans lay.

"By the merest chance, the messenger divined the presence not far off of his comrades and hailed them just before he stepped into the patch of moonlight on which I had my rifle leveled. He passed safely through the lines."

"Major Whittlesey appeared highly displeased at the messenger and rebuked him severely. The messenger then took his place among us.

"For some time after arriving at our rendezvous we were under fire of both our own [French] *and the enemy artillery. We lost several of our men from this source. Major Whittlesey sent back all the carrier pigeons we had with us with messages to our artillery to cease firing on that point. I was only a few feet away when the major sent back the*

last pigeon. All the others, apparently, were killed before reaching their destination, for the shells from our guns kept falling in the vicinity. As the major adjusted the message to the leg of the last pigeon [named Cher Ami], *he remarked:*

"'Now then you little devil, if you don't get through, I don't know what's going to happen to us.

"The bird got through safely, we learned later, and the artillery fire lifted. That last message also resulted in our rescue."

…Where the detachment of the 77th was surrounded [was] *called… "the pocket," there was a small spring which furnished the only fresh water the Americans could reach. The German artillery had the exact range of the spring and German outposts had a clear view of the spot. Whenever one or more Americans tried to reach the spring, the enemy laid down a barrage. It was here the Lost Battalion suffered its heavy casualties, Private Irvin said. Machine guns manned by Germans were stationed on three sides of the American position and a constant storm of lead was directed on the spot. The little band was nearly famished when found.*

[Few of the] *men who composed the detachment were taken out alive, Private Irvin said. A majority went directly to a hospital and remained there several weeks recuperating. Private Irvin and a half dozen other volunteered for duty the following day and resumed the advance, but the Billings man was forced by weakness to drop out.*

"I marched until I couldn't stand up any longer, carrying the regulation pack which a soldier takes into the front lines. This pack weights 110 pounds. I stumbled along for a couple of miles and suddenly everything went black. When I woke up I was in a hospital, and I was still there when the armistice was signed."[163]

MONTANANS IN RELIEF

At 1:00 a.m. on October 6, a patrol of ten men from Company D, 308th Infantry, was sent forward to attempt to break through German lines to reach Major Whittelsey and the Lost Battalion. The attempt failed, and half of the patrol was killed, including Montanan Private Mike Preputin of Loma, Company D, 308th Infantry.

Among the first relief troops finally to reach the Lost Battalion on October 8 were members of Company K, 308th Infantry, including two Montanans: Private Homer J. Brown of Zurich and Private Herman N. Ausenhus of Nashua, Valley County. Private Ausenhus was killed four days later, while Private Brown died of spinal meningitis on January 22, 1919.[164]

Siblings at the Front

On October 3, during the early assault on the Argonne Forest, Second Lieutenant Owen Perry of Helena suffered severe wounds in action. Lieutenant Perry's regiment, the 307th, was part of the 77th Division, which was fighting to reach the Lost Battalion. When Lieutenant Perry was wounded, he was removed to a base hospital, where he underwent an operation to remove steel splinters from his legs. When he came out from under the effect of the ether, he found his sister, Margaret Perry, sitting by his side. "God, it was good to find her," he exclaimed in a letter received by his father in Helena.

Margaret Perry was one of the many Montana women who had found a way to participate actively in the war. She went abroad in May 1918 as secretary for Mabel Boardman, a leader in the American Red Cross. "It was worth coming all the way over here for last night alone," Margaret wrote, describing an air raid on Paris. She went on about the long-range German gun that bombarded the French capital, writing, "The country we saw and Paris itself look as peaceful as can be, but when you hear the long-distance gun you realize that the Germans are around some place. Two nights ago, it was fired a few times, and when I heard it first I am willing to admit that my heart stopped for a moment."

From Paris, Margaret moved on to a base hospital to help with clerical work—the hospital happened to be located where wounded men from the 77th Division were being brought. She asked that the nurses notify her if her brother came in wounded, and so the stage was set for this remarkable sibling reunion.[165]

Two Startling Developments

The decisive Meuse-Argonne Offensive began on September 26 and continued throughout October and on to Armistice Day, November 11. It was the largest U.S. military offensive in history, fought by 1.2 million Yanks—a remarkable achievement just eighteen months after the United States entered the war with a regular army of fewer than 200,000 men. By October 10, General Hunter Liggett's I Corps had achieved an immense milestone. The Yanks of I Corps had driven the Germans out of the Argonne Forest at great cost. Tellingly, peace feelers began to emerge from Germany.

On that same date, October 10, General Pershing, overburdened with the exhausting daily command of both the First Army and the entire AEF, promoted General Liggett to command the First Army. In another sign of the growth in AEF strength, as the number of American soldiers in France neared 2 million, General Pershing created the American Second Army under General Robert Lee Bullard.[166]

The Pandemic Sweep

In the midst of this great Allied offensive, a deadly wave of influenza pandemic swept through the ranks of American soldiers, killing more men than all the bombs and bullets combined during the war. For this virulent strain, there simply was no vaccine or cure. By early October, the wave was sweeping the nation. In Montana, from four hundred to five hundred cases of influenza had hit the Scobey area, twenty-five cases at Malta and forty cases in Wolf Point. The small ranching town of Cascade was struck with thirteen cases, while the pandemic raged at Libby, in northwestern Montana; in Choteau, in northern Montana; at Billings and Scobey, in eastern Montana; and at Whitehall and Twin Bridges, in southern Montana.

The widespread epidemic and devastating nature of this wave of flu caused the cancellation of political campaign meetings and the closure of public schools. The influenza pandemic was raging throughout Montana.[167]

NEW CHOUTEAU COUNTY LIBRARY

Even the much-anticipated dedication of the new Chouteau County Free Library was disrupted by the influenza wave:

The Chouteau County Free Library was opened to the public on Thursday, October 4, in its new Carnegie building, but was closed within a few days by order of the county health officer, on account of the Spanish influenza.

The building is very attractive and conveniently arranged and its possession by the county is a matter of congratulation to all who have been able to make use of it. It is thought by the county commissioners and the librarian that there should be a dedication—a formal opening and presentation of the building to the people of the county—and a very fine program is being arranged for that occasion, which, it is hoped, will be given during the first week in November.

The principal speaker of the day is to be Dr. E.C. Sisson, president of the Montana State University, a very delightful speaker, and a man whom the people of the state are everywhere glad to hear. He has spoken in many parts of the state, and always to large and appreciative audiences. He will

Chouteau County Free Library, designed by Helena architect George H. Carsley and built by contractor James Sherry, opened and closed temporarily during the influenza epidemic in October 1918. *Author's collection.*

speak, on this trip, at Great Falls and Lewistown, also, although the real occasion of his visit to this part of the state is the dedication of the library. His subject, as he announces it, will be "A War of Ideas." It is hoped that the fact of his coming will be known throughout the county, so that a representative crowd of Chouteau county citizens will be there to hear him. The program will be given in the lecture room of the new library.

In case the epidemic which is now raging continues until the date set for the dedication, it will have to be postponed, and in that case the date will be announced later.[168]

The new library dedication fell victim of the influenza pandemic, at the time postponed and never held.

Army Impact

So great was the threat of the influenza wave that draft calls in Montana were temporarily suspended, delaying the call up of 1,300 men, including 400 draft registrants due to report to the Montana State University for training as mechanics.[169]

During the month of October, at least fifty-eight Montana soldiers died of influenza or the resulting pneumonia in the United States, including Privates Silver Reams of Carbon County and Viggo J. Nielsen of Blaine County, in the Students Army Training Corps (SATC) at the University of Colorado, and Private John P. Skladany of East Helena, in SATC Section B at the Montana State University.

Second Lieutenant Paul E. De Mass/De Moss of Billings died on October 2, ending a promising career. He had enlisted in the Army Quartermaster Corps in May 1917, achieved rapid promotion to sergeant and was assigned army liaison officer onboard navy transport ships. By the summer of 1918, he had been promoted to second lieutenant, serving as liaison officer on the USS *Scotian* [NFI], and sailed for Europe on August 15. When his ship was torpedoed by a German U-boat, Lieutenant De Mass was cited for bravery in saving the life of another officer and recommended for promotion to captain. The end came for Lieutenant De Mass when he died of pneumonia following influenza.[170]

By mid-September, the influenza had become a "mild epidemic" among recruits at Camp Lewis, with 108 cases reported at the base hospital, including 11 Montanans. At Camp Grant, Illinois, the camp commander, Colonel Charles B. Hagadorn, committed suicide in his quarters from insomnia and the strain on him resulting from the epidemic in his camp causing more than 500 deaths.[171]

While American troops abroad neared 2 million in October, the influenza pandemic in the camps began to disrupt the transport of more men, as the War Department adopted the policy of not sending any man overseas who had been exposed or showed symptoms of the disease.

Meanwhile, in France, an estimated 20 to 40 percent of troops of all nationalities suffered from the pandemic.[172]

MONTANA CHINESE

The Great War was fought by Montanans from dozens of ethnic backgrounds. Among them were at least thirteen Chinese Americans serving their adopted country, including Private Hon Wing, who died at Camp Grant, Illinois, of influenza-induced pneumonia. Private Hon Wing had come from China several years earlier and settled in Butte, becoming a popular businessman. He was buried with military honors at Mount Mariah Cemetery in Butte.

Fifteen-year-old China-born Sing On came to America in 1875, was adopted by Montana rancher Jesse Taylor and, by an act of the 1879 Montana legislature, was given the name George Washington Taylor. After operating hotels in Dupuyer and Browning, he acquired a 480-acre ranch in Teton County. Marrying Swedish-born Lena Bloom, the Taylors raised seven children. Their eldest son, Albert H. Taylor, age twenty-two, joined the Valier Company, 2nd Montana Guard, and served on the Mexican border in 1916. When the United States entered the Great War, Private Taylor deployed to France with the 163rd Infantry, earning promotion to sergeant, and served overseas until February 1919. The Taylors' second-oldest son, Jesse E. Taylor, enlisted in the army on his twentieth birthday in June 1918 and served as a mechanic in the Quartermaster Corps.

At a time when the Chinese faced discrimination in Montana and total exclusion in Great Falls, the need for fighting men drove their inclusion in the U.S. military. On Sunday, June 30, 1918, Reverend G.G. Bennett of the Church of the Incarnation in Great Falls spoke to a crowd of about 1,500 at Gibson Park after spending a month with the conscripts at Camp Lewis. His message, in part, urged tolerance for the Chinese:

Montage of the Chinese War Saving Society of Big Timber, Sweet Grass County, including army soldier Tom Hang. *From the* Fallon County Times, *July 3, 1919.*

REV. DR. BENNETT'S TALK ON CAMP LEWIS...
An especially interesting part of his speech was an incident which he related about a Chinaman who, because of his own merit, had been commissioned a sergeant and when one day he was sent out in charge of two American soldiers to do some work, the Americans had determined not to obey the Chinaman, so when they arrived at the place for work they sat down under a tree and started to smoke. The Chinaman watched them for a few minutes and then walked up to them and said: "God made me a Chinaman and the United States made me a sergeant; now you get to work." They went to work.

In connection with this, Mr. Bennett said: "Are you men and women willing to exclude from your city men who are willing to take up arms for your country and by virtue of their ability have been appointed to positions of trust in the United States army because of their race? Think it over; it is worth your consideration."[173]

Under the headline "Sweet Grass County Has Only Chinese War Savings Organization in the State," the *Fallon County Times* reported on war support from Big Timber Chinese:

The war savings and thrift stamp administration of Montana is very proud of a unique thrift society which was organized last April in Big Timber. The Chinese residents of the town constitute its membership. It is the only organization of its kind in the state…

The head of the Big Timber society is Tom Kue, the wealthiest and most influential man of Chinese blood in the Sweet Grass metropolis. Years ago Tom Kue opened a restaurant in Big Timber. His habits of thrift and industry have had their usual effect and he is on speaking terms with every bank director in the town. Tom Kue has no vote, because he cannot become a citizen of the United States, but he is just as patriotic as though he enjoyed all the privileges of a sovereign elector. He has been in Montana 35 years and has seen the state develop during the past three and one-half decades and has grown with it.

T.J. Edwards, whose Chinese name is forgotten, and who in Anglicizing himself made himself the namesake of the first citizen of the county, Senator John E. Edwards, is a loyal American, although outside the pale of suffrage He tried to enlist as a volunteer in the army when the war was declared on Germany, but was rejected because of physical disability.

Tom Hang…has served 18 months in the army, and is a member of the society.

The Big Timber Chinese have shown themselves to be as public spirited as any other nationality. Any subscription lists passed for any purpose have always a good proportion of Chinese subscriptions. Of the 15 Chinese members, six are citizens of the United States.

The membership of the society has the following roll: Tom Kue, Han Kay, Quong Louie, Tom J. Edwards, Yu Toy, Toy Park, Lon Quong, Wo Long, Lee Ling Ying, Lee Gock Gong, Qwong Hand, Tom Hang, Gock Mon, Joe Thank and Charlie Kuwn.

In addition to those 15 there are three white members, who are employes of Mr. Kue's restaurant and who joined at his request so that each one of his employes would be represented.[174]

The Montana Chinese Americans known to have served in the war include the following:

- Yee Chung of Havre, U.S. guard at the Presidio, San Francisco.
- Tom Hang of Big Timber, served eighteen months.
- Tom Hong of Butte, aviation school, Kelly Field, Texas.
- Ham Y. Koy of Havre, medical department.
- George W. Ling of Scobey, Company G, 362nd Infantry, 91st Division.
- Harry C. Parks of Butte, 340th Field Artillery, 89th Division in France.
- Hom Sung of White Sulphur Springs, Company D, 62nd Infantry.
- Sergeant Albert H. Taylor of Valier, Company E, 163rd Infantry.
- Jesse E. Taylor of Valier, machine repair shop, 304th Quartermaster Corps.
- Tom Wah of Missoula, 166 Depot Brigade.
- Hon Wing of Butte, died of pneumonia.
- Ah Foo Wong of Helena, Company F, 44th Infantry.
- Tom S. Yin of Big Timber, U.S. Army.[175]

ON THE HOMEFRONT

Montana exceeded subscriptions for the Fourth Liberty Loan quota of $16 million, with Silver Bow County alone raising almost one-third of the state total.

As Montana suffered its second year of drought, the *River Press* reported yields about half normal for both spring and winter wheat, with an average yield of only 12.6 bushels per acre and a total wheat production of just over 25 million bushels.

Enforcement of Montana sedition laws continued at an alarming rate, with Louis Effinger of Missoula charged with sedition and found guilty in District Court. Effinger, born in the United States of German immigrant parents, paid an $800 fine. In Chouteau County District Court, Judge John

Tattan dismissed charges of seditious talk against Josef Parthe because federal charges were pending accusing him of being in the United States through violation of immigration laws.

George Hamilton became the first black man in Helena to be arrested for uttering seditious remarks after a night of drinking, stating that the United States was not his country and that he would not fight for it.[176]

Helping Disabled Soldiers

In the fall of 1918, a new opportunity opened for Montana women as reconstruction aides who could instruct and entertain convalescing disabled soldiers. Elizabeth Wear, a former teacher in Fort Benton public schools, was hired for an army position that included teaching convalescent soldiers different classes of handwork for which they were best adapted.

Danish immigrant Sergeant Owen W. Olesen of Kalispell seemed a magnet for German bullets, suffering thirteen wounds while living through the fierce battles of Belleau Wood and Blanc Mont Ridge. On October 5, pieces of a three-inch high-explosive shell tore off his left arm. After operations and an artificial arm, Sergeant Olesen underwent training at the Presidio learning the trade of mechanical draftsman. While promised a government job, Olesen returned to Flathead, where he made a mark on his community, first as a deputy game warden and then as the elected Flathead County clerk of court.

Precocious young artist Ethel Hays served as illustrator for her Billings High School publication, *The Kyote*. Hays graduated in 1911 and studied art in California and New York. During World War I, she volunteered for duty as a reconstruction aide for three months at Camp Lewis, one of the first so assigned. Most

BILLINGS GIRL MAKES SKETCHES AND CARTOONS FOR THE INDEPENDENT

ETHEL HAYS

The cleverest girl artist in America today is Ethel Hays of Billings, Montana. This was the decision of the eleven hundred newspapers served by the Newspaper Enterprise Association. Miss Hays will make sketches for The Helena Independent and associated newspapers. Her "Flapper Fanny" comics have been appearing in The Independent for two weeks, and Sunday she made sketches of the modern girl which were unique, original and unequalled by any other feature in American newspapers today. Look at her sketches. They are pretty and life-like.

A comparatively short time ago she was riding a peppy pinto over the eastern Montana prairies. She attracted attention by making covers designs for some sheet music including the old favorite "Out Where the West Begins." She was asked to come to Cleveland by the editors of the Newspaper Enterprise Association and her employment followed as soon as she submitted some of her sketches. Watch for the pictures Miss Hays makes for The Independent. They will appear almost daily. Watch for Flapper Fanny—she's the berries all right.

Ethel Hays, of Billings, who rose from artist helping disabled soldiers to one of America's great cartoonists. *From the* Independent Record, *February 10, 1925.*

Sergeant Owen W. Olesen, Danish immigrant, with his rifle on the left, lost an arm but made his mark on the Flathead Valley. *Ryan Dardis.*

of the soldiers remained at the camp but a short time, so her work teaching art seemed just a time-killer, but it became more than that. Moving on to join the staff of teachers at Government Tuberculosis Hospital No. 21 in Denver, she used art not only as a pastime but also in a curative way both mentally and physically. She taught charcoal drawing and pastel coloring in a studio as well as in the wards for those only able to sit up a few moments at a time.

By December 1923, Ethel Hays was under contract to the *Cleveland Press* for daily cartoons to accompany her madcap adventure articles. The stories and cartoons were an immediate hit, and Ethel Hays was on her way to a trailblazing career as America's first great female cartoonist.[177]

THE PANDEMIC STRIKES THE NAVY

On August 27, at Boston Commonwealth Pier, the receiving ship reported three cases of influenza admitted to sick call at Chelsea Naval Hospital. Rapidly spreading in the following days, the young sailors frequently within an hour or two passed from a healthy condition into a state of prostration.

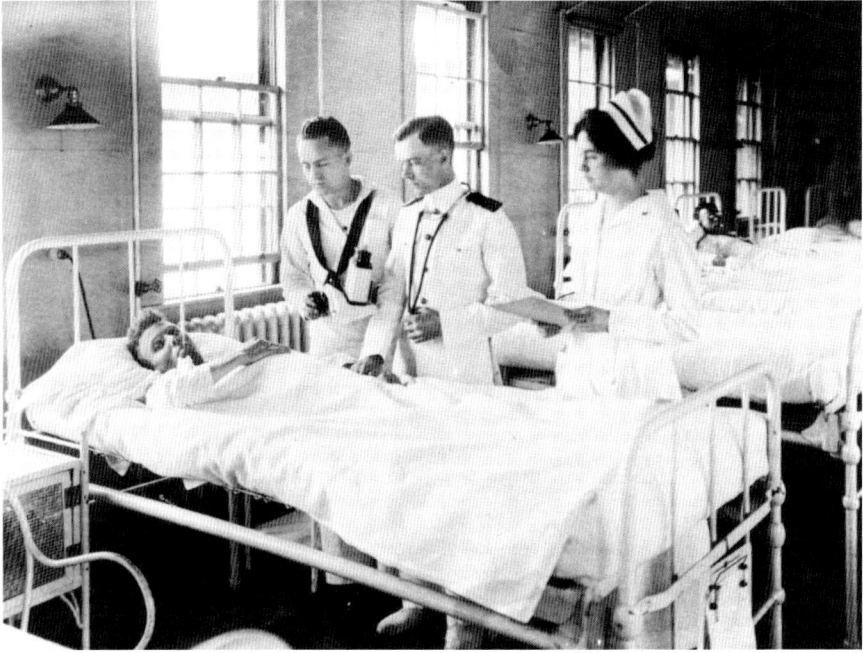

Navy surgeon, nurse and corpsman examine a patient in Ward 6, Group 1, in Chelsea Naval Hospital. *U.S. Naval History and Heritage Command.*

By September 11, the deadly disease had spread to Boston, and from there, the wave raged around the nation. Ten sailors from Montana died of the epidemic during the next two months.

Young navy physician J.J. Keegan at the Naval Hospital and others considered measures and experiments to fight the silent enemy. Seaman Daniel Judd Hedges, age eighteen of Ekalaka, Montana, was one sailor who volunteered to subject himself to experiments at Naval Hospital Chelsea to determine the cause and mode of transmission and prevention of the influenza, and he was later commended by the secretary of the navy for his brave actions.[178]

"WILD WEST" DIVISION TO FLANDERS

By the night of October 4, the "Wild West" Division had been relieved by the 32nd and began a long march to the Cheppy Woods. The officers and men were in the grip of dysentery and weakness and rested the next day in exhausted slumber. The 182nd Brigade, consisting of the 363rd and 364th Infantry, moved out for rest area billets in the rear. Sudden orders were received directing that the 181st Brigade, 361st and 362nd Regiments, return to the front lines to join the 1st Division for further fighting in the Argonne Forest.

Despite being weak in strength and severely depleted in numbers, the 181st Brigade marched wearily back in darkness and pelting rain along the same road it had come. The brigade was ordered to take cover in a small forest near Eclisfontaine as the situation began to clarify—the 181st Brigade was needed urgently to cover a gap that was widening between the flank units of the 1st and 32nd Divisions. As the lead regiment, the 361st faced the same deadly combination of machine gun and artillery shell fire as it had left. The brigade remained under fire until the night of October 12, when at last it was relieved and began marching to the rear.

Reaching Revigny, the brigade learned that there would be no rest and replacements, but rather a rapid boarding of trains and a rushed trip northward. Reaching Flanders, eight days were spent resting and receiving 1,235 replacements. On October 28, the division moved toward the front, and the Battle of the Argonne was replaced by a new battle, this time under King Albert of Belgium, to aid the French in Flanders in driving the Germans beyond the Scheldt River.

91st "Wild West" Division truck towed artillery moving to the front. Note the bucking horse and rider emblem on both truck and artillery. *Author's collection.*

As night fell on October 29, the 362nd Infantry marched toward the front for the Battle in the Turnip Patches. By morning, it had relieved the 164th French Division, and the "Wild West" Division was on the front line in Flanders. Unlike the Argonne, where Boche airplanes ruled the air, here British and French airmen controlled the skies overhead.

At 5:35 a.m. on the thirty-first, the assault wave went over the top in slowly fading darkness through a storm of machine gun fire. Despite stiff German resistance and heavy casualties, by nightfall the objective, Spitalls Bosschen, was taken. The "Wild West" Division's battle cry, "Powder River, Let 'Er Buck," now resonated over the fields of Flanders.[179]

Chapter 8

NOVEMBER 1918

The Armistice—End of the Great War; America Celebrates; Prisoners of War Return

To the End of the Great War

The Meuse-Argonne Offensive, begun on September 26, was a key element in the final Allied drive that led, forty-seven days later, to the general armistice at the eleventh hour of November 11, 1918. The German army—exhausted, demoralized, depleted by the influenza epidemic and facing an ever-increasing number of American divisions—was forced to retreat and could not continue its resistance.

After initial success in the German Spring Offensive, by the early summer of 1918, the Germans were forced on the defensive along their strongly fortified Hindenburg Line. In early August, as the buildup of American forces accelerated, the Allies launched the Hundred Days Offensive, and by September/October, Allied forces were breaking through the length of the Hindenburg Line along the north, center and south sectors. British, French and Belgian advances in the north, combined with French-American successes at St. Mihiel and Argonne Forest, set the stage for German capitulation.

The Meuse-Argonne Offensive was fought in three phases, with the first phase launched toward Sedan on September 26, and over the next week, the 91st, 79th, 35th and 37th Divisions and French forces that included the American 93rd Buffalo Soldiers fought, in the words of General Pershing, "a direct frontal attack against strong, hostile positions fully manned by a determined enemy." At the same time, British and Belgian forces attacked toward Ghent, Belgium, while British and French armies attacked across northern France. The attack along the entire front put great pressure on defending German forces.

The second phase of the Meuse-Argonne Offensive extended from October 4 to October 28, with fresh American forces from the 1st, 3rd, 32nd and 77th Divisions replacing the initial assault force. A successful advance by the 1st Division created a gap in the front lines that led to the problem with the Lost Battalion of the 77th Division, which was rescued by elements of the 77th together with fresh attacks by the 28th and 82nd Divisions. By October 14–17, American assaults had broken through the main German defensive line at Driemhilde Stellung during the Battle of Montfaucon. By the end of October, the Argonne Forest was cleared.

Phase three began October 28 and continued until the Armistice. French and AEF forces continued to advance, with the French reaching the Aisne River. The AEF First and Second Armies faced remaining portions of thirty-one German divisions and overran German defenses at Buzancy. This allowed the French to cross the Aisne River. In the final days of battle, the French captured Sedan, with its critical rail hub, while AEF forces took the surrounding hills.

Meanwhile in the north, AEF troops from the 27th and 30th Divisions fought under British command, joining twelve British and Australian divisions in attacking and capturing the St. Quentin Canal, breaching the Hindenburg Line. In Flanders, the 91st "Wild West" Division was fighting in the Battle of the Turnip Patches. On November 11, the announcement of the German armistice brought an end to the fighting all along the Western Front.

"Peace" headline on Armistice Day. *From the* Great Falls Leader, *November 11, 1918.*

Armistice Day in Miles City, "Peace Forever." *Author's collection.*

Overall, AEF casualties in the final Forty-Seven Days offensive proved costly for several reasons: Meuse-Argonne was the largest AEF battle of the war; several divisions entered combat for the first time; some poor tactics were used in the early phases; determined German resistance from their heavily fortified lines; and the onset of the deadly influenza outbreak.[180]

German Capitulation

In a series of three short articles, the *River Press* reported three immensely important developments: the Armistice, the German kaiser's abdication and the chaos in Germany as the people revolted. The Great War was at an end, and the future of Germany was uncertain.

> Germany Signs Armistice
> *Hostilities Suspended Monday Morning by Prompt Acceptance of Terms Dictated by Gen. Foch*
>
> *Washington, Nov. 11.—The world war will end this morning at 6 o'clock Washington time, 11 o'clock Paris time. The armistice was signed by the German representatives at midnight. This announcement was made by the state department at 2:50 o'clock this morning.*

The terms of the armistice, it was announced, will not be made public until later. Military men here, however, regard it as certain that they include:

Immediate retirement of the German military forces from France, Belgium and Alsace-Lorraine.

Disarming and demobilization of the German army, occupation by the allied and American forces of such strategic points in Germany as will make impossible a renewal of hostilities.

Delivery of the German high seas fleet and a certain number of submarines to the allied and American naval forces.

Disarmament of all other German warships under supervision of the allied and American navy, which will guard them.

Occupation of the naval bases by victorious nations.

Release of the allied and American soldiers, sailors and civilians held prisoners in Germany without such reciprocal action by the associated governments.

KAISER ABDICATES

Kaiser Seeks Safety in Holland. Amsterdam, Nov. 10.—William Hohenzollern, former emperor of Germany, arrived this morning in Holland and is proceeding to Middachten castle, in the town of Desteg.

The Kaiser signed a letter of abdication Saturday morning at the German grand headquarters in the presence of Crown Prince Frederick William and Field Marshal Hindenburg, according to a dispatch from Amsterdam to the Exchange Telegraph company. The German crown prince signed his renunciation to the throne shortly afterward.

Every dynasty in Germany is to be suppressed and all the princes deposed, according to Swiss advices.

Both the former German emperor and his eldest son, Frederick William, crossed the Dutch frontier Sunday morning.

GERMANS REBEL

German People Revolt. London, Nov. 10.—Severe fighting took place in Berlin last night following the establishment of the people's government in the capital Saturday. Violent cannonading was heard from the heart of the city during the night.

The revolution is in full swing in Berlin and the forces occupy the greater part of the German capital, according to a Copenhagen dispatch to the Exchange Telegraph company, quoting Berlin advices sent from there this morning.

Many persons were killed and wounded before the officers surrendered. The red forces are in control and have restored order.[181]

AMERICA CELEBRATES

News of the Armistice reached America and the nation, and Montana celebrated as the great development arrived. Towns large and small across Montana rejoiced, with the *River Press* reporting the festivities in Fort Benton:

FORT BENTON CELEBRATED. Noisy Demonstration of Delight Over the German Surrender.

The millions of people in all parts of the world who participated in armistice celebrations Monday morning included several hundred residents of Fort Benton....The demonstration resembled an accumulation of four years of Fourth of July noise and enthusiasm, and established a local record in this respect.

...Crowds of local residents and visitors took part in the jubilation during the day, the festivities increasing in hilarity during the afternoon. Motor trucks and automobiles, gaily decorated with the national colors, sped up and down Front street heavily loaded with contingents of wildly cheering celebrants, and parties of young people carrying flags and other emblems paraded the sidewalks and expressed their gratification in various ways.

Nearly every residence and business house in town was decorated with flags, some of the designs placing the emblems of Great Britain, France, Belgium and Italy alongside the Stars and Stripes. The combination made a most attractive and appropriate setting.

...The evening session of the celebration eclipsed all the earlier efforts in spectacular effect and deafening tumult. The army cannon that formed part of the equipment of the old fort some fifty years ago was again brought into service, and barked with a vigor that has never been equaled on former occasions. A big bonfire near the north end of the Missouri river bridge indicated the center of celebration activities, a crowd of over a thousand people being congregated at that point.

The culmination of the festivities came soon after 8:00 o'clock, when a procession headed by a band of Fort Benton and Pleasant Valley musicians paraded along Front street, and was vociferously cheered. The procession included a delegation of Red Cross women workers carrying an out-stretched American flag, a company of Camp Fire girls, a number of torch bearers and other marchers. The itinerary ended at the side of the bonfire, the program concluding with community singing of the Star-Spangled Banner, with accompaniment by the band.

An effigy of the Kaiser, which had formed part of a display during the celebration, found a final resting place in the bonfire—this fate giving realistic expression to the anathema that has become popular throughout the civilized world.

Most of the celebrants were a tired bunch of patriots toward the latter part of the evening, but that did not prevent their attendance at a public dance at the Grand Union hotel, which closed the biggest red letter day in local history.[182]

ON TO THE POSTWAR

While the Armistice implemented a ceasefire, it would take months and even years to bring signed peace treaties, the return of the 2 million American troops from overseas duty and some semblance of normalcy. Meanwhile, from October to December 1918, nearly forty thousand influenza cases were reported in Montana, leading to the deaths of more than three thousand.

TRIBUTE TO THE YANKS

The Great War was over. For the United States, it had been a brutal, short war—for our Allies, it had been four long years of horror and immense sacrifice and loss. Perhaps no finer tribute was paid to the American Expeditionary Forces in France than this editorial in the first issue of *Stars and Stripes* after the Armistice:

ALL FOR YOU, UNCLE SAM
At 4 o'clock yesterday afternoon advanced troops of the First American Army took part of the city of Sedan which lies on the west bank of the Meuse....The enemy's principal lateral line of communication between the fortress of Metz and his troops in northern France and Belgium is by the success of the American Army no longer open to him.

In such words the American communique published last Friday morning announced the cutting in two of the German army on the western front, the accomplishment of one of the principal objectives of the great attack at the enemy's vitals which the American Army launched on September 26 between the Meuse and the Argonne, the post of honor in the last grand offensive of the war.

Another prime objective of the American attack, the greatest battle in American history, both in intensity and number of troops engaged, was the penetration of the German positions in the Meuse-Argonne region to a depth sufficient to bring about the capture of the enemy forces between the Argonne and the sea, or, by the threat of such capture, to compel the withdrawal of the enemy holding that portion of the line from France and the greater part of Belgium.

A third important objective of the American attack was to wrest from the Boche the precious Briey basin, the source of three-fourths of Europe's iron supply.

Despite the desperate efforts of the enemy to keep us from cutting his army in two, we cut it in two. With equal determination, we were driving the enemy's divisions before us in the sure achievement of all our objectives when the finger of Time on Monday morning pointed to 11 o'clock, and fighting ceased all along the front under the terms of the armistice dictated to and accepted by the enemy.

But the hand of time can never erase from the pages of history what American divisions did at the post of honor in the world war of 1914–1918 from September 26 to November 11, 1918. The story of American valor along the Meuse and in the Argonne will shine radiantly through the ages. It will glow in the printed word as long as men read of the deeds of their fathers, as long as the passion of liberty swells in the bosom of mankind. And the glory of that story will be none the less refulgent because of the knowledge that only a year before they went forth with boyish smiles and boyish confidence to face the flower of the German host, massed to hurl them back and under orders to hold their positions at all costs, by far the greater part of the personnel of the American divisions had been childishly ignorant of the A B C of war.

"Green troops" we were sneeringly called by the enemy. Green troops our Allies could rightly have classified us, and probably did, before those terrible nightmare days of the war last spring and summer. And green troops we knew ourselves to be, compared with Poilu and Tommy, Jock, Aussie and Canuck [soldiers, respectively, from France, England, Scotland, Australia, and Canada]. *But, bringing youth to the war-worn battle hosts, we believed in our youth. We believed in the holiness of our cause and the job given to our hands to do. We knew that in our keeping were the liberties of the Republic. We believed in America unconquerable. And that is why today the words Marne,*

Belleau Wood, Chateau-Thierry, Oureq, Vesle, St. Mihiel, Argonne, Meuse, Montfaucon, Fismes, Montsec, Cantigny, Bellicourt, Hamel, Seicheprey, Sedan are shining in deathless splendor in Columbia's diadem.[183]

POW Homecoming

With the Armistice, Allied prisoners were released from German prison camps. The *River Press* reported this important development:

Yank POWs Released
Paris, Nov. 14.—More than 2,532 American prisoners in German camps were released immediately by the signing of the German armistice, according to the latest figures prepared by the American Red Cross in Switzerland. This number includes all the Americans captured to November 1. It is estimated that only a few hundred more Americans were captured after that date. Of the total number of prisoners to be released 2,380 are army men, 12 are from the navy and 140 are civilians. In the camps were 241 army officers and 2,139 non-commissioned officers and nine sailors.[184]

Sixteen Montanans were among the American prisoners of war released from German prison camps. The first two Montanans, and among the first Americans captured, were Christian A. Sorensen of Verona in Chouteau County and Edward M. "Bob" Roberts of Miles City, both serving with Company A, 16th Infantry Regiment, 1st Division. The story of their capture on the night of February 7–8, when their night patrol was ambushed, is told in *World War I Montana: The Treasure State Prepares.*

Christian A. Sorensen was released from Tuchel Prison Camp in West Prussia after the Armistice and sent to the British Hospital at Leith, Scotland. On January 7, 1919, he embarked the USS *Louisville* at Liverpool to return to the United States, and after a short period at Army Camp Dix, New Jersey, he was discharged in early February and returned to Big Sandy.[185]

Private Bob Roberts returned to Missoula after gaining his freedom. There, more of his remarkable story was related by fellow World War I combat veteran Al Schak:

On November 21, Roberts, accompanied by a Mr. Huffman, a YMCA worker, left Rastatt enroute for Berne, Switzerland. Huffman arrived with

First train of released American prisoners from Rastatt prison camp arriving at Basle, Switzerland. *Library of Congress.*

his charge at a little border town, where Roberts was inspected by German officers. After the inspection the two men were allowed to cross the border into Switzerland.

"I was certainly happy to be free again," said Roberts, "and the first place I went to was a restaurant. I ate steak and chicken till I grew feathers."

He arrived at Berne a short time later, and was cared for by the Red Cross and YMCA. He found that he weighted 146 pounds. His weight when captured as it is now, was 206 pounds.

The Swiss government gave him a beautiful silver watch while he was at Berne. It is a heavy piece of mechanism, beautifully engraved....The most novel thing about the watch is that it is equipped with chimes telling the hour and minute.

Remaining in Berne long enough to eat his Thanksgiving dinner in a castle in the Alps, he went to Paris, where he was placed in Hospital No. 1. Army medical officers there who examined him reported that his right eye had been removed by a surgical operation...and that his left eye had been scratched both ways with some kind of needle, rendering the victim entirely blind.

THE POST OF HONOR

MEUSE-ARGONNE FRONT

(See Editorial entitled "The Post of Honor")

"The Post of Honor" honoring the AEF during the final Meuse-Argonne Offensive. *From* Stars and Stripes, *November 8, 1918.*

Roberts left Paris for Brest…and sailed on the New Amsterdam, a Dutch vessel which arrived in New York after a nine-day voyage. He says that it seemed quite nice to be again among [Americans], *but that he was greatly surprised to find that many people still sympathized with Germany.*

"They would change their minds if they made the trip that I made into Germany and received the manhandling that I got."[186]

Remarkably, Bob Roberts overcame his loss of sight. By 1922, he was attending Law School at the Montana State University. Eight years later, Roberts lived in Tulsa, Oklahoma, with his third wife, and both were practicing chiropractors.[187]

NAVY NURSE CANON

Nurse Alice M. Canon, of Lewistown and Great Falls, graduated in nursing at California Hospital in Los Angeles in 1914. She volunteered for service when the United States entered the war and is the only known

Montana navy nurse to serve overseas. Assigned to Naval Base Hospital No. 3, at Leith, Scotland, Nurse Canon cared for American and British sailors and soldiers.

Toward the end of her tour at Leith, Nurse Canon became a patient in her own hospital on October 14, 1918, suffering from influenza. She survived and was discharged on November 2. When Hospital No. 3 closed later that month, Nurse Canon transferred to the Naval Base Hospital at Brest, France, and served there until she returned to the United States on the USS *Agamemnon* in April 1919.

Nurse Canon worked at the Naval Hospital in Brooklyn, New York, until late October 1919, when she returned to Lewistown for a one-month furlough before moving to Los Angeles. She was discharged from the navy and remained as a civilian nurse in Los Angeles for the rest of her life.

During World War I, 293 navy nurses served in hospitals and bases overseas. Nurse Alice Canon was one of those 293 and proud of it. In a letter written just before she left Leith, Scotland, she provided highlights of her life overseas with the navy as the war was ending.

> *Leith, Scotland, Dec. 1, 1918.*
> *At last the censorship is off our mail and I can tell you where I am and more about what I am doing.*
>
> *…So many wonderful things have happened lately I hardly know where to begin to tell you about them all, but guess the first one should be "Peace Day," that wonderful day that came on us so suddenly that we can't even quite realize that it is true yet.*
>
> *I can imagine how people at home took it—the noise, excitement, crowds, etc. But not so here. As you probably know, the people are very undemonstrative here. They took the war as a matter of course, a burden that had to be borne, and there was no grumbling or complaining about it. They paid the price and kept still.*
>
> *So now with peace—they don't take it in a spirit of pride or vainglory in what they have accomplished but rather in a spirit of prayer and thanksgiving that it is finally over and they can have their loved ones, who are left back again. So we find them slipping off to church to pray. Of course, there was a crowd down town that evening—some noise, drunks singing and dancing on the streets, but nothing like you would expect.*
>
> *…The real big event happened—the surrender of the German navy— right out in front of our hospital. It was foggy or we could have seen the whole thing. As it was the fog lifted for an hour at noon and we did see the*

U.S. Naval Base Hospital No. 3, Leith, Scotland. *U.S. Navy.*

ships. Four of our doctors had the rare privilege of going out on the USS
New York and seeing the whole thing.

They said it was perfectly wonderful. The British fleet led by our five
U.S. battleships—the New York (flagship). Texas, Florida, Arkansas and
Wyoming, went out to the mouth of the Forth and formed two parallel lines
six miles apart, then prepared for action—guns loaded, gas masks on, etc.

At the appointed time the Germans ships appeared over the horizon,
flying the German flag and the white one of surrender. They seemed to
be coming from all directions, at once, then formed into four lines and
sailed in between our two lines. They were then searched and at sundown
their flag was lowered never to be up again unless so ordered. Theirs
the humiliation, ours the glory, but who can say they didn't deserve it
and more. They never could pay, no, not in centuries for all that they
have done.

The first thing a German gob said was, "When does the meat boat
come out." The next day they went up to Scapa Flow where they are
to be interned, the Germans sent on home and the ships manned [by]
English sailors.

Nurse Canon enjoyed Thanksgiving dinner onboard the USS *Nevada* (BB-36). *U.S. Navy.*

PRISONERS RETURNING

Prisoners of war are now coming back by the thousands. Just last Sunday 17,000 passed through here on their way to rest camps for a month before being sent on to their homes. Some looked well and say they were well treated, others look thin and pale, still others had in be clothed before they could be seen, and some poor chaps had been tattooed all over their faces and necks with German emblems and mottoes, just disfigured for life.

…The British want their hospital back now and Admiral Sims just wired us to not take any more patients as the hospital is to be closed. Our C.O. is in London now, so when he returns we will know our fate. We may be right home and we may be stationed some other place.

We also had a terrible epidemic of the flu. At one time had 800 patients. At the time we thought we were losing a lot but our percentage was small, about eight, I understand; while one of the British hospitals lost 60 per cent.

Best Christmas greetings and wishes for a happy New Year.[188]

AN ANGEL OF BATAAN

Nurse Mina Andy Aasen graduated from the Columbus Hospital School of Nursing in Great Falls and joined the army in 1918. She remained in the Army Nurse Corps after the Great War, serving at Walter Reed Hospital. In 1941, Second Lieutenant Aasen served at Sternberg Hospital in Manila until the Japanese attack, at which time she was sent to Bataan. When Bataan and Corregidor fell, she was one of sixty-six "Angels of Bataan and Corregidor" captured by the Japanese and held at Santo Tomas in Manila until liberated in 1945.[189]

AMONG THE AEF

While the peace process moved forward and the occupation of Germany commenced, the AEF began to return units home and to account for American casualties and honor the dead on the former fields of battle, as reported in the *River Press*:

FIRST TROOPS TO ARRIVE
New York, Dec. 1.—The British steamship Mauretania, *returning to the United States with the first large body of American overseas troops, anchored in Gravesend Bay at 7:40 o'clock tonight. The* Mauretania *was met by navy and army tugs. She will probably remain at her anchorage until early tomorrow, when she is expected to dock at Hoboken. The hospital ship Northern Pacific docked at Hoboken tonight with 1,100 wounded soldiers and marines onboard, including officers. For the returning heroes there was none of the martial pomp, which sent them away. A few of the walking wounded lined the rail of the vessel as she came abreast of the Statue of Liberty and there was a feeble cheer as Bartholdi's emblem of freedom welcomed them to the harbor. The work of removing the wounded to hospitals will begin tomorrow. The Red Cross has mobilized every available ambulance to carry them.*[190]*

CASUALTY LIST INCREASED
Additional Names of American Killed and Wounded Aare Received.
Washington, Nov. 30.—Four divisions in their entirety and major units of eight other divisions of the American Army in France have been designated by General Pershing for an early return home These troops, with other

special units, General March, chief of staff, announced today, total 3,451 officers and 70,663 men. The complete divisions which will return at an early date, General March said are the Thirty-ninth, Seventh-sixth, Eighty-seventh, and Ninety-second.

New figures on the American casualties, announced by the chief of staff, showed a total of 262,693, exclusive of prisoners. The total, which exceeds by 28,000 that made public a week ago, covers all losses to November 26. The principal change in the revised list is the addition of 13,100 men missing in action…

General Pershing reported the following official casualties to November 26:

Killed in action 28,363
Died of wound. 12,101
Died of disease 16,034
Died, other causes 1,980
Missing in action 14,290
Wounded, 189,955, divided as follows:
Severely wounded 51,751
Undetermined 43,168
Slightly wounded 92,036

…Orders have been issued, the chief of staff also said, for the demobilization of 649,000 men in the camps and cantonments in the United States.[191]

Montana Casualties

Montana men served in greater numbers and suffered more casualties per capita than any other state:

Killed/Died of Wounds in Action	681
Died Other Causes	253
Total Dead	**934**
Wounded in Action	2,469
Missing in Action	52
Total Casualties	**3,455**[192]

Chapter 9

POSTWAR ERA

Watch on the Rhine—German Occupation; The Peace Conference; Burying the Dead; An Elusive Peace

New Watch on the Rhine
There's a new watch on the Rhine,
A lank, lean-visaged man,
Well knit and straight
And brisk of gait—
Each inch American.

There's a new flag on the Rhine,
Red, white and blue with stars.
Without a smack
Of pirate black;
Just freedom's glorious bars.

There's a new song on the Rhine,
"My Country, 'Tis of Thee,"
A chorus grand
Enthralls the land.
Our hymn of Liberty.

There's a new watch on the Rhine,
White-souled American—
"Come be ye free!"—
Wide flings his plea
To the brotherhood of man.

—New York Sun[193]

GERMAN OCCUPATION

By the time the war ended, more than 2 million American soldiers were serving on the battlefields of Western Europe. Demobilization began in late 1918, but the last AEF combat divisions did not leave Europe until September 1919. Even then, an occupation force of sixteen thousand U.S. soldiers remained until 1923, based in the town of Coblenz (Koblenz), Germany, as part of the postwar Allied presence in the Rhine Valley determined by the terms of the Treaty of Versailles.

The occupation of the Rhineland from December 1, 1918, until June 30, 1930, consisted of four "bridgeheads" around Cologne, Koblenz, Mainz and Hehl, according to the complex treaty terms. The occupation was designed to give France security against a renewed German attack and serve as a guarantee for reparations payments.

The occupation was viewed by Germans as a national disgrace and fostered bitter feelings, fueling revision of the treaty, the rise of the Nazi Party and the certainty of a second world war.

The United States originally provided nearly one-third of the total occupying force, some 240,000 men in nine divisions. General Pershing established the Third Army for this purpose, commanded by Major

Germany Occupation Zones 1–4 after the Armistice, during 1919: 4, Belgium; 3, British; 2, American; and 1, French. *Museums Victoria, public domain. http://collections.museumvictoriaa.com. au/items/1989353.*

General Joseph T. Dickman. The Third Army occupied the northern sector of the Coblenz bridgehead. The 1st Division, with its 2nd Field Signal Battalion (FS Bn), was one of the occupying units. The 2nd FS Bn had been in France since deployment of the 1st Division in late June 1917, fulfilling the critical role of establishing and maintaining AEF communications throughout France, from the combat front lines to the rear areas. Thousands of Montanans were assigned as replacements to the 1st Division, joining the 16th, 18th, 26th and 28th Infantry Regiments; the 5th through 7th Field Artillery Regiments; and the 2nd FS Bn. Montanans in the 2nd FS Bn fought in every major battle throughout the war. At least twenty-four Montanans served in Company C, 2nd FS Bn, including Sergeant Waldo Thompson of Anaconda, who was awarded the Distinguished Service Cross: "For extraordinary heroism in action near Exermont, France, October 5, 1918. He voluntarily went forward in the face of a most destructive bombardment and kept in repair the telephone line connecting the infantry and artillery, thereby assuring the close cooperation between these two elements."[194]

President Sails for Europe

The "war to end all wars" ended with a peace conference that seemed almost endless. In early December 1918, President Woodrow Wilson sailed for Europe aboard the liner SS *George Washington*, arriving at Brest, France, on December 13 on his way to the Versailles Conference. Along the way, President Wilson received a memorable hero's welcome in Paris from a crowd estimated at 2 million, as reported in the *River Press*:

> *French Greeting to American Executive Surpasses Former Receptions*
> *Dec. 14.—President and Mrs. Wilson made their entry into Paris this morning, greeted by well nigh half the population, not only of the city, but the surrounding districts. They were attended by President Poincare, Premier Clemenceau and others among the most prominent figures of France. Flowers were dropped around their carriage, airplanes winged overhead, guns sounded. But observers were impressed with something more than the magnitude and beauty of the reception by some quality of warmth that made it different from the visits to Paris by other sovereigns.*

This is a greater night in Paris than armistice night. The city is ablaze with illuminations; the boulevards are thronged with crowds, dancing and singing and throwing confetti. The Place de la Concorde has been turned into a great dancing pavilion, where American soldiers are favorite partners. America is the predominating word here tonight.

The interest of France has been stirred by the president of the United States as no other leader beyond the borders. All classes and parties in this country have united to pay honor to the United States through its president. They greet him as the representative of ideals now dawning upon Europe.

Thirty-six thousand soldiers, the flower of the French army, lined the avenues from Dauphine gate to the Murat mansion, which during their stay in Paris will be the home of the president and his wife.

Alpine chasseurs and Zouaves, fresh from the battlefields of Champagne, and colonial troops from whose uniforms the mud of the Somme had only a few days ago been removed, occupied the post of honor. They gently, but firmly, kept order among the enormous crowds, which ever pressed forward in eagerness to have a closer look at the guests of France.

The president entered Paris amid the boom of a hundred guns in salute, greeting at the railway station and along the route to his temporary residence by enthusiastic throngs and estimated to total nearly two million persons, whose cheers set the air vibrating.[195]

Wilson Departs for Europe

Before leaving Washington, D.C., President Wilson explained his quest for peace, named his delegation and described the peace parley:

President Tells Congress His Reasons for Going to Peace Conference

Washington, Dec. 2.—In an address to congress in joint session today, President Wilson formally announced his intention to go to Paris for the peace conference, saying the allied governments have accepted principles enunciated by him for peace and it is his paramount duty to be present.

The president said he will be in close touch by cable and wireless and that congress will know all that he does on the other side.

…He expressed the hope that he would have the co-operation of the public and of congress, saying through the cables and wireless constant counsel and advice would be possible.

...The president's annual address was read before a crowd that filled the floors and galleries. He reviewed at length the country's accomplishments in the war, paying tribute to the armed forces and to loyal workers at home....[196]

PRESIDENT SELECTS FOUR ASSOCIATES FOR ALLIED CONFERENCE
Washington, Nov. 29.—President Wilson himself will head the American delegation to the peace conference. This was announced officially, tonight, at the White House.

The other members of the delegation will be: Robert Lansing, secretary of state; Col. E.M. House, and Henry White, former ambassador to France and Italy; General Tasker H. Bliss,...American military representative on the Supreme War Council at Versailles.

...The premiers of Great Britain, France and Italy are expected to attend the peace conference as representatives of their governments, but like the president, may not remain throughout the conferences. The general understanding here is that present plans are to have the conference first agree to the broad principles for the treaty and leave the working out of details to further sittings.

This would enable the president and the entente premiers speedily to return to the capitals of their respective countries, so as to give their personal attention to affairs of state.[197]

WILL DISCUSS TERMS DECEMBER 17, AND HOLD CONGRESS EARLY IN JANUARY
Paris, Dec. 6.—President Wilson will be informed by wireless of the plans for the assembling of the interallied conference December 16 or 17, and the meeting of the peace congress, set for the first week in January. He will also be advised concerning the recent gathering of the Supreme War Council at London.

...The plans concerning the peace meetings are the results of Colonel Edward M. House's long talk with Premier Clemenceau, following a conference with Baron Sonnino, the Italian foreign minister, and the Earl of Derby, the British ambassador to France...the peace conference [will begin] *the first week in January...*

Translators in 23 languages, including...French, Italian, Greek, Japanese, Spanish, Montenegrin, Norwegian, Bulgarian, German, Hungarian, Turkish, Chinese, Portuguese, Polish, Swedish, Persian, Russian, Serbian, Armenian, Czech, Rumanian, Danish and Arabic [and English, were called for].[198]

Montana "Hello Girl" a Star

A key element in American preparations for the conference involved telephone communications from the Palace of Versailles to world leaders. Chosen to occupy the key position of chief operator for the American Peace Commission at the palace was Merle Egan of Helena. From her arrival in France with the Army Telephone Operators, Merle Egan became a "star," highly respected for her knowledge and organizational ability.[199]

Montanans read of Merle Egan's exciting, challenging adventure in the *Big Sandy Bear Paw Mountaineer*:

Montana Girl Picked for Important Post at Paris
"Hello, Central! This is General Pershing. Please connect me with Premier Lloyd George."

Ting-a-ling-a-ling. Ting-a-ling-a-ling.

"Hello! This is Central. Is this the office of the premier of Great Britain? Thank you. General Pershing desires to speak to the premier. Is this Mr. Lloyd George? General Pershing is on the wire and desires to speak to you. There you are."

This is an imaginary conversation, as it may take place in the Palace of Versailles, just out of Paris, during the peace conference. Montanans will be interested because of the fact that a pretty Helena girl, Miss Merle Egan, will be in charge, as chief telephone operator in the palace of Versailles, and when President Wilson, or David Lloyd George, or Premier Clemenceau, or the Akound of Swat, or the grand vizier of Guam, desires to call some other dignitary in this historic palace he—or they—will have to be very polite to this little girl from Helena, Montana, U.S.A.

Miss Egan is an expert operator. Also, she is very proficient in the French language. So, when she volunteered to serve her country abroad in the telephone service, she was sent to Paris immediately. In a very short time she was made chief operator of the telephone exchange at general headquarters. Now word comes that

Merle Egan, Helena Girl who was put in charge of the telephone exchange at Versailles during the Peace Commission. *National World War I Museum and Memorial.*

she has been appointed to this important post, and will be the medium of communication between the great men of the many nations and states represented at the most important conference since the world began.[200]

THE PEACE CONFERENCE

The Versailles Peace Conference brought the victorious Allies together to set the peace terms for the defeated Central Powers—Germany, Austria-Hungary, the Ottoman Empire and Bulgaria. The Central Powers had mobilized more than 25 million soldiers and suffered more than 15 million casualties, a devastating 66 percent. While the Great War was halted by the Armistice, one by one the Central Powers ended their war in de facto "unconditional surrender." The end, for each, had come with revolution to overthrow kaisers, sultans and tsars alike. The stage was set for fundamental change in Europe and around the world.

President Wilson had won the hearts and minds of many throughout Europe with his Fourteen Points, and now this American president was on the scene to guide the peace negotiations. His optimism was shared by many, but by no means all, as the president led American foreign policy toward interventionism.

While the conference involved diplomats from thirty-two nations, the "Big Four" of Prime Ministers Georges Clemenceau of France, David Lloyd George of the United Kingdom, Vittorio Emanuele Orlando of Italy and President Wilson controlled the conference and made all major decisions. From January 18 until June 1919, the senior statesmen were personally involved, yet the peace process continued on until July 1923. The major results involved five peace treaties, drawing many new national boundaries, imposing major reparations on Germany, realigning German and Turkish foreign possessions and creating a League of Nations. The Treaty of Versailles with Germany laid the blame for the war squarely on aggression of Germany and its allies.

President Wilson soon learned that the historic undercurrents of European rivalries and claims presented powerful obstacles to enactment of his Fourteen Points, and his dreams of democracy, sovereignty and self-determination for Europe and the Middle East ultimately faded, just as his attempts to "sell" the American public on interventionism through the League of Nations.

Council of Four at the Paris Peace Conference, May 27, 1919. *Left to right*: British prime minister David Lloyd George, Italian prime minister Vittorio Orlando, French prime minister Georges Clemenceau and President Woodrow Wilson. *U.S. Signal Corps.*

The United States would neither ratify the Treaty of Versailles nor join the League of Nations. As Wilson's health declined precipitously after a major stroke, so would his personal popularity as the cheering ended. Under his successor, President Warren Harding, in 1921 the United States eventually signed separate treaties with Germany, Austria and Hungary.

By mid-February 1919, President Wilson departed from France on the steamer *George Washington*, landing at Boston on February 24 satisfied that he had done what he could to promote his program for peace. Arriving with the president were 2,304 troops of the Presidential and Peace Commission Guard, including Sergeant George F. Gilman of Lewistown, Montana, serving with the Commission Guard. Another Montanan, Private Hugh J. Larkin of Anaconda, serving with Peace Commission Guard Company No. 2, remained in France until the senior American statesmen of the commission returned to the United States in July 1919.[201]

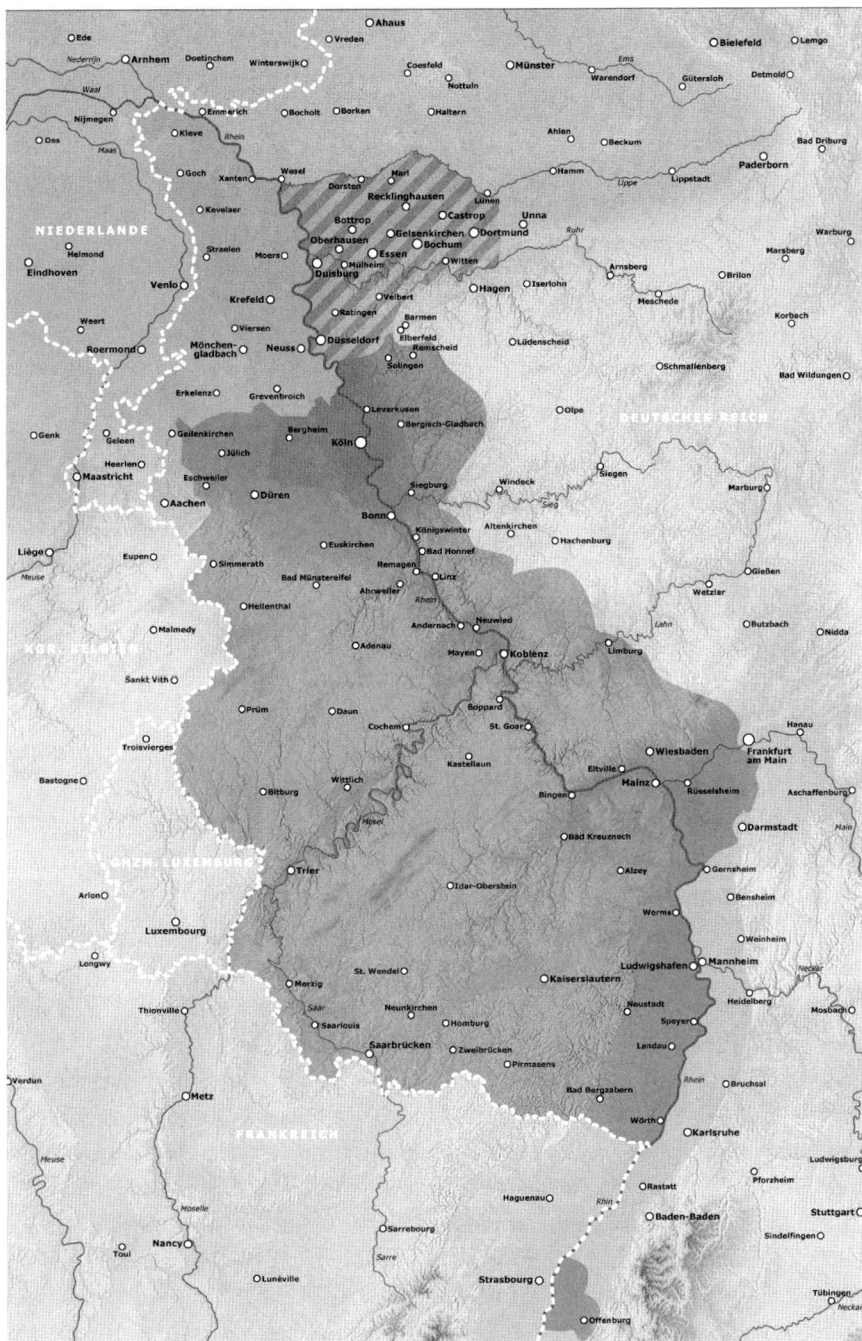

Germany after Versailles. Flags show the areas administered by the League of Nation; annexed or transferred to neighboring countries by the treaty, or later via plebiscite and League of Nation action; and Weimar Germany. *Creative Commons Attribution—Share Alike.*

DALY GOES WITH ARMY OVER RHINE

Sergeant Joseph E. Daly of Great Falls served with Company C, 2nd Signal Battalion. Daly, born in Rockwall, Iowa, came to Great Falls in 1914 as a telegraph operator and later worked for the Mutual Oil Company. Slightly wounded twice during the many battles in which the 2nd Signals served, Sergeant Daly was awarded the Silver Star and the French Croix de Guerre for distinguished bravery. On December 20, 1918, he wrote to friends at Mutual Oil from Dernback, Germany, about his experiences during the war and the German Occupation:

Hello everybody.

Just a line from Germany. We arrived here a couple of days ago as we are now troops of occupation and this little village of Dernback is where we are going to do guard duty for a while. It has been such a long time since I have had the opportunity to write to any of you, but I sincerely hope you will forgive me for the 1st Division has been very busy. We have been what they call "shock troops." The German called us "The Black Snake Division" because we struck so often and unexpected and they evidently knew the fighting ability of the 1st, as well as French and Americans.

We returned from the front about October 15th for a rest and went back in France to real rest billets and expected to remain there for sometime but was called back again after about ten days and hiked full pack back to the front thru mud and rain, sleeping in tents and barns. We went in and experienced a few days hard fighting along the Meuse river and were relieved and started back. We arrived in a large wood about 50 kilometers from Sedan, the big railroad center we captured on Nov. 11th, and it was there we heard the good news of the armistice. We surely were a happy bunch and celebrated the occasion by building large bonfires and getting warm and dry for the first time in over two weeks.

The next day we started on our way to Germany as troops of occupation via Verdun

Great Falls Soldier Decorated by French for Great Bravery

JOSEPH E. DALY

Sergeant Joseph E. Daly awarded the Silver Star and Croix de Guerre. *From the* Great Falls Tribune, *October 26, 1919.*

thru Alsace Lorraine, Luxemburg and on up the Moselle river to the Rhine. It was a long hard hike (full packs) but never the less it was a great change from continuous fighting.

…We stopped in Grenenmacher, a large town and also spent Thanksgiving there and then on across the border and into Germany and up the Moselle River.

The receptions were much different from there on, although we have had no trouble and have gotten along very nicely so far with the German people. We stopped in many of the towns along the river. The scenery was great, it consisted of vineyards, mountains, old castles, etc. We finally arrived in Coblenz which is another very interesting little city; we stopped there over night. From there we came up the Rhine a few miles to this quiet little village [Dernback] and are living in hopes that our stay here will be short as I am curious to get started for the good old U.S.A. now that it is all over with.…

My best regards to all, and a very Merry Xmas. JOE.[202]

A Postwar Montana Mystery

While the Armistice brought an end to the fighting, the AEF continued to suffer deaths, mostly through the raging influenza pandemic. Among the last Montanans to give his life in World War I was Sergeant John L. Griffin of Williams in Teton County. His death is cloaked in mystery, with the U.S. Army reporting that he drowned on February 20, 1919, in the river at Coblenz, Germany. Yet the press reported a far more sinister cause of death: "killed by a German sniper" at Coblenz. The *Great Falls Tribune* reported the incident:

> *Funeral of John L. Griffin, Killed in Coblenz, Germany, to Be Held Here.*
>
> *The first body of an American soldier killed in Germany during the world war to be brought to Montana was landed in New York, Thursday, according to information received by Dan Griffin, a member of the Great Falls fire department. His brother, former Sgt. John L. Griffin, was killed by a German sniper at Coblenz, Germany, on February 20, 1919, over three months after the signing of the armistice. The body will arrive at the chapel of the W.H. George company within a week.*

Sergeant Griffin was a member of Co. L, 4ᵗʰ Infantry, and in the battle of the Marne was severely wounded. After spending four months in a base hospital he was sent to the army of occupation and billeted at Coblenz. It was there in February 1919, that he was killed by a German sniper, and he was buried in the American cemetery near that town…

Dan Griffin his brother was a member of the 9ᵗʰ Machine Gun Company, 3ʳᵈ Division.[203]

A Sad Case

The fog of war left some casualties whose fates would remain unclear for many months after the Armistice. One tragic case is a soldier who is still honored as namesake for Veterans of Foreign Wars Post 1087, Royal A. Caufield Post, Great Falls.

Royal Alvin Caufield was born on March 28, 1895, in Great Falls. His parents came to Montana from Canada in 1890 to settle in the new town of Great Falls. In April 1917, Royal enlisted in Company L of the 2ⁿᵈ Montana Infantry Regiment as President Wilson mobilized the state National Guards. By December, the 163ʳᵈ U.S. Infantry had boarded the transport *Leviathan*

Sergeant Royal A. Caufield.
Veterans of Foreign Wars Post 1087, Royal A. Caufield Post.

As the AEF built up and trained in France, Royal was promoted to sergeant and often wrote letters back to his parents in Great Falls. Impatient for action, Sergeant Caufield and other Montanans from his company transferred to Company E of the 23ʳᵈ Infantry Regiment. In mid-July, the 23ʳᵈ Infantry, 2ⁿᵈ Division, led the bloody but successful American offensive near Château-Thierry, and on July 18 in the Battle of Soissons, Sergeant Royal Caufield was killed in action when his position was overrun by Germans.

Sadly, Sergeant Caufield's fate became blurred for many months. The U.S. Army initially reported him missing in action. In September, the Caufield family received a letter from a comrade in Royal's company advising them that their son had been killed. More months later, the army reported him wounded, and it was not until late January 1919 that the army finally advised the family that Royal had been killed in action.

In May 1921, Sergeant Royal A. Caufield was buried at Old Highland Cemetery with full military honors. Two years later, a new veterans post was organized in Great Falls, Veterans of Foreign Wars Post 1087, Royal A. Caufield Post, and that name remains to this day.[204]

MONTANAN SERVED IN 94ᵀᴴ AERO SQUADRON

The 94th Aero Squadron gained fame during 1918 for the skill of its aviators and the sterling leadership of its commander, Captain Edward V. "Eddie" Rickenbacker, whose exploits in achieving twenty-six "victories" (twenty German aircraft and six balloons) became legendary. Serving in the 94th was Montanan First Lieutenant Raymond J. Saunders of Billings.

Saunders was born in Oklahoma in 1895, enlisted in the army in August 1917 and attended the School of Military Aeronautics at Columbus, Ohio, before deploying to France in October. In June 1918, PFC Saunders accepted

Captain Eddie Rickenbacker, commander of the 94th Aero Squadron with his SPAD-XIII-C.1 aircraft. *Library of Congress.*

a commission in the Aviation Service and assignment to the 185th Aero Squadron. Just as the Meuse-Argonne Offensive began, First Lieutenant Saunders transferred to Captain Rickenbacker's 94th Aero Squadron. On October 22, Lieutenant Saunders was reported missing in action during that major offensive. After the war, his parents, Mr. and Mrs. Don E. Saunders, and sister of Billings embarked on a journey to discover the fate of their son and brother and details about what had happened, as well as to locate his grave if he had been killed. After four challenging months in France and Washington, D.C., the Saunderses returned to Billings after successfully, though sadly, locating their son's crashed plane and his grave in France.[205]

GRAVES REGISTRATION SERVICE

Throughout the Great War, Montanans were involved in every aspect, and now the grim task of burial and honoring the dead moved to the forefront. Young Bessie Little of Helena arrived in France in 1918 to assist the Red Cross in clerical work. In April 1919, Bessie was promoted to manage the main office of the Graves Registration Service near Paris, which recorded the graves of all American soldiers in France, England, Switzerland, Ireland, Belgium and Germany.

By early 1920, the Graves Registration Service was completing its task, with every record checked against the army's casualty list. Each white cross—or six-pointed star over Jewish graves—had an embossed aluminum strip placed on the back duplicating the name, rank and organization already painted on the marker.

Nearly 70,000 American soldiers were buried in the eleven districts of France, the Belgian battlefields and the Duchy of Luxembourg. Some thirty-eight cemeteries of 300 or more graves were cared for by discharged Allied soldiers. The largest of these was Romagne, north of Verdun, where 23,000 American men were interred. Next in size was Thiaucourt Cemetery, with 4,500 graves. Many other Yanks rested in British and French military or French communal cemeteries.[206]

Montana soldiers with the Graves Registration Service were in the field carrying out this important task, including Sergeant First Class Joseph H. Gillis of Sand Coulee and Sergeant Guy Stucky of Missoula. Upon his return home, Sergeant Stucky talked about this grim but necessary work:

BURIED SOLDIERS ON FRENCH FRONT
Sergeant Guy Stucky Tells of Grave Registration Work Overseas.
"It was gruesome work and hard work and I'm glad it's over. Somebody had to do it, and I don't think that there were any to whom the task was given, who complained," Sergeant Guy Stucky, recently returned from France, where for a year he served with the grave registration section of the quartermaster's corps, made this statement to a Missoulian *reporter yesterday while speaking of that branch of service.*

"There is little I can say of the work now," he continued, "for reason of army regulations. Most of what the grave registration service did will have to remain unsaid until such time as censorship may be lifted. I can say this much, though, it was not the pleasant side of war, if there is such.

"Generally stated, our work consisted of burying the American soldiers who died in battle, and those of the allied countries. We gave no attention to German bodies. Ordinally we tended only United States soldiers, but as the war progressed, this led to much complication and we later took care of the bodies of our allies as well.

"Much of our work had to be done under shell fire at night. We would go beyond the trenches, or to such places as men may have died, and there in the dark of night we would dig temporary graves and bury our dead. We would mark the graves in any way that we could. Sometimes it would be with a bayonet or a gun; sometimes only branches of trees. Again we would use helmets or parts of clothing stuck on a stick. But always we were careful to make identification of the grave certain.

"Then as the opportunity was give us by change in the battle front, we would erect crosses over the graves and map the battlefield showing the location of each. This too, was only temporary work, and as the Germans abandoned the country we gradually took up the task of gathering bodies of all American dead and burying them in permanent cemeteries. Here we would place the bodies in boxes and bury them in graves six feet deep, over which we would erect white crosses, bearing the name of the soldier."

…Sergeant Stucky is well known in Missoula. He was formerly employed in the Lucy undertaking place here. Mrs. Guy Stucky has been active in her war work in Missoula since the outbreak of the war. [In 1918, Mrs. Stucky, a nurse, conducted a state survey for the Montana Association for the prevention of tuberculosis.][207]

WORLD WAR COLLEGE WARRIORS

Seven hundred college men and women of Montana's institutions of higher learning entered the service during the war. Montana State University Missoula enrolled 400 in the service. Montana State College Bozeman had 227, while the smallest, School of Mines Butte, had 62 soldiers enlisted for the duration of the war. Every major sport captain in each of the three schools enlisted for duty, many of them taking the larger part of their teams with them.

Paul Logan Dornblaser graduated from the University Law School before enlisting in the Marine Corps, leading most of his football team into service. Corporal Dornblaser suffered severe wounds in combat on October 8 in the Argonne Forest and died two days later. In tribute to the university men and women who died in service, thirty-two Ponderosa pines, Montana's state tree, were planted on Arbor Day on May 13, 1919. At the main west entrance to Brick Breeden Fieldhouse at the State College is a plaque reading "THESE STUDENTS OF MONTANA STATE COLLEGE OF AGRICULTURE AND MECHANIC ARTS GAVE THEIR LIVES IN DEFENSE OF HUMANITY IN THE GREAT WORLD WAR OF 1914–1918," followed by sixteen names of students who died in service, four in combat.

Three Montana college men were honored with the Distinguished Service Cross earned in action by heroic service: Ernest Anderson, School of Mines (killed in action); Charles McAuliffe, School of Mines; and Major Charles L. Sheridan, State College. Many others received French decorations and American citations.[208]

CORPORAL FLETCHER'S OCCUPATION VIEWS

The Great War began for Chicago-born twenty-three-year-old Arthur E. Fletcher (of Stevensville in the Bitterroot Valley) when he departed for France on November 26, 1917. Assigned to Company C, 2nd Field Signal Battalion, his war ended in September 1919, just short of two years since his induction. Corporal Fletcher often wrote home to his parents during the long period of occupation. His letters provide excellent insight into the environment during this postwar period and reflect the views of many young Yanks, impatient to leave Europe and the war behind to rebuild their lives at home.

In his letter of March 31, 1919, from Montabaur, Corporal Fletcher wrote:

Dear Folks.…We crushed the Kaiser and Militarism and should have sailed home. I don't believe in Wilson's policy of joining the League of Nations and making every war our war. The time for such a league is not here yet.

Some time ago when [General] *Pershing reviewed the 1ˢᵗ Division he made a speech. A mighty warm reception he received. From all over the field one could hear the boys saying, "I want to go home." There was so much whimpering he could not be heard. Of course this is not military but what did the boys care.*

United States is going on the bum because of the love for France. Could they see how dirty the French are they might change. England is showing much more sense than our country. She is providing better for her soldiers and also getting them home quicker. Those in her Army of Occupation have the privilege of going home often.

…There was a dandy write-up in the Stars & Stripes of this division in the Argonne. It stated we struck the strongest section of the Enemy's front between the Meuse-Argonne and that we captured 1,407 prisoners and had lost a total of 9,387 officers and men, the greatest casualties suffered by any American division in the Meuse-Argonne offensive. During its seven days in the line the 1ˢᵗ had advanced seven kilometers against the Germans.

…I don't understand why the drafted man in the Regular Army must wait until all the others who came over later, go home.

…With love and best wishes. Arthur[209]

Three weeks later, Corporal Fletcher wrote home on April 22:

Dear Folks.…Was very much pleased at noon when I received your letter of Mar. 24ᵗʰ. I am glad you wrote when you did instead of waiting for my letters.

Last Sunday was Easter and do you know it was the first time since I left home that I heard a Robin. I woke at 4.30 am Sunday and listened to the Robins for about an hour. It sure sounded good to hear them. You see last year we were at the front and you can bet the birds knew it is not a pleasant place.

I went to church Easter morning, in fact I go most every Sunday.

Lately some pretty strong rumors have been going the rounds. They are such as that this division's sailing date is on July 7th, and that the 1st and 2nd Divisions would parade in Washington, D.C. on July 4th which would mean that we would leave here in June. Sounds pretty good don't it?…

One month and four days and I will have three service stripes [for eighteen months' service]. *When I first came to France I believed it would be only a matter of a few months and we would be returning to U.S.A. But now I have a right to believe it will only be a matter of a few months.*

The [German] *people with whom I used to stay invited me to come to their home last Saturday as they would have some wine and cake for me. I was in the show when I remembered of the invitation but remained until it was over. I suppose I will have to explain to them the next time I see them. They were very good to me and hated to see me go. Don't think that the people I stay with are different. Yesterday the woman brought in some coffee and cake and insisted on my taking it.*

Recently an order came out that if there were anyone who had a complaint to make about the Y. they should send it in to their commanding officer. We would rather wait though and be sure that it reached the people without any part cut out. There is much that concerns the officers when telling of the YMCA. Something should have happened long ago when the Y. was appealing to the people, "How much will your mother-love give to your boy who is in the battle"; and at the same time enjoying themselves with the money which the givers honestly believed was for a good cause. The man in the S.O.S. got more than he whom they were speaking for. There is an investigation being made but you can bet nothing will come from it as there would be some big men exposed who are wound up in it.

With love and best wishes. Arthur[210]

Corporal Fletcher wrote home again on July 10, with little news except that his division was receiving a large number of replacement soldiers to fill the ranks. He made note also of a circus to entertain the troops:

Dear Folks.…The 1st Division will soon receive 5708 replacements. I do hope I am lucky enough to go home.

Tomorrow and the next day the 1st is to hold a circus at Montabaur.

All welfare workers are to leave here soon. This is a good sign that we will start for home soon…

Best wishes and lots of love to all. Arthur[211]

A tribute to the 1st Division circus at Montabaur. *Author's collection.*

The return to the United States still did not develop for the 1st Division, and on July 24, Corporal Fletcher wrote home:

> *Dear Folks, I moved to Neuwied Monday July 21st. I have a very nice room and bed at 66 Schloss Strasse. On one end of the same street is our telephone central while on the other end is a castle or mansion in which 2nd Brigade Headquarters have their offices. This mansion belongs to the Prince of Wied.* [Many generations earlier, in the early 1830s, Prince Maximilian of Wied brought artist Karl Bodmer along on an expedition to the Upper Missouri and Fort McKenzie, precursor trading post to Fort Benton.] *Neuwied is much larger and better located than Montabaur.*
>
> *…Our switch-board is in the same room with the division board. Across the hall is a German Telegraph Office and next to it a German Telephone Central.*
>
> *Tuesday I went through the old mansion belonging to the Prince of Wied. It certainly is nicely furnished and in the rear is a private theatre which will seat about two hundred people. I also went through his stables*

where he has some thorough bred horses. He has more harness and saddles than most harness shops. He has a park, a riding barn and everything one cares for.

*   ...Best wishes and love to all. Arthur*[212]

WELCOME HOME, CORPORAL FLETCHER

The 2nd Field Signal Battalion finally returned to the United States in August 1919, and on September 6, Corporal Fletcher wrote home from Camp Mills on Long Island, New York:

Dear Folks, Wednesday night I went to New York with a friend. They are building stands on Fifth Avenue and are getting ready for the parade. I believe it will be the biggest parade ever held. From New York we go to Washington, D.C. where we will parade on the 17th. There are rumors of our parading in Philadelphia and Chicago, but I hope we will not have to do so.

World War I veterans parade. *Library of Congress.*

Last night I brought a uniform to Hempstead to have it tailored. This is the first new uniform I received for a long time.

Camp Mills has changed a great deal since 1917. I am staying in a barrack about 300 yards from the spot where our tent stood in 1917. The sanitary conditions are much better although the camp gets pretty muddy when it rains.

Am in good health and hope you are all well. Lots of love to all. Arthur[213]

VICTORY PARADES

Before the AEF's combat units left service in 1919, the War Department gave citizens the chance to honor their troops. The parade in New York occurred on September 10, and according to the *New York Times*, an enthusiastic crowd cheered the twenty-five thousand men of the 1st Division as they marched down Fifth Avenue from 107th Street to Washington Square in Greenwich Village, wearing full combat gear and trench helmets. The *Times* noted, "It was the town's first opportunity to greet the men of the 1st Division, and to let them know it remembered their glorious part in the American Army's smashing drives at Toul, at Cantigny, at Soissons, at St. Mihiel, and at the Meuse and the Argonne." The greatest cheers were given for General John J. Pershing.

General Pershing then led a similar parade down Pennsylvania Avenue in Washington, D.C., on September 17. Two days later, General Pershing addressed a joint session of Congress, sporting his new rank, "General of the Armies."[214]

BEYOND THE GREAT WAR

The Great War had ended at last, the influenza pandemic continued unabated in communities large and small for many months, a troubled peace was arranged, a toothless League of Nations was born without U.S. participation, the hyper-patriotism of the war years evolved seamlessly into anti-Bolshevism, the United States returned inwardly toward its traditional isolationism and the military shrank to peacetime levels. Millions of soldiers returned to communities, as did thousands of women from their wide-ranging war work.

Montana women returned from their jobs in industry and with governmental and nongovernmental organizations in large part to their traditional roles in homes. None would ever forget her wartime experience. Their sisters in many states finally gained the right to vote in 1920. (Montana women received the right to vote in 1916.)

Black soldiers returned to their homes to find Jim Crow still firmly entrenched, while Chinese citizens would remain excluded from Great Falls for two more decades.

Montana continued in its third year of severe agricultural drought, bringing on depression a decade before the rest of the nation. Monuments to the Great War rose in tribute in Fort Benton, Kalispell and Missoula, while Montana soldiers, men and women, formed a new American Legion.

A Tomb of Honor

Three years after the Armistice, thousands gathered at Arlington Cemetery on Armistice Day to dedicate the Tomb of the Unknown Soldier, selected in anonymity from the 1,652 Americans too damaged to be identified. This soldier symbolically represented the 116,000 Americans slain in the Great War's devastation. One Montanan represented America's Indian nations. Chief Plenty Coups, of the Crow Nation, placed a war bonnet and a coups stick on the Tomb that day. From the coups stick hung Plenty

"Plenty Coups" (Crow Nation chief Aleek-chea-ahoosh) at the burial of the Unknown Soldier of World War I at Arlington National Cemetery. *Library of Congress.*

Coups's first feather, won by accompanying a war party on some forgotten raid against Piegan Blackfeet marauders, symbolic of the start on the long and difficult trail to head chieftainship. On this occasion, Chief Plenty Coups said, "I hope the great spirit will grant that all this nation's noble warriors have not given up their lives in vain, and that there will be peace to all men hereafter. That is the Indian hope and prayer."[215]

Three years later, citizenship was granted to America's native peoples.

CLOSING WITH LOVE

Florence Sheridan Spaulding of Bozeman composed this loving tribute for all servicemen returning home from overseas, including her brother, Major Charles L. Sheridan:

THE VETERAN
Shadowy eyes, eyes that have seen
so much
Dear weary hands too holy, most, to
touch
Slow trudging feet, their path through
scenes untold,
Through days of weariness, of hunger,
pain and cold.

It is such joy Dear One, as at your
feet I sit
To see your war tired eyes with happy
home fires lit.
For Love well knows and true heart
can read so well;
The horrors they have seen your lips
will never tell.

The record on your sleeve, written in
Bars of old.
Is also in your eyes, so young and
Yet so old.[216]

247

NOTES

Chapter 1

1. *Story of the War and Family War Service Record*, 89–96; Wikipedia, "Operation Michael"; Dunn, *Narrow Gauge*; Carroll, *My Fellow Soldiers*, 170–73; Davenport, *First Over There*, 80–82.
2. *Fort Benton River Press*, March 27, 1918.
3. *Montana Standard*, March 20, 1918.
4. *Missoulian*, March 26, 1918.
5. *River Press*, March 20, 1918.
6. Carroll, *My Fellow Soldiers*, 87–90; Davenport, *First Over There*, 87–90.
7. *River Press*, April 3, 1918.
8. *River Press*, April 10, 1918.
9. Ibid.
10. *Great Falls Tribune*, March 3, September 28, November 10, 1918.
11. *River Press*, March 27, 1918; *Great Falls Tribune*, April 14, 1918.
12. *Great Falls Tribune*, April 16, 1918.
13. *Missoulian*, November 27, 1914. See www.kenrobisonhistory.com/world-war-1 for more of this adventure.
14. *Great Falls Tribune*, April 27, 1918. For more of Chaplain Pippy's letter, see www.kenrobisonhistory.com/world-war-1.
15. *River Press*, April 10, 1918.
16. *River Press*, April 17, 1918.
17. Ibid.

18. *River Press*, April 10, 1918.
19. Montana enlistments cards, Montana Memory Project; *Montana Standard*, March 16, 1918; *Great Falls Tribune*, December 29, 1918; *Anaconda Standard*, March 1, 1918, June 19, 1919; See more details on all casualties at www.kenrobisonhistory.com/world-war-1.
20. *River Press*, May 1, 1918.
21. Montana enlistments cards, Montana Memory Project; Royal Navy and Naval History, "Chronology of the United States Marine Corps."
22. *Great Falls Tribune*, April 27, 1919; Montana enlistments cards, Montana Memory Project.
23. *River Press*, April 24, 1918.
24. Blackpast.org, "Horace W. Bivins"; *Salisbury (MD) Times*, September 19, 1950; Find A Grave website.
25. *River Press*, April 24, 1918; Work, *Darkness Before Dawn*, 199.
26. *River Press*, April 17, 1918; Work, *Darkness Before Dawn*, 194–96.
27. *River Press*, January 2, May 1, 1918; *Sanders County Independent-Ledger*, November 14, 1918.

Chapter 2

28. Robison, *World War I Montana*, 223–26; *Missoulian*, April 16, 1922.
29. *Great Falls Tribune*, April 23, 1918.
30. *River Press*, May 1, 1918.
31. Wikipedia, "Spruce Production Division."
32. *Butte Miner*, November 10, 1918.
33. *Hardin Tribune*, May 10, 1918. The rest of Lena Roy's story appears at www.kenrobisonhistory.com/world-war-1.
34. *River Press*, May 1, 1918; *Great Falls Tribune*, July 17, 1918; *Anaconda Standard*, April 30, 1918.
35. *Great Falls Tribune*, July 21, 1918.
36. Montana enlistments cards, Montana Memory Project. Details on all casualties appear at www.kenrobisonhistory.com/world-war-1.
37. *Montana Standard*, September 14, 1917.
38. *River Press*, May 29, 1918.
39. *Great Falls Tribune*, December 29, 1918; Montana enlistments cards, Montana Memory Project. An account of the *Moldavia*'s final moments from a history of the 4th Division appears at www.kenrobisonhistory.com/world-war-1.

40. Robison, *World War I Montana*, 193–98; *River Press*, May 8, 1918. For a complete listing of Montana women who served as Yeoman (F), see www. kenrobisonhistory.com/world-war-1.

41. *River Press*, April 10, May 15, 1918.

42. *Democrat-News (Lewistown)*, April 23, 1917; "Mob Action in Lewistown, 1917–1918: Patriots on the Rampage," http://mhs.mt.gov/Portals/11/ education/WWI/Mob%20Action%20in%20Lewistown.pdf.

43. Wikipedia, "Fort Keogh"; Harper, "Real War Horses of America."

44. *Butte Miner*, July 19, 1922.

45. *Missoulian*, May 13, 1919.

46. *Glasgow Courier*, July 19, 1918.

47. *History of the First Division*, 82–83; Davenport, *First Over There*, 87–90.

48. Montana enlistments cards, Montana Memory Project; *Montana Standard*, June 29, 1918.

49. Montana enlistments cards, Montana Memory Project; *River Press*, June 26, 1918. For details on all casualties, see www.kenrobisonhistory.com/ world-war-1.

50. *Missoulian*, September 2, 1918.

51. Montana enlistments cards, Montana Memory Project; *Anaconda Standard*, December 11, 1918.

52. *River Press*, May 15, 22, 1918.

Chapter 3

53. Davenport, *First Over There*, 244–46.

54. Marshall, *Memoirs of My Services*, 96.

55. *Great Falls Tribune*, March 11, 1919.

56. Richard, "Battle of Chateau Thierry, 1–4 June 1918"; Eggleston, *5th Marine Regiment Devil Dogs*, 57–65.

57. Harold M. Mady letter, May 26, 1918, SC337 Box 1, Folder 7, The History Museum.

58. Mady letter, June 15, 1918.

59. *Ronan Pioneer*, October 19, 1917; *Conrad Independent*, November 29, 1917; Montana enlistments cards, Montana Memory Project.

60. *River Press*, January 17, 1934; Gibbons, "*And They Thought We Wouldn't Fight*," 304.

61. Wikipedia, "Daniel Daly."

62. *River Press*, February 19, 1919; *Missoulian*, February 9, 1919. See www. kenrobisonhistory.com/world-war-1.
63. *Great Falls Tribune*, September 20, 1919; March 4, 1922; see Robison, *World War I Montana*, 58–60, for more of HM-1 McGee's Story.
64. *River Press*, June 19, 1918.
65. *Missoulian*, July 28, 1918.
66. *Great Falls Tribune*, June 23, 1918.
67. *Hardin Tribune*, July 7, 1918.
68. *River Press*, May 22, 1918.
69. *River Press*, May 15, 1918.
70. *Great Falls Tribune*, October 19, 1919.
71. *Great Falls Tribune*, May 20, 1918.
72. *Billings Weekly Gazette*, June 11, 1918.
73. For Representative Rankin's speech in August 1917, see Robison, *World War I Montana*, 91–93.

Chapter 4

74. *Flathead Courier*, June 27, 1918; the original painting, *Smoking 'Em Out*, was sent to the Remount Station by Charlie Russell to bolster troop morale and is today at the Wichita Art Museum. See also Robison, *World War I Montana*, 156–58.
75. Archambault, "Camp Lewis Remount Rodeo."
76. United States World War One Centennial Commission, "Veterinary Corps"; Montana enlistments cards, Montana Memory Project.
77. *Great Falls Tribune*, June 15, 1918; Internet Archives, "Montana Primary Sources," 67–73.
78. *River Press*, July 3, 1918.
79. *Conrad Independent*, September 19, 1918.
80. *Billings Gazette*, July 7, 1919.
81. *Great Falls Tribune*, July 16, 1918.
82. *River Press*, July 3, 1918.
83. *Billings Gazette*, July 5, 1918.
84. *River Press*, July 17, 1918.
85. *Great Falls Tribune*, March 2, 1919.
86. Kelton, "Miracle of Chateau-Thierry," 106–9. Colonel Kelton's complete article is carried on www.kenrobisonhistory.com/world-war-1, as is a listing of known Montanans who served with the 3rd Infantry at the Marne.

87. *History of the 362ⁿᵈ Infantry*, 13–15; *Story of the 91ˢᵗ Division*, 3.
88. *Great Falls Tribune*, March 2, 1919.
89. Gibbons, *"And They Thought We Wouldn't Fight,"* 366, 373–75.
90. *River Press*, July 10, 24, 1918.
91. *River Press*, July 3, 24, 1918.
92. *River Press*, July 24, 1918.
93. Montana Sedition Project.
94. *River Press*, July 24, 1918.
95. *Great Falls Tribune*, July 24, 1918; Work, *Darkness Before Dawn*, 139–40.
96. *Great Falls Tribune*, June 20, 1918; *Anaconda Standard*, June 23, 1918.

Chapter 5

97. *Billings Gazette*, March 3, 1919. For Private Andrews's complete article, see www.kenrobisonhistory.com/world-war-1.
98. *River Press*, August 14, 1918.
99. *River Press*, August 7, 1918.
100. Ibid.
101. *River Press*, July 24, 1918; *Great Falls Leader*, August 2, 1918.
102. *River Press*, July 31, 1918; *Olathe Kansas Register*, August 1, 1918; *Great Falls Tribune*, August 11, 1918.
103. *River Press*, August 28, 1918.
104. *Great Falls Tribune*, July 6, September 8, 1918; United States World War One Centennial Commission.
105. *River Press*, September 19, 1918; Robison, *World War I Montana*, 104–6.
106. *Anaconda Standard*, August 22, 1918.
107. *River Press*, August 14, 1918.
108. *Butte Miner*, September 16, 1918; Robison, *World War I Montana*, 86–88.
109. *Carolina Mountaineer and Waynesville (NC) Courier*, May 15, 1919.
110. *Anaconda Standard*, October 26, 1919.
111. *River Press*, August 21, 1918.
112. Ibid.
113. *River Press*, August 7, December 18, 1918; Wikipedia, "Reserve Officers' Training Corps: Student Army Training Corps."
114. Adler, "Meuse-Argonne First Phase."
115. Montana enlistments cards, Montana Memory Project; Wikipedia, "339ᵗʰ Infantry Regiment (United States)."
116. *River Press*, September 18, 1918.

117. Robison, *World War I Montana*, 143–44, 199–200; *Great Falls Tribune*, April 9, 1919; *Helena Independent*, July 19, 1919; *Conrad Independent*, July 10, 1919.

118. Wiley, *Montana and the Sky*, 97–98; *Butte Miner*, September 9, 1918. During the Battle of Chateau-Thierry, Lieutenant Harwood experienced astonishing aerial combat featuring a thrilling escape. His long account of this aerial battle appears at www.kenrobisonhistory.com/world-war-1.

119. Oberdorfer, *Senator Mansfield*.

120. *River Press*, August 22, 1918; Virginia Flanagan Diary, 14–15. See also Robison, *World War I Montana*, 43–44.

121. *River Press*, August 21, 1918.

122. *Great Falls Tribune*, September 15, 1918.

123. *Anaconda Standard*, January 30, 1919.

124. *Butte Miner*, September 24, 1918.

125. Hall of Valor, "Sergeant Arthur Aamot."

126. *32nd Division in the World War*, 71.

127. Ibid., 69, 71.

Chapter 6

128. Montana enlistments cards, Montana Memory Project; *Great Falls Tribune*, September 11, 1918.

129. *Anaconda Standard*, September 9, 1918.

130. Montana enlistments cards, Montana Memory Project.

131. Ibid.

132. Letter, Russell to Bumpsky, September 6, 1918. "Bumpsky" was Abe Lawrence Goodman, owner of Goodman's Cigar Store.

133. *Billings Gazette*, August 15, 1918. For more from Captain Vidal's letter, see www.kenrobisonhistory.com/world-war-1.

134. *Great Falls Tribune*, October 13, 1918. Captain Vidal continues his letter with more about how the attack unfolded; the complete letter can be found at www.kenrobisonhistory.com/world-war-1.

135. *Great Falls Tribune*, October 27, 1918. For Lieutenant Vidal's complete letter to Governor Sam Stewart, see www.kenrobisonhistory.com/world-war-1.

136. *Montana Standard*, January 17, 1991; *Missoulian*, March 26, 1995; Vrooman, *Whole Country Was…"One Robe,"* 312.

137. *River Press*, September 4, 1918. For President Wilson's Fourteen Points, see Robison, *World War I Montana*, 200–202.

138. *Butte Miner*, September 29, 1918.

139. *Missoulian*, February 3, 1918; *Conrad Independent*, November 29, 1917.

140. *Anaconda Standard*, October 26, 1919.

141. *Sanders County Independent-Ledger*, January 8, 1920; *River Press*, August 29, 1917; Montana enlistments cards, Montana Memory Project; Montana History Compass, "Montana Native Warriors."

142. *Washington, D.C., Evening Star*, July 5, 1917; Carpenter, "Detecting Indianness," 139–59.

143. Montana enlistments cards, Montana Memory Project Cards; Robison, *World War I Montana*, 215. All known Montana native warriors are listed at www.kenrobisonhistory.com/world-war-1.

144. Scott, *Scott's Official History*.

145. *Great Falls Tribune*, October 11, 1918; October 31, 1967; Scott, *Scott's Official History*. All known Montana African Americans serving in the war are listed at www.kenrobisonhistory.com/world-war-1.

146. Montanans known serving with the 14th Infantry are listed at www. kenrobisonhistory.com/world-war-1.

147. *River Press*, September 18, 1918.

148. *Missoulian*, May 19, 1919. For the complete narrative of Sam Caras's *Experiences*, see www.kenrobisonhistory.com/world-war-1.

149. *Missoulian*, May 26, 1919.

150. *Missoulian*, June 2, 1919.

151. World War I/The Great War, 1914–1918, "Big Show."

152. Ibid., "Meuse-Argonne Offensive: Part II; Pershing's Report"; Wikipedia, "Meuse-Argonne Offensive."

153. Mullen and Nelson, "Montanans and 'The Most Peculiar Disease,'" 50–61.

154. Harwell, Holzman and Helgerson, "No More War, No More Plague," 27–44.

155. *Great Falls Tribune*, September 28, 1918.

156. Montana enlistments cards, Montana Memory Project. Navy enlistment cards did not record cause of death.

157. Wikipedia, "372nd Regiment"; Montana enlistments cards, Montana Memory Project; *Denver (CO) Post*, November 27, 1912; June 14, 1916; Charles L. Holmes, Montana World War I draft registration card; *Anaconda Standard*, June 8, December 21, 1917; September 15, 1918; July 14, 1919; *Colorado Springs (CO) Gazette*, December 8, 1918; *Butte Daily Bulletin*, July 14, 1919; U.S. Census, 1930, 1940. For more on Lieutenant Charles L. Holmes, see www.kenrobisonhistory.com/world-war-1.

158. *River Press*, September 11, 1918.

Chapter 7

159. *River Press*, October 9, 1918; October 1, 1919; Prisoners of the First World War, 1914–1918, ICRC Historical Archives.

160. *St. Louis Post-Dispatch*, February 11, 1919.

161. Montana enlistments cards, Montana Memory Project; American Red Cross POW File. See www.kenrobisonhistory.com/world-war-1 for additional information on each POW.

162. Gaff, *Blood in the Argonne*; Laplander, *Finding the Lost Battalion*; *Missoulian*, October 17, 1937; Montana enlistments cards, Montana Memory Project. Private Marvin B. Long of Glasgow later recalled his experiences as one of the Americans who went through the hell of starvation and exposure to war's worst elements. Nineteen years later, living in Hamilton, Private Long vividly recalled the horror of the siege. See www.kenrobisonhistory.com/world-war-1 for Private Long's account.

163. *Great Falls Tribune*, May 30, 1919.

164. See www.kenrobisonhistory.com/world-war-1 for all known Montanans serving in the Lost Battalion and in the 77th Infantry Regiment.

165. *Butte Miner*, June 17, 1918; *Anaconda Standard*, May 11, 1918; *River Press*, November 6, 1918; *Conrad Independent-Observer*, November 14, 1918.

166. Carroll, *My Fellow Soldiers*, 301–2.

167. National Center for Biotechnology Information, "U.S. Military and the Influenza Pandemic"; *River Press*, October 9, 16, 1918.

168. *River Press*, October 16, 1918.

169. Ibid.

170. *Billings Gazette*, August 25, 1918; *Larned (KS) Chronoscope*, January 23, 1919; Gail, *Yellowstone County, Montana*.

171. *River Press*, October 16, 1918; *Helena Independent*, September 22, 1918.

172. *River Press*, October 9, 1918.

173. Montana enlistments cards, Montana Memory Project; *Great Falls Tribune*, January 8, 1917; June 26, July 1, 1918.

174. *Fallon County Times*, July 3, 1919.

175. *Big Timber Pioneer*, May 9, 1935; *Great Falls Tribune*, June 23, 1918.

176. *River Press*, October 16, 1918.

177. *River Press*, October 9, 16, 1918; *Billings Gazette*, January 11, 1920.

178. American Experience, "Flu in Boston." See www.kenrobisonhistory.com/world-war-1 for all known Montana navy influenza casualties; J.J. Keegan, Montana enlistments cards, Montana Memory Project.

179. *History of the 362nd Infantry*, 58–60.

Chapter 8

180. Yockelson, *Forty-Seven Days*, 247.

181. *River Press*, November 13, 1918.

182. Ibid.

183. *Stars and Stripes*, November 15, 1918.

184. *River Press*, November 20, 1918.

185. *Bear Paw Mountaineer*, January 30, 1919; *River Press*, January 9, 1919, 9.

186. *Missoulian*, April 16, 1922.

187. *Montana Standard*, November 11, 1929.

188. *Great Falls Tribune*, January 16, 1919. See also Robison, *World War I Montana*, 181–84, for more about Nurse Canon. The rest of Nurse Canon's remarkable letter appears at www.kenrobisonhistory.com/world-war-1, including the visit of King George and his family and a naval Thanksgiving onboard the USS *Nevada*.

189. Brunh, *Memories of Mina*.

190. *River Press*, December 11, 1918.

191. Ibid.

192. Stout, *Montana: Its Story and Biography*, vol. 1, 652; United States World War One Centennial Commission, Doughboy MIA Database.

Chapter 9

193. *River Press*, December 11, 1918.

194. Montana enlistments cards, Montana Memory Project.

195. *River Press*, December 18, 1928.

196. *River Press*, December 4, 1918. See www.kenrobisonhistory.com/world-war-1 for the complete article.

197. *River Press*, December 4, 1918.

198. *River Press*, December 11, 1918.

199. *Great Falls Tribune*, January 4, 1919.

200. *Bear Paw Mountaineer*, January 16, 1919.

201. *Great Falls Tribune*, February 26, 1919; Montana enlistments cards, Montana Memory Project.

202. *Great Falls Tribune*, October 26, 1919. See www.kenrobisonhistory.com/world-war-1 for Sergeant Daly's complete letter.

203. *Great Falls Tribune*, July 21, 1920.

204. *Great Falls Tribune*, September 26, November 16, December 1, 1918; January 26, 1919; May 15, 1921; October 2, 1923.

205. *Billings Weekly Gazette*, September 2, 1920. Read the full story at www.kenrobisonhistory.com/worldwarI.

206. *Butte Miner*, January 5, 1920; *Anaconda Standard*, April 12, 1919.

207. *Missoulian*, August 2, 1918; August 3, 1919; Montana enlistments cards, Montana Memory Project.

208. *Bear Paw Mountaineer*, August 7, 1919; *Missoulian*, May 11, 1919; Martin, "Sixteen Names on a Plaque."

209. Fletcher Letters, March 31, 1919. For Corporal Fletcher's complete letters, see www.kenrobisonhistory.com/world-war-1.

210. Ibid., April 22, 1919.

211. Ibid., July 10, 1919.

212. Ibid., July 24, 1919.

213. Ibid., September 6, 1919.

214. History, "1919: New York City Parade."

215. *Billings Gazette*, November 20, 29, 1921.

216. Gallatin County Museum, undated newspaper clipping. Three of Mrs. Spaulding's brothers and her husband were serving in France.

BIBLIOGRAPHY

Online Resources

Ancestry.com.

Fold 3. http://www.fold3.com.

Military enlistment cards, Montana Memory Project. http//mtmemory. org/cdm.

Montana World War I draft registration cards. Family Search. familysearch. org/search/collection.

U.S. Army Transport Service, passenger lists, 1910–39. Ancestry.com.

U.S. Census Records. https://www.census.gov/history/www/genealogy/ decennial_census_records/census-records_2.html.

Wikipedia. wikipedia.org.

Newspapers

Note: These are Montana periodicals unless otherwise noted.

Anaconda Standard.

Bear Paw Mountaineer.

Big Timber Pioneer.

Billings Gazette.

Buffalo (NY) Sunday Express.

Butte Daily Bulletin.
Butte Miner.
Carolina Mountaineer and Waynesville (NC) Courier.
Choteau Acantha.
Colorado Springs (CO) Gazette.
Conrad Independent.
Denver (CO) Post.
Evening Star (Washington, D.C.).
Fairbanks (AK) Daily News-Miner.
Fergus County Democrat.
Flathead Courier.
Fort Benton River Press.
Great Falls Leader.
Great Falls Tribune.
Helena Herald.
Helena Independent.
Indianapolis (IN) News.
Kansas (Olathe, KS) Register.
Kansas City (KS) Journal.
Larned (KS) Chronoscope.
Lewistown Democrat-News.
Lewistown Democrat.
Mineral Independent.
Missoulian.
Montana Standard.
New York Sun.
Powder River County Examiner and the Broadus Independent.
Ronan Pioneer.
Sanders County Independent-Ledger.
Sanders County Signal.
Stars and Stripes.
St. Louis (MO) Post-Dispatch.

Additional Sources

Active History. "An American Legion in the Canadian Expeditionary Force." http://activehistory.ca/2015/02/an-american-legion-in-the-cef-crossing-borders-during-canadas-first-world-war.

Adler, Julius Ochs. "The Meuse-Argonne First Phase." History of the 306th Infantry. Longwood Central School District. http://longwood.k12.ny.us/cms/One.aspx?portalId=2549374&pageId=7374596.

American Experience. "The Flu in Boston." https://www.pbs.org/wgbh/americanexperience/features/influenza-boston.

Americans at War in Foreign Forces. Battalion 211, American Legion. http://www.americansatwarinforeignforces.com/named-americans-in-the-american-legion-cef.html.

Archambault, Alan. "The Camp Lewis Remount Rodeo, 1917–1918." *Banner Friends of the Fort Lewis Military* 22, no. 3 (Summer 2008).

———. "A Cowboy Painting for Camp Lewis." *Banner Friends of the Fort Lewis Military* 22, no. 3 (Summer 2008).

Bach, Christian A., and Henry Noble Hall. *The Fourth Division: Its Services and Achievements in the World War.* Garden City, NY: Country Life Press, 1920.

Barry, John M. *The Great Influenza: The Epic Story of the Deadliest Plague in History.* New York: Penguin Books, 2004.

BlackPast. "Horace W. Bivins." blackpast.org.

Blackwell-Frazier American Legion Post 142. "The Sinking of the RMS Moldavia." https://americanlegion142.org/noted-local-vets/andrew-blackwell/the-sinking-of-the-rms-moldavia.

Botkin, Jane Little. *Frank Little and the IWW: The Blood that Stained an American Family.* Norman: University of Oklahoma Press, 2017.

Bruhn, Gladys E. *Memories of Mina.* N.p.: self-published, 1982.

Buschlen, J.P. comp. *Big Horn County (Montana) in the World War.* Hardin, MT: Hardin Tribune, 1919.

Caras, Sam. *My Experiences in My Third War.* Pamphlet. N.p.: self-published, 1919.

Carpenter, Cari. "Detecting Indianness: Gertrude Bonnin's Investigation of Native American Identity." *Wicazo Sa Review* 20, no. 1 (2005): 139–59.

Carroll, Andrew. *My Fellow Soldiers: General John Pershing and the Americans Who Helped Win the Great War.* New York: Penguin Press, 2017.

Chacon, H. Rafael. *Over There! Montanans in the Great War.* Missoula: Montana Museum of Art & Culture, 2017.

Clark, George B. *Devil Dogs: Fighting Marines of World War I.* Novato, CA: Presidio Press, 1999.

———. *The Fourth Marine Brigade in World War: Battalion Histories Based on Official Documents.* Jefferson, NC: McFarland & Company, 2015.

Cole, Ralph D., and W.C. Howells. *The Thirty-Seventh Division in the World War, 1917–1918.* Columbus, OH: F.J. Beer Printing Company, 1926.

Croix Rouge Farm Memorial Foundation. "42nd (Rainbow) Division— History." http://croixrougefarm.org/history-42nd.

Davenport, Matthew J. *First Over There: The Attack on Cantigny America's First Battle of World War I*. New York: St. Martin's Press, 2015.

Dickon, Chris. *Americans at War in Foreign Forces: A History, 1914–1945*. Jefferson, NC: McFarland & Company, 2014.

Dunn, Richard. *Narrow Gauge to No Man's Land. First Army 60cm Gauge Railways of the First World War in France*. Los Altos, CA: Benchmark Publications, 1990.

Ebbert, Jean, and Marie-Beth Hall. *The First, the Few, the Forgotten: Navy and Marine Corps Women in World War I*. Annapolis, MD: Naval Institute Press, 2002.

Eggleston, Michael A. *The 5th Marine Regiment Devil Dogs in World War I: A History and Roster*. Jefferson, NC: McFarland & Company, 2016.

Evans, Martin Marix, ed. *American Voices of World War I: Primary Source Documents 1917–1920*. Chicago: Fitzroy Dearborn Publishers, 2001.

Faulkner, Richard S. *Pershing's Crusaders: The American Soldier in World War I*. Lawrence: University of Kansas Press, 2017.

Ferrell, Robert H. *Unjustly Dishonored: An African American Division in World War I*. Columbia: University of Missouri Press, 2011.

Flanagan, Virginia. Diary, The History Museum, Great Falls, Montana.

Fletcher, Arthur E. Letters. Author's collection.

Gaff, Alan D. *Blood in the Argonne: The "Lost Battalion" of World War I*. Norman: University of Oklahoma Press, 2005.

Gahm, Margaret, comp. *Tuscania* passenger list. Privately maintained.

Gail, W.W. *Yellowstone County, Montana, in the World War 1917–1918–1919*. Billings, MT: War Book Publishing Company, 1919.

Gavin, Lettie. *American Women in World War I: They Also Served*. Niwot: University Press of Colorado, 1997.

George, Albert E., and Edwin H. Cooper. *Pictorial History of the Twenty-Sixth Division United States Army*. Boston, MA: Ball Publishing Company, 1920.

Gibbons, Floyd. *"And They Thought We Wouldn't Fight."* New York: George H. Doran Company, 1918.

Gleaves, Albert. *A History of the Transport Service: Adventures and Experiences of United States Transports and Cruisers in the World War*. New York: George H. Doran Company, 1921.

Godson, Susan H. *Serving Proudly: A History of Women in the U.S. Navy*. Annapolis, MD: Naval Institute Press, 2001.

Gordon, Dennis. *Lafayette Escadrille Pilot Biographies*. Missoula, MT: Doughboy Historical Society, 1991.

Greenwood, John T., ed. *My Life Before the World War, 1860–1917: A Memoir General of the Armies John J. Pershing*. Lexington: University of Kentucky Press, 2013.

The Hall of Valor. "Sergeant Arthur Aamot." https://valor.militarytimes.com/hero/10354.

Harold M. Mady Letters. SC 337 Box 1, The History Museum, Great Falls, Montana.

Harper, Michelle. "The Real War Horses of America." *Readex Blog*, January 5, 2012. https://www.readex.com/blog/real-war-horses-america.

Harris, Bill. *The Hellfighters of Harlem: African-American Soldiers Who Fought for the Right to Fight for Their Country*. New York: Carroll & Graf Publishers, 2002.

Harris, Stephen L. *Rock of the Marne: The American Soldiers Who Turned the Tide Against the Kaiser in World War I*. New York: Penguin Random House, 2015.

Harwell, Todd S., Greg S. Holzman and Steven D. Helgerson. "'No More War, No More Plague': The Spanish Influenza Pandemic Toll on Montana." *Montana: The Magazine of Western History* 37, no. 2 (Spring 1987): 27–44.

Henderson, Alice Palmer. *The Ninety-First: The First at Camp Lewis*. Tacoma, WA: John C. Barr, 1918.

History. "1919: New York City Parade Honors World War I Veterans." November 16, 2009. https://www.history.com/this-day-in-history/new-york-city-parade-honors-world-war-i-veterans.

History and Roster Cascade County Soldiers and Sailors, 1919. Great Falls, MT: War Book Publishing Company, n.d.

History of the First Division during the World War, 1917–1919. Philadelphia, PA: John C. Winston Company, 1922.

History of the Seventy-Seventh Division, August 25th, 1917–November 11th, 1918. New York: Wynkoop Hallenbeck Crawford Company, n.d.

A History of the 362nd Infantry. N.p.: T. Ben Meldrum, 1920.

Hynes, Samuel. *The Unsubstantial Air: American Fliers in the First World War*. New York: Farrar, Straus and Giroux, 2014.

Internet Archives. "Montana Primary Sources from the National Archives Rocky Mountain Region." Lesson 6: Montana Artist Charles Russell Contributes to the War Effort, 67–73. https://www.archives.gov/files/denver/education/materials/lessons-montana.pdf.

Johnson, Douglas V., II, and Rolfe L. Hillman Jr. *Soissons 1918*. College Station: Texas A&M University Press, 1999.

Kelton, Colonel R.H.C. "The Miracle of Chateau-Thierry." *The Century*, May 1919, 106–9.

Kennedy, David M. *Over Here: The First World War and American Society*. Oxford: Oxford University Press, 2004.

Kilford, Lieutenant Colonel Christopher R. *On the Way! The Military History of Lethbridge, Alberta (1914–1945)*. Victoria, BC: Trafford Publishing, 2004.

Laplander, Robert J. *Finding the Lost Battalion: Beyond the Rumors, Myths and Legends of America's Famous WWI Epic*. Waterford, WI: Lulu Press, 2017.

Letter, Russell to Bumsky, September 6, 1918. Private collection (anonymous).

Lewis and Clark County in the World War: A Record of the Achievements of Those Who Sacrificed Abroad and at Home. N.p., n.d.

Library and Archives Canada, Online Research. Canadian Expeditionary Forces (CEF) Service Files. https://www.bac-lac.gc.ca/eng/discover/military-heritage/first-world-war/Pages/introduction.aspx.

Liggett, Hunter. *Commanding an American Army: Recollections of the World War*. Boston: Houghton Mifflin Company, 1925.

Lopach, James J., and Jean A. Luckowski. *Jeannette Rankin: A Political Woman*. Boulder: University Press of Colorado, 2005.

Marsh, Francis A. *History of the World War*. 2 vols. Chicago: United Publishers, 1919.

Marshall, George C. *Memoirs of My Services in the World War, 1917–1918*. Boston: Houghton Mifflin Company, 1976.

Martin, Dale. "Sixteen Names on a Plaque: The Mortal Toll of the First World War at Montana State College." *Bozeman Magazine*, November 1, 2018. http://bozemanmagazine.com/articles/2018/11/01/28637_sixteen_names_on_a_plaque.

Montana Council of Defense Records. RS 19, Box 1, Folder 12, Montana Historical Society Research Center Archives.

Montana Historical Society. "Montana and the Great War." http://montana.maps.arcgis.com/apps.

Montana History Compass. "Montana Native Warriors." http://mthistory.pbworks.com/w/page/100686922/Facts%3A%20Native%20Warriors%3A%20K-L.

Montana Memory Project. Silver Bow County in the World War.

The Montana Sedition Project. http://www.seditionproject.net/master spreadsheet.html.

Mueller, George D. "Pandemic: The Flu Epidemic of 1918 in Central Montana." Montana Memory Project.

Mullen, Pierce C., and Michael L. Nelson. "Montanans and 'The Most Peculiar Disease': The Influenza Epidemic and Public Health, 1918–

1919." *Montana: The Magazine of Western History* 37, no. 2 (Spring 1987): 50–61.

Munroe, Jack. *Mopping Up! Through the Eyes of Bobbie Burns.* New York: H.K. Fly Company, 1918.

National Center for Biotechnology Information. "The U.S. Military and the Influenza Pandemic of 1918–1919." *Public Health Report*, April 2010, 125 Suppl 3:82–91. https://www.ncbi.nlm.nih.gov/pubmed/20568570.

Naval Historical Center. "Nurses and the U.S. Navy, 1917–1919." https://www.ibiblio.org/hyperwar/OnlineLibrary/photos/prs-tpic/nurses/nrs-e.htm.

Nelson, James Carl. *The Polar Bear Expedition: The Heroes of America's Forgotten Invasion of Russia, 1918–1919.* New York: William Morrow, 1919.

Nelson, Peter N. *A More Unbending Battle: The Harlem Hellfighters' Struggle for Freedom in WW I and Equality at Home.* New York: Basic Civatas Books, 2009.

Oberdorfer, Don. *Senator Mansfield: The Extraordinary Life of a Great American Statesman and Diplomat.* Washington, D.C.: Smithsonian Books, 2003.

Owen, Peter F. *To the Limit of Endurance: A Battalion of Marines in the Great War.* College Station: Texas A&M University Press, 2007.

Pershing, John J. *My Experiences in the World War.* 2 vols. New York: Frederick A. Stokes Company, 1931.

Prisoners of the First World War, 1914–1918, ICRC Historical Archives. International Committee of the Red Cross. https://grandeguerre.icrc.org/en/File/Search#/2/2/48/0/American%20(USA)/Military/Lara.

Red Cross Magazine. November 1918.

[Regimental Chaplain]. *The Story of the Sixteen Infantry in France.* Frankfurt, DE: Martin Flock Montabaur, 1919.

Reilly, Henry J. *Americans All, The Rainbow at War: Official History of the 42nd Rainbow Division in the World War.* Columbus, OH: F.J Beer Printing Company, 1936.

Richard, J. "Battle of Chateau Thierry, 1–4 June 1918." Military History Encyclopedia on the Web. www.historyofwar.org/articles/battles_chateau_thierry1918.html.

Robison, Ken. *World War I Montana: The Treasure State Prepares.* Charleston, SC: The History Press, 2018.

Rogan, Eugene. *The Fall of the Ottomans: The Great War in the Middle East.* New York: Basic Books, 2016.

Royal Navy and Naval History. "Chronology of the United States Marine Corps in the World War." http://www.naval-history.net/WW1NavyUSMC-aChronology.htm.

Rubin, Richard. *Back Over There*. New York: St. Martin's Press, 2017.

Saunders, Edward E. *Knapsacks and Roses: Montana's Women Veterans of World War I*. N.p.: self-published, 2018.

Schak, Al. *Soul Wounds: A Novel of the World War*. Missoula, MT: Missoulian, 1934.

Scott, Emmett J. *Scott's Official History of the American Negro in the World War*. N.p.: self-published, 1919.

The Second Division American Expeditionary Force in France, 1917–1919. New York: Hillman Press, 1937.

600 Days' Service: A History of the 361st Infantry Regiment. N.p., n.d.

Smith, Norma. *Jeannette Rankin America's Conscience*. Helena: Montana Historical Society Press, 2002.

Stonehouse, Frederick. *Combat Engineer!: The History of the 107th Engineering Battalion, 1881–1981*. N.p.: 107th Engineer Association, 2001.

The Story of the 91st Division. San Francisco, CA: H.S. Crocker Company, 1919.

A Story of the War and Family War Service Record, 1914–1919. St. Paul, MN: Mackey, Smith & Stiles, 1919.

Stout, Tom, ed. *Montana: Its Story and Biography: A History of Aboriginal and Territorial Montana and Three Decades of Statehood*. 3 vols. Chicago: American Historical Society, 1921.

Svingen, Orlan J., ed. *Splendid Service: The Montana National Guard, 1867–2006*. Pullman: Washington State University Press, 2010.

The 32nd Division in the World War, 1917–1919. Milwaukee, WI: Wisconsin Printing Company, 1920.

The Times History of the War. "Chapter CCXLIV: America's First Year at War." *Times of London*. https://fileupload.timesdev.tools/uploads/2b80a8 b839dcd83ed09e8afccea5b671-America%20chapter.pdf.

Toole, K. Ross. *Twentieth Century Montana: A State of Extremes*. Norman: University of Oklahoma Press, 1972.

The United States World War One Centennial Commission. "American Indians in World War I Branches of Service." https://www. worldwar1centennial.org/index.php/american-indians-in-ww1-branches-of-service/american-indians-in-ww1-branch-navy.html.

———. "Doughboy MIA Database, 1917–1920." https://www. worldwar1centennial.org/index.php/doughboy-mia-database-1917-1920.html.

———. "The Veterinary Corps: Caring and Curing." https://www. worldwar1centennial.org/index.php/brookeusa-veterinary-corps.html.

Vrooman, Nichols C.P. *"The Whole Country Was…'One Robe'": The Little Shell Tribe's America*. Helena, MT: Drumlummon Institute, 2012.

Wawro, Geoffrey. *Sons of Freedom: The Forgotten American Soldiers Who Defeated Germany in World War I*. New York: Basic Books, 2018.

Wikipedia. "Daniel Daly." https://en.wikipedia.org/wiki/Daniel_Daly.

———. "Fort Keogh." https://en.wikipedia.org/wiki/Fort_Keogh.

———. "The Meuse-Argonne Offensive." https://en.wikipedia.org/wiki/Meuse-Argonne_Offensive.

———. "Operation Michael." https://en.wikipedia.org/wiki/Operation_Michael.

———. "Reserve Officers' Training Corps: Student Army Training Corps." https://en.wikipedia.org/wiki/Reserve_Officers%27_Training_Corps#Student_Army_Training_Corps_(SATC).

———. "Spruce Production Division." https://en.wikipedia.org/wiki/Spruce_Production_Division.

———. "The 372nd Regiment." https://en.wikipedia.org/wiki/372nd_Infantry_Regiment_(United_States).

———. "339th Infantry Regiment (United States)." https://en.wikipedia.org/wiki/339th_Infantry_Regiment_(United_States).

Wiley, Frank W. *Montana and the Sky*. Minneapolis, MN: Holden Printing Company, 1966.

Work, Clemens P. *Darkness Before Dawn: Sedition and Free Speech in the American West*. Albuquerque: University of New Mexico Press: 2005.

World War I/The Great War, 1914–1918. "The Big Show: The Meuse-Argonne Offensive." Doughboy Center: The Story of the AEF. http://www.worldwar1.com/dbc/bigshow.htm.

———. "The Meuse-Argonne Offensive: Part II; Pershing's Report." http://www.worldwar1.com/dbc/bigshow2.htm.

Yockelson, Mitchell. *Forty-Seven Days: How Pershing's Warriors Came to Defeat the German Army in World War I*. New York: New American Library, 2016.

Zelick, Anna. "Mob Action in Lewistown, 1917–1918: Patriots on the Rampage." *Montana: The Magazine of Western History*. http://mhs.mt.gov/Portals/11/education/WWI/Mob%20Action%20in%20Lewistown.pdf.

INDEX

ABOUT THE AUTHOR

Ken Robison is a chronicler of neglected western history who lives in Great Falls, Montana. Ken, a Montana native, is historian at the Overholser Historical Research Center in Fort Benton, the Sun River Valley Historical Society and the Great Falls/Cascade County Historic Preservation Commission. His books include *World War I Montana: The Treasure State Prepares*; *Montana Territory and the Civil War: A Frontier Forged on the Battlefield*; *Confederates in Montana Territory: In the Shadow of Price's Army*; and *Yankees and Rebels on the Upper Missouri: Steamboats, Gold and Peace*. He has contributed to *Black Americans in the Civil Rights Movement in the West*; *Montana, a Cultural Medley: Stories of Our Ethnic Diversity*; *Beyond Schoolmarms and Madams: Montana Women's Stories*; and *The Mullan Road: Carving a Passage through the Frontier Northwest, 1859 to 1862*. Ken is a retired U.S. Navy captain after a career in naval intelligence. The Montana Historical Society has honored Ken as a "Montana Heritage Keeper."

Visit us at
www.historypress.com